Robert Burns

Poems and songs complete

Vol. 3

4

Robert Burns

Poems and songs complete
Vol. 3

ISBN/EAN: 9783337264949

Printed in Europe, USA, Canada, Australia, Japan

Cover: Foto ©Thomas Meinert / pixelio.de

More available books at **www.hansebooks.com**

ROBERT BURNS

POEMS AND SONGS COMPLETE

VOLUME
THIRD

PUBLISHED BY
JAMES THIN 🐦
EDINBURGH 1896

LIST OF ILLUSTRATIONS

CONTENTS OF VOLUME THIRD.

(An asterisk is prefixed to those pieces that, either wholly or in part, are here first embraced in a popular edition of the author's works.)

A.D. 1791.

III.   *b*

Contents.

Contents. xi

POEMS AND SONGS.

—o—

INTRODUCTORY NOTE.

THE close of Volume Second, fragrant with the perfume of wild flowers gathered by our Author in his charming "Posie," has brought the reader forward to the spring or early summer of 1791. The poet is still at Ellisland, but the last of his cereal harvests there will soon be reaped. No more is he to drudge at barn or byre ; for the soil of the South has proved to him as ungrateful as the soil of the West. "If once I was clear of this farm, I should respire more at ease. It has undone my enjoyment of myself." Such were his observations a year and more prior to this period; and after some further practical experience of the everlasting truth, "A man cannot serve two masters," he resolved to untie the couplings which fettered him to the soil, that he might the more resolutely seek advancement in his new calling. Dr Currie has pictured the "high-minded poet pursuing the defaulters of the Revenue among the hills and vales of Nithsdale, his roving eye wandering over the charms of Nature, and 'muttering his wayward fancies' as he moved along." But "riding two hundred miles every week through ten moorland parishes" was rough work, and he longed to have his Excise district changed for that of a seaport town, where the field of his labours would be less expanded, and perhaps more agreeable, and more remunerative.

In this closing Volume of the poetical works of Burns, the poems, strictly so called, must be few and far between, and these comparatively short and unimportant. That want, however, is fully compensated by a copious flow of undying song, which he continued to give forth during the remaining five years of his life ; and not even on his death-bed was his harp silent, some of its sweetest notes being then emitted. Near the close of 1791 he removed to Dumfries, where the efforts of his muse were chiefly directed to the self-imposed labour of supplying songs for Johnson's fourth volume, which appeared in August 1792. Shortly after that date, the correspondence with George Thomson commenced, and to him he furnished upwards of sixty new songs, besides supplying Johnson with other lyrics that were published after the poet's death in the fifth and sixth volumes of the *Musical Museum.*

III.   A

ON GLENRIDDELL'S FOX BREAKING HIS CHAIN.

A FRAGMENT, 1791.

THOU, Liberty, thou art my theme;
Not such as idle poets dream,
Who trick thee up a heathen goddess
That a fantastic cap and rod has;
Such stale conceits are poor and silly;
I paint thee out, a Highland filly,
A sturdy, stubborn, handsome dapple,
As sleek's a mouse, as round's an apple,
That when thou pleasest can do wonders;
But when thy luckless rider blunders,
Or if thy fancy should demur there,
Wilt break thy neck ere thou go further.

These things premised, I sing—a Fox
Was caught among his native rocks,
And to a dirty kennel chained,
How he his liberty regained.

Glenriddell! a Whig without a stain,
A Whig in principle and grain,
Could'st thou enslave a free-born creature,
A native denizen of Nature?
How could'st thou, with a heart so good,
(A better ne'er was sluiced with blood)
Nail a poor devil to a tree,
That ne'er did harm to thine or thee?

The staunchest Whig Glenriddell was,
Quite frantic in his country's cause;
And oft was Reynard's prison passing,
And with his brother-Whigs canvassing

The Rights of Men, the Powers of Women,
With all the dignity of Freemen.

Sir Reynard daily heard debates
Of Princes', Kings', and Nations' fates,
With many rueful, bloody stories
Of Tyrants, Jacobites, and Tories :
From liberty how angels fell,
That now are galley-slaves in hell ;
How Nimrod first the trade began
Of binding Slavery's chains on Man ;
How fell Semiramis—G—d d-mn her !
Did first, with sacrilegious hammer,
(All ills till then were trivial matters)
For Man dethron'd forge hen-peck fetters ;
How Xerxes, that abandoned Tory,
Thought cutting throats was reaping glory,
Until the stubborn Whigs of Sparta
Taught him great Nature's Magna Charta ;
How mighty Rome her fiat hurl'd
Resistless o'er a bowing world,
And, kinder than they did desire,
Polish'd mankind with sword and fire :
With much, too tedious to relate,
Of ancient and of modern date,
But ending still, how Billy Pitt
(Unlucky boy !) with wicked wit,
Has gagg'd old Britain, drain'd her coffer,
As butchers bind and bleed a heifer.

Thus wily Reynard, by degrees,
In kennel listening at his ease,
Suck'd in a mighty stock of knowledge,
As much as some folks at a College ;
Knew Britain's rights and constitution,
Her aggrandisement, diminution,

How fortune wrought us good from evil ;
Let no man, then, despise the Devil,
As who should say, ' I ne'er can need him,'
Since we to scoundrels owe our freedom.

*   *   *   *

CALEDONIA—A BALLAD.

Tune—" Caledonian Hunts' Delight" of Mr Gow.

THERE was once a time, but old Time was then young,
    That brave Caledonia, the chief of her line,
From some of your northern deities sprung,
    (Who knows not that brave Caledonia's divine?)
From Tweed to the Orcades was her domain,
    To hunt, or to pasture, or do what she would :
Her heav'nly relations there fixèd her reign,
    And pledg'd her their godheads to warrant it good.

A lambkin in peace, but a lion in war,
    The pride of her kindred, the heroine grew :
Her grandsire, old Odin, triumphantly swore,—
    " Whoe'er shall provoke thee, th' encounter shall rue !'
With tillage or pasture at times she would sport,
    To feed her fair flocks by her green rustling corn ;
But chiefly the woods were her fav'rite resort,
    Her darling amusement, the hounds and the horn.

Long quiet she reigned ; till thitherward steers
    A flight of bold eagles from Adria's strand :[1]
Repeated, successive, for many long years,
    They darken'd the air, and they plunder'd the land :
Their pounces were murder, and terror their cry,
    They'd conquer'd and ruin'd a world beside :
She took to her hills, and her arrows let fly,
    The daring invaders, they fled or they died.

---

[1] The Romans.

The Cameleon-Savage disturb'd her repose,
  With tumult, disquiet, rebellion, and strife ;
Provok'd beyond bearing, at last she arose,
  And robb'd him at once of his hopes and his life :[1]
The Anglian lion, the terror of France,
  Oft prowling, ensanguin'd the Tweed's silver flood ;
But, taught by the bright Caledonian lance,
  He learnèd to fear in his own native wood.

The fell Harpy-raven took wing from the north,
  The scourge of the seas, and the dread of the shore ;[2]
The wild Scandinavian boar issued forth
  To wanton in carnage and wallow in gore :[3]
O'er countries and kingdoms their fury prevail'd,
  No arts could appease them, no arms could repel ;
But brave Caledonia in vain they assail'd,
  As Largs well can witness, and Loncartie tell.[4]

Thus bold, independent, unconquer'd, and free,
  Her bright course of glory for ever shall run :
For brave Caledonia immortal must be ;
  I'll prove it from Euclid as clear as the sun :
Rectangle-triangle, the figure we'll chuse :
  The upright is Chance, and old Time is the base ;
But brave Caledonia's the hypothenuse ;
  Then, ergo, she'll match them, and match them always.[5]

[The poet directs this song to be united with Gow's set of the "Caledonian
Hunts' Delight," and hopes the words will be found to " suit the excellent
air they are designed for."]

---

[1] The Picts.   [2] The Saxons.   [3] The Danes.
  [4] Two famous battles in which the Scandinavians were defeated.
  [5] This singular figure of poetry, taken from the mathematics, refers to
the famous proposition of Pythagoras, the 47th of Euclid. In a right-
angled triangle, the square of the hypothenuse is always equal to the
squares of the two other sides.—*Currie.*

POEM ON PASTORAL POETRY.

HAIL, Poesie ! thou Nymph reserv'd !
In chase o' thee, what crowds hae swerv'd
Frae common sense, or sunk enerv'd
      'Mang heaps o' clavers : *
And och ! o'er aft thy joes hae starv'd,
      'Mid a' thy favors !

Say, Lassie, why thy train amang,
While loud the trump's heroic clang,
And sock or buskin skelp † alang
      To death or marriage ;
Scarce ane has tried the shepherd-sang
      But wi' miscarriage ?

In Homer's craft Jock Milton thrives ;
Eschylus' pen Will Shakespeare drives ;
Wee Pope, the knurlin, ‡ till him rives
      Horatian fame ;
In thy sweet sang, Barbauld, survives
      Even Sappho's flame.

But thee, Theocritus, wha matches ?
They're no herd's ballats, Maro's catches ;
Squire Pope but busks his skinklin § patches
      O' heathen tatters :
I pass by hunders, nameless wretches,
      That ape their betters.

In this braw age o' wit and lear,‖
Will nane the Shepherd's whistle mair

---

* gossip.   † move quickly.   ‡ of stunted growth.
§ wishy-washy.   ‖ learning.

Blaw sweetly in its native air,
          And rural grace ;
And, wi' the far-fam'd Grecian, share
          A rival place?

Yes ! there is ane ; a Scottish callan !*
There's ane ; come forrit,† honest Allan !
Thou need na jouk ‡ behint the hallan, §
          A chiel sae clever ;
The teeth o' time may gnaw Tantallan,[1]
          But thou's for ever.

Thou paints auld Nature to the nines, ‖
In thy sweet Caledonian lines ;
Nae gowden stream thro' myrtles twines,
          Where Philomel,
While nightly breezes sweep the vines,
          Her griefs will tell !

In gowany glens thy burnie strays,
Where bonie lasses bleach their claes,
Or trots by hazelly shaws ¶ and braes,
          Wi' hawthorns gray,
Where blackbirds join the shepherd's lays,
          At close o' day.

Thy rural loves are Nature's sel' ;
Nae bombast spates ** o' nonsense swell ;
Nae snap †† conceits, but that sweet spell
          O' witchin love,
That charm that can the strongest quell,
          The sternest move.

---

* youth.	† forward.	‡ hide.	§ outside porch.
‖ perfection.	¶ low woods.	** floods.	†† smart.

[1] A strong fortress on a high sea-rock in East Lothian.

[The authorship of this poem is involved in some uncertainty. It was found in the hand-writing of Burns after his decease, and printed by Dr Currie without remark.

The language and concentrated force of some of the lines in this poem are quite in Burns's manner; yet we feel constrained to observe that in his earlier epistles he never loses an opportunity, while naming Ramsay and Fergusson together, of shewing a preference to the latter; but in this poem, Fergusson's name is not even hinted at. This fact gives rise to a suspicion that the poem, if not by Fergusson himself, was composed prior to the era of that poet; and we conceive that Wm. Hamilton of Gilbertfield, who addressed several complimentary Epistles to Ramsay, might have been the author of this poem.]

VERSES ON THE DESTRUCTION OF THE WOODS NEAR DRUMLANRIG.

As on the banks of winding Nith,
  Ae smiling simmer morn I stray'd,
And traced its bonie holms and haughs,
  Where linties sang and lammies play'd,
I sat me down upon a craig,
  And drank my fill o' fancy's dream,
When from the eddying deep below,
  Up rose the genius of the stream.

Dark, like the frowning rock, his brow,
  And troubled, like his wintry wave,
And deep, as sughs the boding wind
  Amang his caves, the sigh he gave—
"And come ye here, my son," he cried,
  "To wander in my birken shade?
To muse some favourite Scottish theme,
  Or sing some favourite Scottish maid?

"There was a time, it's nae lang syne,
  Ye might hae seen me in my pride,
When a' my banks sae bravely saw
  Their woody pictures in my tide;

When hanging beech and spreading elm
   Shaded my stream sae clear and cool :
And stately oaks their twisted arms
   Threw broad and dark across the pool ;

" When, glinting thro' the trees, appear'd
   The wee white cot aboon the mill,
And peacefu' rose its ingle reek,
   That, slowly curling, clamb the hill.
But now the cot is bare and cauld,
   Its leafy bield for ever gane,
And scarce a stinted birk is left
   To shiver in the blast its lane."

"Alas ! " quoth I, "what ruefu' chance
   Has twin'd ye o' your stately trees?
Has laid your rocky bosom bare—
   Has stripped the cleeding aff your braes?
Was it the bitter eastern blast,
   That scatters blight in early spring?
Or was 't the wil'fire scorch'd their boughs,
   Or canker-worm wi' secret sting?"

" Nae eastlin blast," the sprite replied ;
   " It blaws na here sae fierce and fell,
And on my dry and halesome banks
   Nae canker-worms get leave to dwell :
Man ! cruel man ! " the genius sighed—
   As through the cliffs he sank him down—
" The worm that gnaw'd my bonie trees,
   That reptile wears a Ducal crown."

[The Duke of Queensberry's object in felling the trees on his beautiful estates—for the woods around Neidpath in Peeblesshire shared the same fate—was to raise money to provide a princely dowry for the Countess of Yarmouth, his *supposed* natural daughter.]

THE GALLANT WEAVER.

WHERE Cart rins rowin to the sea,
By mony a flower and spreading tree,
There lives a lad, the lad for me,
    He is a gallant Weaver.
O I had wooers aught or nine,
They gied me rings and ribbons fine ;
And I was fear'd my heart wad tine,*
    And I gied it to the Weaver.

My daddie sign'd my tocher-band,†
To gie the lad that has the land,
But to my heart I'll add my hand,[1]
    And give it to the Weaver.
While birds rejoice in leafy bowers,
While bees delight in opening flowers,
While corn grows green in summer showers,
    I love my gallant Weaver.

[The poet may have composed this song as a humorous reference to a portion of Jean Armour's history in 1786, when she was sent to Paisley to keep her out of his way.]

EPIGRAM AT BROWNHILL INN.

AT Brownhill we always get dainty good cheer,
And plenty of bacon each day in the year ;
We've a' thing that's nice, and mostly in season,
But why always Bacon—come tell me the reason?

[This Inn, in the neighbourhood of Thornhill, was a convenient resting-place for the poet on his homeward journey in some of his Excise rounds.]

* be lost.   † marriage settlement.

[1] " And in the lustre of her youth, she gave
    Her hand, with her heart in it, to Francesco."—*Roger's Italy.*

YOU'RE WELCOME, WILLIE STEWART.

Chorus.—You're welcome, Willie Stewart,
　　　You're welcome, Willie Stewart,
　　　There's ne'er a flower that blooms in May,
　　　That's half sae welcome's thou art !

COME, bumpers high, express your joy,
　　The bowl we maun renew it,
The tappet hen, gae bring her ben,
　　To welcome Willie Stewart,
　　　You're welcome, Willie Stewart, &c.

May foes be strang, and friends be slack,
　　Ilk action, may he rue it,
May woman on him turn her back
　　That wrangs thee, Willie Stewart !
　　　You're welcome, Willie Stewart, &c.

[The original of this little song was inscribed by the poet himself on a
crystal tumbler. The relic was acquired by Sir Walter Scott, and is still
preserved at Abbotsford The subject of the verses was the factor at Close-
burn. He died in 1812.]

LOVELY POLLY STEWART.

Chorus.—O lovely Polly Stewart,
　　　O charming Polly Stewart,
　　　There's ne'er a flower that blooms in May,
　　　That's half so fair as thou art !

THE flower it blaws, it fades, it fa's,
　　And art can ne'er renew it ;
But worth and truth, eternal youth
　　Will gie to Polly Stewart,
　　　O lovely Polly Stewart, &c.

May he whase arms shall fauld thy charms
   Possess a leal and true heart !
To him be given to ken the heaven
   He grasps in Polly Stewart !
    O lovely Polly Stewart, &c.

[The "charming Polly," daughter of the factor at Closeburn, having been born in 1775, could be only about sixteen years old when she became a theme for the Muse of Burns. Her after-career in life was not an enviable one. She married her cousin, by whom she had three sons: he fell into some scrape which compelled him to abscond, and "Polly" afterwards contracted a matrimonial alliance with a man named Welsh, but as she did not live happily with him, a separation soon took place. In 1806, she resided in Maxwelltown with her father, who was no longer factor at Close-burn.]

FRAGMENT,—DAMON AND SYLVIA.

Tune—"The Tither Morn."

YON wandering rill that marks the hill,
   And glances o'er the brae, Sir,
Slides by a bower, where mony a flower
   Sheds fragrance on the day, Sir ;
There Damon lay with Sylvia gay,
   To love they thought no crime, Sir,
The wild birds sang, the echoes rang,
   While Damon's heart beat time, Sir.

[These eight lines form the central portion of a completed production of Burns, entitled an "Ode to Spring," which appears in a letter addressed to George Thomson, dated early in January 1795 (the last New year season, save one, which the bard was fated to see). It appears in the same letter in which he transcribed his world-famous "A man's a man for a' that."]

JOHNIE LAD, COCK UP YOUR BEAVER.

WHEN first my brave Johnie lad came to the town,
He had a blue bonnet that wanted the crown ;
But now he has gotten a hat and a feather,
Hey, brave Johnie lad, cock up your beaver !

Cock up your beaver, and cock it fu' sprush,
We'll over the border, and gie them a brush ;
There's somebody there we'll teach better behaviour,
Hey, brave Johnie lad, cock up your beaver !

[The second stanza only of this little fragment can be considered as the work of Burns. The original was a London production framed in ridicule of the Scottish settlers who made their way into England after James VI. of Scotland succeeded to the throne of Queen Elizabeth.]

MY EPPIE MACNAB.

O SAW ye my dearie, my Eppie Macnab ?
O saw ye my dearie, my Eppie Macnab ?
　　She's down in the yard, she's kissin the laird,
She winna come hame to her ain Jock Rab.

O come thy ways to me, my Eppie Macnab ;
O come thy ways to me, my Eppie Macnab ;
　　Whate'er thou hast dune, be it late, be it sune,
Thou's welcome again to thy ain Jock Rab.

What says she, my dearie, my Eppie Macnab ?
What says she, my dearie, my Eppie Macnab ?
　　She let's thee to wit that she has thee forgot,
And for ever disowns thee, her ain Jock Rab.

O had I ne'er seen thee, my Eppie Macnab !
O had I ne'er seen thee, my Eppie Macnab !
　　As light as the air, and as fause as thou's fair,
Thou's broken the heart o' thy ain Jock Rab.

[This was composed as a substitute for old words which, the poet tell us, "had more wit than decency."]

ALTHO' HE HAS LEFT ME.

ALTHO' he has left me for greed o' the siller,
   I dinna envy him the gains he can win ;
I rather wad bear a' the lade o' my sorrow,
   Than ever hae acted sae faithless to him.

[These four lines by Burns were added in the process of retouching an old
song for Johnson which first appeared in Herd's Collection, entitled, " I'll
never lay a' my love upon ane."]

MY TOCHER'S THE JEWEL.

O MEIKLE thinks my luve o' my beauty,
   And meikle thinks my luve o' my kin ;
But little thinks my luve I ken brawlie
   My tocher's the jewel has charms for him.
It's a' for the apple he'll nourish the tree,
   It's a' for the hiney he'll cherish the bee,
My laddie's sae meikle in luve wi' the siller,
   He canna hae luve to spare for me.

Your proffer o' luve's an airle-penny,
   My tocher's the bargain ye wad buy ;
But an ye be crafty, I am cunnin,
   Sae ye wi' anither your fortune may try.
Ye're like to the timmer o' yon rotten wood,
   Ye're like to the bark o' yon rotten tree,
Ye'll slip frae me like a knotless thread,
   And ye'll crack your credit wi' mair nor me.

[The four closing lines and also the fifth and sixth lines of the first stanza
of this song are old ; the remainder is the poet's own. In 1787 he included
the old fragment among several others, chiefly of the ballad kind, which he
transcribed for Mr Wm. Tytler of Woodhouselee, as "samples of the old
pieces that are still to be found among our peasantry in the West."]

O FOR ANE AN' TWENTY, TAM.

Chorus.—An' O for ane an' twenty, Tam !
And hey, sweet ane an' twenty, Tam !
I'll learn my kin a rattlin sang,
An' I saw ane an' twenty, Tam.

THEY snool * me sair, and haud † me down,
An' gar ‡ me look like bluntie,§ Tam ;
But three short years will soon wheel roun',
An' then comes ane an' twenty, Tam.
An' O for, &c.

A glieb ‖ o' lan', a claut ¶ o' gear,
Was left me by my Auntie, Tam ;
At kith or kin I need na spier,**
An' I saw ane an' twenty, Tam.
An' O for, &c.

They'll hae me wed a wealthy coof,††
Tho' I mysel' hae plenty, Tam ;
But, hear'st thou laddie ! there's my loof,‡‡
I'm thine at ane an' twenty, Tam.
An' O for, &c.

[Here the playful comic genius of Burns is most happily displayed. The
song speaks to the heart of man and woman of every tongue and kindred.
A maiden of eighteen has a handsome tocher waiting for her when she shall
reach her majority : a wealthy suitor asks her hand ; but she reserves that
for the lad who has already secured her heart, and the avaricious "coof"
is rejected.

" I'd rather take *Tam*, wi' his staff in his hand,
Before I'd hae Sandy wi' houses and land."]

---

* snub, suppress. † hold. ‡ make. § a cowed person.
‖ a piece of land attached to a mansion. ¶ hoard.
** consult. †† blockhead. ‡‡ palm of the hand.

THOU FAIR ELIZA.

TURN again, thou fair Eliza !
  Ae kind blink before we part ;
Rew on thy despairing lover,
  Can'st thou break his faithfu' heart ?
Turn again, thou fair Eliza !
  If to love thy heart denies,
Oh, in pity hide the sentence
  Under friendship's kind disguise !

Thee, sweet maid, hae I offended ?
  My offence is loving thee ;
Can'st thou wreck his peace for ever,
  Wha for thine would gladly die ?
While the life beats in my bosom,
  Thou shalt mix in ilka throe :
Turn again, thou lovely maiden,
  Ae sweet smile on me bestow.

Not the bee upon the blossom,
  In the pride o' sinny noon ;
Not the little sporting fairy,
  All beneath the simmer moon ;
Not the Minstrel, in the moment
  Fancy lightens in his e'e,
Kens the pleasure, feels the rapture,
  That thy presence gies to me.

[This elegant lyric was composed in fulfilment of a promise made by the author to Mr James Johnston, the engraver and publisher of the *Musical Museum*. In a letter to him, dated 15th November 1788, after expressing himself in a highly complimentary strain regarding that publication, he thus concludes :—" Have you never a fair goddess that leads you a wild-goose chase of amorous devotion ? Let me know a few of her qualities, such as whether she be rather black or fair, plump or thin, short or tall, &c. ; and choose your air, and I shall task my muse to celebrate her."]

MY BONIE BELL.

" In those vernal seasons of the year, when the air is calm and pleasant,
it were an injury and sullenness against Nature not to go out and see her
riches, and partake in her rejoicing with Heaven and Earth."
                         JOHN MILTON.—*Letter on Education.*

THE smiling Spring comes in rejoicing,
 And surly Winter grimly flies ;
Now crystal clear are the falling waters,
 And bonie blue are the sunny skies.
Fresh o'er the mountains breaks forth the morning,
 The ev'ning gilds the ocean's swell ;
All creatures joy in the sun's returning,
 And I rejoice in my Bonie Bell.

The flowery Spring leads sunny Summer,
 The yellow Autumn presses near ;
Then in his turn comes gloomy Winter,
 Till smiling Spring again appear :
Thus seasons dancing, life advancing,
 Old Time and Nature their changes tell ;
But never ranging, still unchanging,
 I adore my Bonie Bell.

[No one has ever ventured to suggest the identity of the fair one who inspired this exquisite song. In the *Museum*, it stands on the page opposite
"Afton Water," and it may fairly be assumed that both were composed
about the same period.]

SWEET AFTON.

" I charge you, O ye daughters of Jerusalem, that ye stir not, nor awake
my love—my dove, my undefiled ! The flowers appear on the earth, the
time of the singing of the birds is come, and the voice of the turtle is heard
in our land."

FLOW gently, sweet Afton ! among thy green braes,
Flow gently, I'll sing thee a song in thy praise ;
My Mary's asleep by thy murmuring stream,
Flow gently, sweet Afton, disturb not her dream.

III.   B

Thou stock dove whose echo resounds thro' the glen,
Ye wild whistling blackbirds, in yon thorny den,
Thou green crested lapwing* thy screaming forbear,
I charge you, disturb not my slumbering Fair.

How lofty, sweet Afton, thy neighbouring hills,
Far mark'd with the courses of clear, winding rills;
There daily I wander as noon rises high,
My flocks and my Mary's sweet cot in my eye.

How pleasant thy banks and green vallies below,
Where, wild in the woodlands, the primroses blow;
There oft, as mild Ev'ning weeps over the lea,
The sweet-scented birk shades my Mary and me.

Thy crystal stream, Afton, how lovely it glides,
And winds by the cot where my Mary resides;
How wanton thy waters her snowy feet lave,
As, gathering sweet flowerets, she stems thy clear wave.

Flow gently, sweet Afton, amang thy green braes,
Flow gently, sweet river, the theme of my lays;
My Mary's asleep by thy murmuring stream,
Flow gently, sweet Afton, disturb not her dream.

[A kind of holy calm pervades the soul of the reader who peruses, or the
auditor who listens to the music of this unique strain. The "pastoral
melancholy," which Wordsworth felt at St Mary's Loch, steals over his heart,
and laps him in a dreamy Elysium of sympathetic repose.

What can we say in regard to the heroineship of this pastoral song? Did
the living Mary Campbell inspire it? Or was it composed in 1791, five
years after her death, in a reverie of retrospective admiration of her sleeping
image enshrined "within his bosom's core"? Did he, in that still valley,
amuse his fond fancy by reflecting what might have been his fate had not
Death seized her as his prey? And did he there, in imagination only,

". . . . wander as noon rises high,
My flocks and my Mary's sweet cot in my eye"?]

* peaseweep or pewit.

ADDRESS TO THE SHADE OF THOMSON,

ON CROWNING HIS BUST AT EDNAM, ROXBURGHSHIRE, WITH A WREATH OF BAYS.

WHILE virgin Spring by Eden's flood,
   Unfolds her tender mantle green,
Or pranks the sod in frolic mood,
   Or tunes Eolian strains between.

While Summer, with a matron grace,
   Retreats to Dryburgh's cooling shade,
Yet oft, delighted, stops to trace
   The progress of the spikey blade.

While Autumn, benefactor kind,
   By Tweed erects his aged head,
And sees, with self-approving mind,
   Each creature on his bounty fed.

While maniac Winter rages o'er
   The hills whence classic Yarrow flows,
Rousing the turbid torrent's roar,
   Or sweeping, wild, a waste of snows.

So long, sweet Poet of the year !
   Shall bloom that wreath thou well hast won ;
While Scotia, with exulting tear,
   Proclaims that THOMSON is her son.

[In August 1791, Burns received a letter from the Earl of Buchan, inviting him to be present at Ednam near Kelso on 22nd September, to take part in the ceremony of inaugurating a monumental erection he had reared there, to be unveiled on Thomson's birthday.

Burns replied in courteous fashion ; but said that "a week or two's absence, in the very middle of harvest, is what I much doubt I dare not venture on. Your lordship hints at an Ode for the occasion ; but who would write after Collins?   I read over his verses to the memory of Thomson, and despaired.   I got indeed to the length of three or four stanzas, in the way of address to the shade of the bard, on crowning his bust.   I shall trouble your lordship with the subjoined copy of them, which, I am afraid, will be but too convincing a proof how unequal I am for the task."]

NITHSDALE'S WELCOME HAME.

THE noble Maxwells and their powers
    Are coming o'er the border,
And they'll gae big * Terreagles' towers,
    And set them a' in order.
And they declare Terreagles fair,
    For their abode they choose it ;
There's no a heart in a' the land
    But's lighter at the news o't.

Tho' stars in skies may disappear,
    And angry tempests gather ;
The happy hour may soon be near
    That brings us pleasant weather :
The weary night o' care and grief
    May hae a joyfu' morrow ;
So † dawning day has brought relief,
    Fareweel our night o' sorrow.

[The song in the text was composed and presented to Lady Winifred Maxwell Constable of Terreagles, as an affectionate tribute of respect for an ancient family in whose fortunes the poet felt a natural interest.]

FRAE THE FRIENDS AND LAND I LOVE.

FRAE the friends and land I love,
    Driv'n by Fortune's felly spite ;
Frae my best belov'd I rove,
    Never mair to taste delight :

---

* build.   † since.

Never mair maun hope to find
　　Ease frae toil, relief frae care ;
When Remembrance wracks the mind,
　　Pleasures but unveil despair.

Brightest climes shall mirk appear,
　　Desert ilka blooming shore,
Till the Fates, nae mair severe,
　　Friendship, love, and peace restore.
Till Revenge, wi' laurel'd head,
　　Bring our banished hame again ;
And ilk loyal, bonie lad
　　Cross the seas, and win his ain.

[The poet in his Glenriddell notes claims only the last four lines of this song, which he says he added "by way of giving a turn to the theme of the poem, such as it is."]

SUCH A PARCEL OF ROGUES IN A NATION.

FAREWEEL to a' our Scottish fame,
　　Fareweel our ancient glory ;
Fareweel ev'n to the Scottish name,
　　Sae fam'd in martial story.
Now Sark rins over Solway sands,
　　An' Tweed rins to the ocean,
To mark where England's province stands—
　　Such a parcel of rogues in a nation !

What force or guile could not subdue,
　　Thro' many warlike ages,
Is wrought now by a coward few,
　　For hireling traitor's wages.
The English steel we could disdain,
　　Secure in valour's station ;
But English gold has been our bane—
　　Such a parcel of rogues in a nation !

O would, ere I had seen the day
 That Treason thus could sell us,
My auld grey head had lien in clay,
 Wi' Bruce and loyal Wallace !
But pith and power, till my last hour,
 I'll mak this declaration ;
We're bought and sold for English gold—
 Such a parcel of rogues in a nation !

[The chief reference in this piece is to the treaty of Union between England and Scotland, which was signed on 22nd July 1707. An old-fashioned
prejudice against this measure was long in dying away, among the Jacobites in particular ; and this seems to have been one of several pieces which
were constructed by Burns for the delectation of his friends whose tastes
lay in that direction.]

YE JACOBITES BY NAME.

YE Jacobites by name, give an ear, give an ear,
Ye Jacobites by name, give an ear,
 Ye Jacobites by name,
 Your fautes I will proclaim,
Your doctrines I maun blame, you shall hear.

What is Right, and what is Wrang, by the law, by the
  law?
What is Right, and what is Wrang, by the law?
 What is Right, and what is Wrang?
 A short sword, and a lang,
A weak arm and a strang, for to draw.

What makes heroic strife, famed afar, famed afar?
What makes heroic strife, famed afar?
 What makes heroic strife?
 To whet th' assassin's knife,
Or hunt a Parent's life, wi' bluidy war?

Then let your schemes alone, in the state, in the state,
Then let your schemes alone, in the state.
  Then let your schemes alone,
  Adore the rising sun,
And leave a man undone, to his fate.

[This powerful political satire, in which some of the bard's favourite sentiments are expressed under the coverture of Jacobitism, might have been produced for the gratification of his neighbour, Lady Winifred Maxwell.]

I HAE BEEN AT CROOKIEDEN.

I HAE been at Crookieden,*
  My bonie laddie, Highland laddie,
Viewing Willie and his men,
  My bonie laddie, Highland laddie.
There our foes that burnt and slew,
  My bonie laddie, Highland laddie,
There, at last, they gat their due,
  My bonie laddie, Highland laddie.

Satan sits in his black neuk,†
  My bonie laddie, Highland laddie,
Breaking sticks to roast the Duke,
  My bonie laddie, Highland laddie.
The bloody monster gae a yell,
  My bonie laddie, Highland laddie,
And loud the laugh gied round a' hell
  My bonie laddie, Highland laddie.

[This familiar ditty is mainly indebted to the hand of Burns for its point and pith. The original title of the tune is "Jinglin John," and after the cruelties of William, Duke of Cumberland, at Culloden, it became one of several quick step tunes known by the title "Bonie laddie, Highland laddie."]

---

* a cant name for *hell*.   † corner.

O KENMURE'S ON AND AWA, WILLIE.

O KENMURE'S on and awa, Willie,
  O Kenmure's on and awa ;
An' Kenmure's lord's the bravest lord
  That ever Galloway saw.
Success to Kenmure's band, Willie !
  Success to Kenmure's band !
There's no a heart that fears a Whig,
  That rides by Kenmure's hand.

Here's Kenmure's health in wine, Willie !
  Here's Kenmure's health in wine !
There's ne'er a coward o' Kenmure's blude,
  Nor yet o' Gordon's line.
O Kenmure's lads are men, Willie,
  O Kenmure's lads are men ;
Their hearts and swords are metal true,
  And that their foes shall ken.

They'll live or die wi' fame, Willie,
  They'll live or die wi' fame ;
But sune, wi' sounding victorie,
  May Kenmure's lord come hame !
Here's him that's far awa, Willie !
  Here's him that's far awa !
And here's the flower that I loe best,
  The rose that's like the snaw.

[The hand of Burns is very visible here ; but it is impossible to say what portions of the song are old and what by him.

The Right Hon. William George, Viscount Kenmure, was Commander-in-chief of the Chevalier's forces in the south-west of Scotland, in 1715. At the head of two hundred horsemen, he formed a junction with the troops under General Forster, and they marched into Preston in Lancashire. Here he was compelled to surrender a prisoner at discretion, on 13th Nov. 1715, and early on the following month, he and many of his unfortunate followers were conducted to London, where they were subjected to great indignities. Lord Kenmure was afterwards tried, and beheaded on Tower-hill, 24th Feb 1716.]

EPISTLE TO JOHN MAXWELL, ESQ. OF TERRAUGHTY,

ON HIS BIRTH-DAY.

HEALTH to the Maxwell's veteran Chief!
Health, ay unsour'd by care or grief:
Inspired, I turn'd Fate's sibyl leaf,
   This natal morn,
I see thy life is stuff o' prief,
   Scarce quite half-worn.

This day thou metes threescore eleven,
And I can tell that bounteous Heaven,
(The second-sight, ye ken, is given
   To ilka Poet)
On thee a tack o' seven times seven
   Will yet bestow it.

If envious buckies view wi' sorrow
Thy lengthen'd days on this blest morrow,
May Desolation's lang-teeth'd harrow,
   Nine miles an hour,
Rake them, like Sodom and Gomorrah,
   In brunstane stoure.

But for thy friends, and they are mony,
Baith honest men, and lasses bonie,
May couthie Fortune, kind and cannie,
   In social glee,
Wi' mornings blythe, and e'enings funny,
   Bless them and thee!

Fareweel, auld birkie! Lord be near ye,
And then the deil, he daurna steer ye:

Your friends ay love, your faes ay fear ye ;
        For me, shame fa' me,
If neist my heart I dinna wear ye,
        While Burns they ca' me.

[John Maxwell, of Terraughty and Munches, near Dumfries, was seventy-one years old when Burns thus addressed him, and although his earthly pilgrimage was not extended by forty-nine years more, according to the poet's wish, he eventually reached the age of ninety-four. Chambers informs us that he was descended, at a comparatively small number of removes, from the gallant and faithful Lord Herries, who on bended knees entreated Queen Mary to prosecute Bothwell, as the murderer of Darnley, and who subsequently fought for her at Langside.

The original MS. of this Epistle is now in the Poet's Monument at Edinburgh, to which it was presented many years ago by the publisher of this Edition.]

SECOND EPISTLE TO ROBERT GRAHAM, ESQ. OF FINTRY.

5TH OCTOBER 1791.

LATE crippl'd of an arm, and now a leg,
About to beg a pass for leave to beg ;
Dull, listless, teas'd, dejected, and deprest
(Nature is adverse to a cripple's rest) ;
Will generous Graham list to his Poet's wail ?
(It soothes poor Misery, hearkening to her tale)
And hear him curse the light he first survey'd,
And doubly curse the luckless rhyming trade ?

Thou, Nature ! partial Nature, I arraign ;
Of thy caprice maternal I complain :
The lion and the bull thy care have found,
One shakes the forests, and one spurns the ground ;
Thou giv'st the ass his hide, the snail his shell ;
Th' envenom'd wasp, victorious, guards his cell ;
Thy minions kings defend, control, devour,
In all th' omnipotence of rule and power ;

Foxes and statesmen subtile wiles ensure ;
The cit and polecat stink, and are secure ;
Toads with their poison, doctors with their drug,
The priest and hedgehog in their robes, are snug ;
Ev'n silly woman has her warlike arts,
Her tongue and eyes—her dreaded spear and darts.

But Oh ! thou bitter step-mother and hard,
To thy poor, fenceless, naked child—the Bard !
A thing unteachable in world's skill,
And half an idiot too, more helpless still :
No heels to bear him from the op'ning dun ;
No claws to dig, his hated sight to shun ;
No horns, but those by luckless Hymen worn,
And those, alas ! not, Amalthea's horn :
No nerves olfact'ry, Mammon's trusty cur,
Clad in rich Dulness' comfortable fur ;
In naked feeling, and in aching pride,
He bears th' unbroken blast from ev'ry side :
Vampyre booksellers drain him to the heart,
And scorpion critics cureless venom dart :

Critics—appall'd, I venture on the name ;
Those cut-throat bandits in the paths of fame :
Bloody dissectors, worse than ten Monroes ;
He hacks to teach, they mangle to expose :

His heart by causeless wanton malice wrung,
By blockheads' daring into madness stung ;
His well-won bays, than life itself more dear,
By miscreants torn, who ne'er one sprig must wear ;
Foil'd, bleeding, tortur'd in th' unequal strife,
The hapless Poet flounders on thro' life :
Till, fled each hope that once his bosom fir'd,
And fled each muse that glorious once inspir'd,
Low sunk in squalid, unprotected age,
Dead even resentment for his injur'd page,

He heeds or feels no more the ruthless critic's rage !
So, by some hedge, the gen'rous steed deceas'd,
For half-starv'd snarling curs a dainty feast ;
By toil and famine wore to skin and bone,
Lies, senseless of each tugging bitch's son.

O Dulness ! portion of the truly blest !
Calm shelter'd haven of eternal rest !
Thy sons ne'er madden in the fierce extremes
Of Fortune's polar frost, or torrid beams.
If mantling high she fills the golden cup,
With sober selfish ease they sip it up ;
Conscious the bounteous meed they well deserve,
They only wonder " some folks " do not starve.
The grave sage hern thus easy picks his frog,
And thinks the mallard a sad worthless dog.
When disappointment snaps the clue of hope,
And thro' disastrous night they darkling grope,
With deaf endurance sluggishly they bear,
And just conclude " that fools are fortune's care."
So, heavy, passive to the tempest's shocks,
Strong on the sign-post stands the stupid ox.

Not so the idle Muses' mad-cap train,
Not such the workings of their moon-struck brain ;
In equanimity they never dwell,
By turns in soaring heav'n, or vaulted hell.

I dread thee, Fate, relentless and severe,
With all a poet's, husband's, father's fear !
Already one strong hold of hope is lost—
Glencairn, the truly noble, lies in dust
(Fled, like the sun eclips'd as noon appears,
And left us darkling in a world of tears) :
O ! hear my ardent, grateful, selfish pray'r !
Fintry, my other stay, long bless and spare !
Thro' a long life his hopes and wishes crown,

And bright in cloudless skies his sun go down !
May bliss domestic smooth his private path ;
Give energy to life ; and soothe his latest breath,
With many a filial tear circling the bed of death !

[The opening lines refer to the fact that about the end of March 1791, the poet had the misfortune to come down with his horse, and break his right arm. He soon recovered from that mishap, but about the close of the following September he experienced a similar accident, by which his leg was broken or sadly bruised. In sending the poem which forms the text he thus wrote :—" Along with two other pieces, I enclose you a sheetful of groans, wrung from me in my elbow-chair, with one unlucky leg on a stool before me."]

THE SONG OF DEATH.

Scene.—A Field of Battle—Time of the day, evening—The wounded and dying of the victorious army are supposed to join in the following song.

FAREWELL, thou fair day, thou green earth and ye skies,
    Now gay with the broad setting sun ;
Farewell, loves and friendships, ye dear tender ties,
    Our race of existence is run !
Thou grim King of Terrors ; thou Life's gloomy foe !
    Go, frighten the coward and slave ;
Go, teach them to tremble, fell tyrant ! but know
    No terrors hast thou to the brave !

Thou strik'st the dull peasant—he sinks in the dark,
    Nor saves e'en the wreck of a name ;
Thou strik'st the young hero—a glorious mark ;
    He falls in the blaze of his fame !
In the field of proud honor—our swords in our hands,
    Our king and our country to save ;
While victory shines on Life's last ebbing sands,—
    O who would not die with the brave ?

[This appears to be the last composition produced by Burns before leaving Ellisland to take up his abode in the town of Dumfries.

In sending this piece to Mrs Dunlop he wrote thus :—"I have just finished the following song, which, to a lady the descendant of Wallace, and many heroes of his illustrious line, and herself the mother of several soldiers,

needs neither preface nor apology." And, under the words, he added—
"The circumstance that gave rise to it was—looking over, with a musical
friend, M'Donald's Collection of Highland airs, I was struck with one, an
Isle of Skye tune, entitled 'Oran an Aoig, or The Song of Death,' to the
measure of which I have adapted my stanzas."]

POEM ON SENSIBILITY.

SENSIBILITY, how charming,
    Dearest Nancy, thou canst tell ;
But distress, with horrors arming,
    Thou alas ! hast known too well !

Fairest flower, behold the lily
    Blooming in the sunny ray ;
Let the blast sweep o'er the valley,
    See it prostrate in the clay.

Hear the woodlark charm the forest,
    Telling o'er his little joys ;
But alas ! a prey the surest
    To each pirate of the skies.

Dearly bought the hidden treasure
    Finer feelings can bestow :
Chords that vibrate sweetest pleasure,
    Thrill the deepest notes of woe.

[For some years the correspondence between Burns and Mrs M'Lehose
had entirely ceased ; for she still retained the unforgiving attitude which
broken hopes and wounded pride forced her to assume on hearing of the
poet's marriage to Jean Armour in April or May 1788. In the autumn of
1791, however, she made overtures towards reconciliation by sending him
some verses she had lately composed. In his reply he says : "I have perused your most beautiful, but most pathetic poem—do not ask me how often,
or with what emotions. You know that 'I dare to *sin*, but not to lie !'
Your verses wring the confession from my inmost soul, that—I will say it,
expose it if you please—I have more than once in my life been the victim of
a damning conjuncture of circumstances; and that to me you must be ever

    'Dear as the light that visits those sad eyes.'

    I have just, since I had yours, composed the following stanzas; let me
know your opinion of them.

        Sensibility, how charming, &c."]

Versicles produced prior to A.D. 1792.

THE TOADEATER.

Of Lordly acquaintance you boast,
　And the Dukes that you dined with yestreen ;
Why, an insect's an insect at most,
　Tho' it crawl on the curl of a Queen !

[Allan Cunningham, in his Biography of our Poet, tells us that "at the table of Maxwell of Terraughty, when one of the guests chose to talk of the Dukes and Earls with whom he had drank or dined, Burns silenced him with an epigram, thus :—

"What of Earls with whom you have supt ?
　And of Dukes that you dined with yestreen ?
Lord ! an insect's an insect at most,
　Tho' it crawl on the curls of a Queen."

These epigrams are differently quoted by the various editors. Thus Chambers, in 1838, gave the following version of this trifle :—

"No more of your titled acquaintances boast,
　And what nobles and gentles you've seen ;
An insect is only an insect at most,
　Tho' it crawl on the curl of a queen."]

DIVINE SERVICE IN THE KIRK OF LAMINGTON.

As cauld a wind as ever blew,
A caulder kirk, and in't but few :
A caulder Preacher never spak—
Ye'se a' be het or I come back.

[Lamington is in Clydesdale, and the poet occasionally tarried for a day or two in that neighbourhood.]

THE KEEKIN GLASS.

How daur ye ca' me " Howlet-face " ?
    Ye blear-e'ed, withered spectre !
Ye only spied the keekin-glass,
    An there ye saw your picture.

[The history of this curious epigram is thus given :—Burns one day visited his landlord, Mr Miller, at Dalswinton house ; and Miss Miller, in answer to some complimentary remark from the poet about her blooming looks, told him that she had been much less commended on the previous evening. One of the Lords of Justiciary from the circuit court at Dumfries happened to be dining with her father, and the gentlemen sat over their cups a considerable time after dinner. When they joined the ladies in the drawing room, his lordship's visual organs were so much affected that, pointing to Miss Miller, he asked her father,—"Wha's yon howlet-faced thing i' the corner."

Burns immediately pulled out his pencil and wrote on a slip of paper the above lines, which he handed to Miss Miller, saying—"There is the answer you should send him."]

A GRACE BEFORE DINNER, EXTEMPORE.

O thou who kindly dost provide
    For every creature's want !
We bless Thee, God of Nature wide,
    For all Thy goodness lent :

And if it please Thee, heavenly Guide,
    May never worse be sent ;
But, whether granted or denied,
    Lord, bless us with content.   Amen !

A GRACE AFTER DINNER, EXTEMPORE.

O Thou, in whom we live and move—
    Who made the sea and shore ;
Thy goodness constantly we prove,
    And, grateful, would adore :

And, if it please Thee, Power above !
Still grant us, with such store,
The friend we trust, the fair we love—
And we desire no more.   Amen !

[Both of these expressions of thankfulness and devotion are happily conceived.

Currie has given us interesting particulars of a visit paid to the poet at
his farm in the summer of 1790, by Mr Ramsay of Ochtertyre, accompanied
by Dr Stuart of Luss. "I was much pleased (related Mr Ramsay) with
his *uxor Sabina qualis*, and the poet's modest mansion, so unlike the
habitation of ordinary rustics. . . . Such was the force and versatility of the
bard's genius, that he made the tears run down Dr Stuart's cheeks, albeit
unused to melting mood. . . . From that time we met no more, and I was
grieved at the reports of him afterwards : poor Burns ! we shall hardly ever
see his like again ! He was, in truth, a sort of comet in literature, irregular
in its motion, which did not do good proportioned to the blaze of light it
displayed."—Fair and softly, Mr Ramsay ! we shall have to " wait a little
longer "—say, a century or two—before philosophers can measure the
"good" of such a spirit as that of Burns.

"So triumphs the Bard ! he hath pass'd from our sight,
    But his thoughts, like the power of the sun,
Shall continue the light of their truth and their might,
    Till the aim of their mission be won."

In the summer of 1791 (that which, with our reader, we have just been
passing through,) he was visited at Ellisland " by two English gentlemen :"
Currie gives the account from the information of one of the party : "He
received them with great cordiality, and asked them to share his humble
dinner—an invitation which they accepted. After dinner, he produced his
punch-bowl, made of Inverary marble, and mixing the spirit from the bottle
which Mrs Burns set on the board, with water and sugar, he filled their
glasses, and invited them to drink. Burns was in his happiest mood, and
the charms of his conversation were altogether fascinating. In the wildest
of his strains of mirth, he threw in touches of melancholy, and spread around
him the electric emotions of his powerful mind. The Highland whisky
improved in its flavour : the marble-bowl was again and again emptied and
replenished : the guests forgot the flight of time and the dictates of prudence :
at the hour of midnight they lost their way in returning to Dumfries, and
could scarcely distinguish the town even when assisted by the morning's
dawn."

Ellisland, with its scaur over the flowing Nith, from the brow of which
the poet used to glower and spell, with a westlin look in the direction of
Corsincone, must now be abandoned. To Dumfries "with darkening or
illusive prospects, and dubious patronage, he must go! Multitudinous
temptations, and uncertain footing" await him there : "sycophants, and

III.   C

spies, and tale-bearers to government, and to posterity," shall encompass his path; but his stay shall be brief—not so much as five years in duration. His genius with its elevating instincts shall bear him through the ordeal, and the music of his minstrelsy shall not cease to be heard—even when the Bard seems "to know existence only by the pressure of the heavy hand of sickness, and to count time by the repercussions of pain."]

The Dumfries Period.

(Nov. 1791, to July 1796.)

" George the Third is Defender of something we call 'the Faith' in those years; George the Third is head charioteer of the Destinies of England, to guide them through the gulph of French Revolutions, American Independencies, &c.; and Robert Burns is Gauger of ale in Dumfries. It is an Iliad in a nutshell. We find a Poet, as brave a man as has been made for a hundred years or so, anywhere under the sun; and do we kindle bonfires, or thank the gods? Not at all. We, taking due counsel of it, set the man to gauge ale-barrels in the Burgh of Dumfries; and pique ourselves on our 'patronage of genius.' "—*Carlyle's* " *Past and Present*," Book 2, Chap. ix.

THE DEAREST O' THE QUORUM.

O MAY, thy morn was ne'er sae sweet
　　As the mirk night o' December !
For sparkling was the rosy wine,
　　And private was the chamber :
And dear was she I dare na name,
　　But I will ay remember :
And dear was she I dare na name,
　　But I will ay remember.

And here's to them that, like oursel,
　　Can push about the jorum !
And here's to them that wish us weel,
　　May a' that's gude watch o'er 'em !
And here's to them, we dare na tell,
　　The dearest o' the quorum !
And here's to them, we dare na tell,
　　The dearest o' the quorum.

[On 23rd November Burns wrote to Clarinda from Dumfries, informing her that he would be in Edinburgh on the first Tuesday thereafter. That lady (as Chambers explains) "was now approaching a critical passage of her own history. She had resolved, though with much hesitation, to accept an invitation from her heartless husband, and join him in Jamaica. A parting interview took place between her and Burns in Edinburgh specially on the 6th of December. That it gave an occasion to an effusion of passionate feeling, is strongly hinted at in a letter of the poet written a twelvemonth after. We may also hesitate little in reading as a record of the scene a series of lyrics, one of which is amongst the most earnest and arresting expressions of intense feeling ever composed in verse." This remark refers to the three songs we next proceed to lay before the reader. That which now forms the text appears to be a dash-off, but warmly coloured, reminiscence of the same private interview, disrobed of the passionately sentimental aspect which pervades the lyrics he communicated to the lady herself.]

PARTING SONG TO CLARINDA.

AE fond kiss, and then we sever ;
Ae farewell, and then forever !
Deep in heart-wrung tears I'll pledge thee,
Warring sighs and groans I'll wage thee.
Who shall say that Fortune grieves him,
While the star of hope she leaves him ?
Me, nae cheerful twinkle lights me ;
Dark despair around benights me.

I'll ne'er blame my partial fancy,
Naething could resist my Nancy :
But to see her was to love her ;
Love but her, and love for ever.
Had we never lov'd sae kindly,
Had we never lov'd sae blindly,
Never met—or never parted,
We had ne'er been broken-hearted.

Fare-thee-weel, thou first and fairest !
Fare-thee-weel, thou best and dearest !
Thine be ilka joy and treasure,
Peace, Enjoyment, Love and Pleasure !

Ae fond kiss, and then we sever !
Ae farewell, alas, for ever !
Deep in heart-wrung tears I'll pledge thee,
Warring sighs and groans I'll wage thee.

[This impassioned lyric was posted to Mrs M'Lehose in a letter from
Dumfries on 27th December 1791, and contained also the two songs which
immediately follow, on the same subject. The latter half of stanza *second*
was used by Byron as a motto for his " Bride of Abydos." Sir Walter Scott
remarked that these four lines " contain the essence of a thousand love
tales ; " and Mrs Jameson eloquently added that the lines are " in themselves
a complete romance—the alpha and omega of feeling. and contain the
essence of an existence of pain and pleasure distilled into one burning
drop."]

BEHOLD THE HOUR, THE BOAT, ARRIVE.

BEHOLD the hour, the boat, arrive !
My dearest Nancy, O fareweel !
Severed frae thee, can I survive,
Frae thee whom I hae lov'd sae weel ?

Endless and deep shall be my grief ;
Nae ray of comfort shall I see,
But this most precious, dear belief,
That thou wilt still remember me !

Alang the solitary shore
Where flitting sea-fowl round me cry,
Across the rolling, dashing roar,
I'll westward turn my wishful eye.

' Happy thou Indian grove,' I'll say,
' Where now my Nancy's path shall be !
While thro' your sweets she holds her way,
O tell me, does she muse on me ? '

[These verses, sent on 27th December 1791 to Clarinda, pleased Burns so
much that in September 1793, he subjected them to some farther polishing
to appear in George Thomson's collection set to a Gaelic air, called " Oran
Gaoil."]

THOU GLOOMY DECEMBER.

ANCE mair I hail thee, thou gloomy December!
   Ance mair I hail thee wi' sorrow and care ;
Sad was the parting thou makes me remember
   Parting wi' Nancy, oh, ne'er to meet mair !

Fond lovers' parting is sweet, painful pleasure,
   Hope beaming mild on the soft parting hour ;
But the dire feeling, O farewell for ever !
   Anguish unmingled, and agony pure !

Wild as the winter now tearing the forest,
   Till the last leaf o' the summer is flown,
Such is the tempest has shaken my bosom,
   Till my last hope and last comfort is gone.

Still as I hail thee, thou gloomy December,
   Still shall I hail thee wi' sorrow and care ;
For sad was the parting thou makes me remember,
   Parting wi' Nancy, oh, ne'er to meet mair.

[Only the two opening stanzas of this song were forwarded to Clarinda in the poet's letter to her of 27th December, which closes with these verses, followed by the words—"The rest of this song is on the wheels." The remainder was added some time after.]

MY NATIVE LAND SAE FAR AWA.

O SAD and heavy, should I part,
   But for her sake, sae far awa ;
Unknowing what my way may thwart,
   My native land sae far awa.

Thou that of a' things Maker art,
   That formed this Fair sae far awa,
Gie body strength, then I'll ne'er start,
   At this my way sae far awa.

How true is love to pure desert !
Like mine for her sae far awa ;
And nocht shall heal my bosom's smart,
While, oh, she is sae far awa !

Nane other love, nane other dart,
I feel but her's sae far awa ;
But fairer never touch'd a heart
Than her's, the Fair, sae far awa.

[This song would almost pass for one of the series composed at this period in reference to the author's parting with Clarinda. Others have been pressed into the same service by some of the poet's editors, such as "My Nannie's Awa," "Wandering Willie," &c.; but the dates of these are considerably later, as may be ascertained from the Thomson correspondence.]

LINES ON FERGUSSON, THE POET.

ILL-FATED genius ! Heaven-taught Fergusson,
What heart that feels and will not yield a tear,
To think Life's sun did set e'er well begun
To shed its influence on thy bright career.

O why should truest Worth and Genius pine
Beneath the iron grasp of Want and Woe,
While titled knaves and idiot-Greatness shine
In all the splendour Fortune can bestow?

[Chambers assigns this little effusion to the early portion of 1792, and informs us that the poet had inscribed the lines on a blank leaf of a publication, called *The World*, which we find he ordered from Peter Hill on 2nd February 1790.]

I DO CONFESS THOU ART SAE FAIR.

ALTERATION OF AN OLD POEM.

I DO confess thou art sae fair,
I wad been o'er the lugs in luve,
Had I na found the slightest prayer
That lips could speak thy heart could muve:

I do confess thee sweet, but find
   Thou art so thriftless o' thy sweets,
Thy favours are the silly wind
   That kisses ilka thing it meets.

See yonder rosebud, rich in dew,
   Amang its native briers sae coy ;
How sune it tines its scent and hue,
   When pu'd and worn a common toy ;

Sic fate ere lang shall thee betide,
   Tho' thou may gaily bloom awhile ;
And sune thou shalt be thrown aside,
   Like ony common weed and vile.

[The poet in his Glenriddell Notes says :—" This song is altered from a
poem by Sir Robert Aytoun, private secretary to Mary and Anne, Queens
of Scotland. I do think that I have improved the simplicity of the sentiments by giving them a Scots dress."]

THE WEARY PUND O' TOW.

Chorus—The weary pund, the weary pund,
      The weary pund o' tow ;
   I think my wife will end her life,
      Before she spin her tow.

I BOUGHT my wife a stane o' lint,
   As gude as e'er did grow,
And a' that she has made o' that
   Is ae puir pund o' tow,
      The weary pund, &c.

There sat a bottle in a bole,
   Ayont the ingle low ;
And aye she took the tither souk,
   To drouk the stourie tow,
      The weary pund, &c.

Quoth I, for shame, ye dirty dame,
Gae spin your tap o' tow !
She took the rock, and wi' a knock,
She brake it o'er my pow,
The weary pund, &c.

At last her feet—I sang to see't !
Gaed foremost o'er the knowe,
And or I wad anither jad,
I'll wallop in a tow,
The weary pund, &c.

[This was a favourite subject among the old song writers. In a later
edition of Herd's Collection (1791) we find the following :-

" If my wife and thy wife
    Were in a boat thegither,
And yon honest man's wife
    Were there to steer the ruther .
And if the boat was bottomless,
    And seven miles to row :
We ne'er would wish them back again
    To spin their taps o' tow."

Burns is undoubtedly the author of the version of the song which forms the
text. The title and music are taken from Oswald's Caledonian Pocket
Companion, Book 8. The tune has been much admired and was selected
to suit Mr Graham of Gartmore's chivalrous words, published by Sir Walter
Scott in the Border Minstrelsy. The first verse will indicate the song.

" If doughty deeds my ladye please,
    Right soon I'll mount my steed ;
And strong his arm and fast his seat,
    That bears from me the meed,
I'll wear thy colours in my cap,
    Thy picture in my heart :
And he that bends not to thine eye
    Shall rue it to his smart,
Chorus.—Then tell me how to woo thee, love,
    O tell me how to woo thee !
For thy dear sake, nae care I'll take,
    Tho' ne'er another trow me."]

WHEN SHE CAM' BEN SHE BOBBET

O WHEN she cam' ben she bobbet fu' low,
O when she cam' ben she bobbet fu' low,
And when she cam' ben, she kiss'd Cockpen,
    And syne she deny'd she did it ava.

And was na Cockpen right saucy witha'?
And was na Cockpen right saucy witha'?
In leaving the daughter o' a lord,
    And kissin' a collier lassie an' a'!

O never look down, my lassie, at a',
O never look down, my lassie, at a',
Thy lips are as sweet, and thy figure complete,
    As the finest dame in castle or ha.'

Tho' thou hast nae silk, and holland sae sma',
Tho' thou hast nae silk, and holland sae sma',
Thy coat and thy sark are thy ain handywark,
    And lady Jean was never sae braw.

[This is certainly more of a dressed-up old ballad than an original song.
Such as it is, however, it was destined to give the hint to Lady Nairne, out
of which issued her famous ballad—

    "The Laird o' Cockpen, he's proud and he's great."

The air of this song is so familiar that it needs not to be given here.]

SCROGGAM, MY DEARIE.

THERE was a wife wonn'd in Cockpen,
        Scroggam ;
She brew'd gude ale for gentlemen ;
    Sing auld Cowl, lay ye down by me,
        Scroggam, my dearie. ruffum.

The gudewife's dochter fell in a fever,
    Scroggam ;
The priest o' the parish he fell in anither ;
    Sing auld Cowl lay ye down by me,
      Scroggam, my dearie, ruffum.

They laid them side by side thegither,
    Scroggam ;
That the heat o' the taen might cool the tither ;
    Sing auld Cowl, lay ye down by me,
      Scroggam, my dearie, ruffum.

[This singular song has Burns's name attached to it in the *Museum*.
We place it here in consequence of its connection with the preceding song,
so far as locality is concerned. Cockpen is a neat village a few miles south
from Edinburgh, with a parish church, of which Lord Dalhousie is the
patron.]

MY COLLIER LADDIE.

WHARE live ye, my bonie lass?
    And tell me what they ca' ye ;
My name, she says, is mistress Jean,
    And I follow the Collier laddie.
         My name, she says, &c.

See you not yon hills and dales
    The sun shines on sae brawlie ;
They a' are mine, and they shall be thine,
    Gin ye'll leave your Collier laddie.
         They a' are mine, &c.

Ye shall gang in gay attire,
    Weel buskit up sae gaudy ;
And ane to wait on every hand,
    Gin ye'll leave your Collier laddie.
         And ane to wait, &c.

Tho' ye had a' the sun shines on,
  And the earth conceals sae lowly,
I wad turn my back on you and it a',
  And embrace my Collier laddie.
                    I wad turn my back, &c.

I can win my five pennies in a day,
  An' spend it at night fu' brawlie ;
And make my bed in the collier's neuk,
  And lie down wi' my Collier laddie.
                    And make my bed, &c.

Loove for loove is the bargain for me,
  Tho' the wee cot-house should haud me ;
And the warld before me to win my bread,
  And fair fa' my Collier laddie !
                    And the warld before me, &c.

[This is one of those songs—never seen or heard in the world before the poet picked it up, both words and music, "from the singing of a country girl."]

SIC A WIFE AS WILLIE HAD.

WILLIE WASTLE dwalt on Tweed,
  The spot they ca'd it Linkumdoddie ;*
Willie was a wabster† gude,
  Could stoun‡ a clue wi' ony body :
He had a wife was dour§ and din,||
  O Tinkler Maidgie was her mither ;
Sic a wife as Willie had,
  I wad na gie a button for her.

She has an e'e, she has but ane,
  The cat has twa the very colour ;

| * an imaginary locality. | † weaver. | ‡ stolen. |
| § sulky. | || ill-coloured. | |

Five rusty teeth forbye a stump,
   A clapper tongue wad deave* a miller :
A whiskin beard about her mou,†
   Her nose and chin they threaten ither ;
Sic a wife as Willie had,
   I wad na gie a button for her.

She's bow-hough'd,‡ she's hen-shin'd, §
   Ae limpin leg a hand-breed shorter ; ‖
She's twisted right, she's twisted left,
   To balance fair in ilka quarter :
She has a hump upon her breast,
   The twin o' that upon her shouther ;
Sic a wife as Willie had,
   I wad na gie a button for her.

Auld baudrans ¶ by the ingle ** sits
   An' wi' her loof †† her face a washin ;
But Willie's wife is nae sae trig,
   She dights her grunzie ‡‡ wi' a hushion : §§
Her walie nieves ‖‖ like midden-creels, ¶¶
   Her face wad fyle *** the Logan Water ;
Sic a wife as Willie had,
   I wad na gie a button for her

[Cunningham tells us that the heroine was the wife of a farmer who lived near Ellisland. Mrs Renwick of New York (the "blue-eyed lassie" of Burns's song) refers to this matter thus : "Cunningham says, the name of Willie Wastle's wife is lost ; I could tell him who she was, but there is no use in opening up old sores."]

---

* deafen.   † mouth.   ‡ crooked in the hip-joint.
§ shot ankles like a hen.
‖ one leg shorter than its fellow by a hand-breadth.   ¶ cat.
** fireside.   †† paw.   ‡‡ pig-shaped mouth.
§§ a stocking leg with the feet cut off, worn over the arms in winter.
‖‖ powerful fists.   ¶¶ baskets for removing manure.   *** pollute.

LADY MARY ANN.

O LADY Mary Ann looks o'er the Castle wa',
She saw three bonie boys playing at the ba',
The youngest he was the flower amang them a',
    My bonie laddie's young, but he's growin' yet.

O father, O father, an ye think it fit,
We'll send him a year to the college yet,
We'll sew a green ribbon round about his hat,
    And that will let them ken he's to marry yet.

Lady Mary Ann was a flower in the dew,
Sweet was its smell and bonie was its hue,
And the longer it blossom'd the sweeter it grew,
    For the lily in the bud will be bonier yet.

Young Charlie Cochran was the sprout of an aik,
Bonie and bloomin' and straught was its make,
The sun took delight to shine for its sake,
    And it will be the brag o' the forest yet.

The simmer is gane when the leaves they were green,
And the days are awa' that we hae seen,
But far better days I trust will come again ;
    For my bonie laddie's young, but he's growin' yet.

[This ballad is said to be founded on a real incident dating about 1634.
The young Urquhart of Craigston, who by the death of his parents had fallen
into the guardianship of the laird of Innes, was married, while yet a youth,
to his daughter Elizabeth Innes, with the object of securing his estates.
The closing verse of the original ballad is thus given:—

    " In his twelfth year, he was a married man,
      In his thirteenth year, there he gat a son,
      In his fourteenth year, his grave was growing green,
      And that was the end of his growing."]

KELLY BURN BRAES.

THERE leevit a carl in Kelly Burn Braes,[1]
　　Hey, and the rue grows bonie wi' thyme;
And he had a wife was the plague o' his days,
　　And the thyme it is wither'd, and rue is in prime.

Ae day as the carl gaed up the lang glen,
　　Hey, and the rue grows bonie wi' thyme;
He met wi' the Deil, wha said, " How do you fen?"
　　And the thyme it is wither'd, and rue is in prime.

" I've got a bad wife, sir, that's a' my complaint,
　　Hey, and the rue grows bonie wi' thyme;
For, saving your presence, to her ye're a saint,
　　And the thyme it is wither'd, and rue is in prime."

" It's neither your stot nor your staig I shall crave,
　　Hey, and the rue grows bonie wi' thyme;
But gie me your wife, man, for her I must have,
　　And the thyme it is wither'd, and rue is in prime."

" O welcome most kindly!" the blythe carl said,
　　" Hey, and the rue grows bonie wi' thyme;
But if ye can match her ye're waur than ye're ca'd,
　　And the thyme it is wither'd, and rue is in prime."

The Devil has got the auld wife on his back,
　　Hey, and the rue grows bonie wi' thyme;
And like a poor pedlar he's carried his pack,
　　And the thyme it is wither d, and rue is in prime.

---

[1] The Kelly Burn is the northern boundary of Ayrshire, and divides the
parish of Largs from Renfrewshire for upwards of two miles, and flows into
the firth of Clyde at Kelly Bridge. Further east, the boundary is marked
by "the Rowtin Burn," and the locality is called "The Back o' the
Warld."

He's carried her hame to his ain hallan door,
    Hey, and the rue grows bonie wi' thyme ;
Syne bade her gae in for a b—, and a w—,
    And the thyme it is wither'd, and rue is in prime.

Then straight he makes fifty, the pick o' his band,
    Hey, and the rue grows bonie wi' thyme ;
Turn out on her guard in the clap o' a hand,
    And the thyme it is wither'd, and rue is in prime.

The carlin gaed thro' them like ony wud bear,
    Hey, and the rue grows bonie wi' thyme ;
Whae'er she gat hands on cam' ne'er her nae mair,
    And the thyme it is wither'd, and rue is in prime.

A reekit wee deevil looks over the wa',
    Hey, and the rue grows bonie wi' thyme ;
" O help, maister, help, or she'll ruin us a'!"
    And the thyme it is wither'd, and rue is in prime.

The Devil he swore by the edge o' his knife,
    Hey, and the rue grows bonie wi' thyme :
He pitied the man that was tied to a wife,
    And the thyme it is wither'd, and rue is in prime

The Devil he swore by the kirk and the bell,
    Hey, and the rue grows bonie wi' thyme ;
He was not in wedlock, thank Heav'n, but in hell,
    And the thyme it is wither'd, and rue is in prime.

Then Satan has travell'd again wi' his pack,
    Hey, and the rue grows bonie wi' thyme ;
And to her auld husband he's carried her back,
    And the thyme it is wither'd, and rue is in prime.

" I hae been a Deevil the feck o' my life,
    Hey, and the rue grows bonie wi' thyme ;

But ne'er was in hell till I met wi' a wife,
  And the thyme it is wither'd, and rue is in prime."

[This ballad displays the genius of Burns, perhaps, as decidedly as his
"Tam o' Shanter." There is a sort of original ballad which suggested it,
an English production called "The Farmer's old Wife," which is given at
length in No. 62 of the Percy Society's Publications.]

THE SLAVE'S LAMENT.

IT was in sweet Senegal that my foes did me enthral,
  For the lands of Virginia, ginia O :
Torn from that lovely shore, and must never see it more;
  And alas ! I am weary, weary O :
Torn from that lovely shore, and must never see it more ;
  And alas ! I am weary, weary O.

All on that charming coast is no bitter snow and frost,
  Like the lands of Virginia, ginia O :
There streams for ever flow, and the flowers for ever blow,
  And alas ! I am weary, weary O :
There streams for ever flow, and flowers for ever blow,
  And alas ! I am weary, weary, O.

The burden I must bear, while the cruel scourge I fear,
  In the lands of Virginia, ginia O ;
And I think on friends most dear, with the bitter, bitter
    tear,
  And alas ! I am weary, weary O :
And I think on friends most dear, with the bitter, bitter
    tear,
  And alas ! I am weary, weary O.

[Both words and melody of this very tender production were communicated
by Burns to Johnson; the air is supposed to be native African. Mr C. K.
Sharpe gives a stall-copy of a somewhat similar subject called "The
Betrayed Maid," which is of the most prosaic character.]

O CAN YE LABOR LEA?

Chorus—O can ye labor lea, young man,
O can ye labor lea?
It fee nor bountith shall us twine
Gin ye can labor lea.

I FEE'D a man at Michaelmas,
Wi' airle pennies three ;
But a' the faut I had to him,
He could na labor lea,
O can ye labor lea, &c.

O clappin's gude in Febarwar,
An' kissin's sweet in May ;
But my delight's the ploughman lad,
That weel can labor lea,
O can ye labor lea, &c.

O kissin is the key o' luve,
And clappin is the lock ;
An' makin o's the best thing yet,
That e'er a young thing gat.
O can ye labour lea, &c.

[It is explained by farmers that to "labour lea" is to plough soil that has lain for a considerable time in grass, and the tearing up of the spretty roots is rather a tough operation. The fine old melody attached to these words was called "The Miller's Daughter," or "Sir Alexander Don's Strathspey," and is now familiar over the whole globe as the air of Burns's "Auld Lang Syne."]

THE DEUK'S DANG O'ER MY DADDIE.

THE bairns gat out wi' an unco * shout,
The deuk's † dang ‡ o'er my daddie, O !
The fien-ma-care,§ quo' the feirrie‖ auld wife,
He was but a paidlin ¶ body, O !

---

* uncommon. † duck. ‡ knocked over. § devil-ma-care.
‖ hale, active. ¶ with shuffling gait.

He paidles out, and he paidles in,
    An' he paidles late and early, O !
This seven lang years I hae lien by his side,
    An' he is but a fusionless * carlie,† O.

O haud your tongue, my feirrie auld wife,
    O haud your tongue, now Nansie, O :
I've seen the day, and sae hae ye,
    Ye wad na been sae donsie,‡ O.
I've seen the day ye butter'd my brose,
    And cuddl'd me late and early, O ;
But downa-do's § come o'er me now,
    And och, I find it sairly, O !

[This picture of senile frailty has its key-note struck in the opening couplet by proclaiming the fact that a duck, in running between the feet of the little old man, has overturned him in the gutter. The tune is old, and was a favourite in England so early as 1657, when it was included in Playford's " Dancing Master," under the title of " The Buff Coat."

THE DEIL'S AWA WI' TH' EXCISEMAN.

THE deil cam fiddlin thro' the town,
    And danc'd awa wi' th' Exciseman,
And ilka wife cries, " Auld Mahoun,
    I wish you luck o' the prize, man."

    Chorus—The deil's awa, the deil's awa,
        The deil's awa wi' th' Exciseman,
        He's danc'd awa, he's danc'd awa,
        He's danc'd awa wi' th' Exciseman.

---

* sapless, feckless.   † little old man.
‡ troublesome, wanton.   § incapacity

We'll mak our maut, and we'll brew our drink,
  We'll laugh, sing, and rejoice, man,
And mony braw thanks to the meikle black deil,
  That danc'd awa wi' th' Exciseman.
          The deil's awa, &c.

There's threesome reels, there's foursome reels,
  There's hornpipes and strathspeys, man,
But the ae best dance ere cam to the land
  Was the deil's awa wi' th' Exciseman.
          The deil's awa, &c.

[Cromek's account of this song is that at a meeting of his brother Excise-men in Dumfries, Burns being called upon for a song, handed these verses extempore to the president, written on the back of a letter. That account (which was earliest given to the public) nearly tallies with the following passage in a letter of Burns addressed to the General Supervisor of Excise at Edinburgh :—" Mr Mitchell mentioned to you a ballad which I composed and sung at one of his Excise-court dinners, here it is—'The deil's awa wi' th' Exciseman,'—Tune, *Madam Cossy.* If you honour my ballad by making it one of your charming *bon-vivant* effusions, it will secure it undoubted celebrity " Lockhart's account is very circumstantial, thus :—"On 27th February 1792, a suspicious-looking brig was discovered in the Solway Firth, and Burns was one of the party whom the superintendent conducted to watch her motions. She got into shallow water, and the officers were enabled to discover that her crew were numerous, armed, and not likely to yield without a struggle." The account, which is rather prolix, goes on to state that Lewars was despatched to Dumfries for a guard of dragoons, and Burns, getting impatient at Lewar's protracted absence, employed himself by striding among the reeds and shingle humming to himself some ditty, which afterwards turned out to be the very song in the text that he had then been in the act of composing. Lewars at length arrived with the soldiers, and "Burns putting himself at the head of the party, waded, sword in hand, to the brig, and was the first to board her. The crew lost heart, and submitted, the vessel was condemned, and with all her arms and stores, sold by auction next day at Dumfries ; upon which occasion, Burns thought fit to bid for and secure four carronades, by way of trophy. But his glee went a step farther : he sent the guns, with a letter, to the French Assembly, requesting that body to accept of them as a mark of his admira-tion and respect. The present and its accompaniment were intercepted at Dover, and this would appear to be the principal circumstance that drew on Burns the notice of his jealous superiors."]

THE COUNTRY LASS.

IN simmer, when the hay was mawn,
   And corn wav'd green in ilka field,
While claver * blooms white o'er the lea
   And roses blaw in ilka bield ! †
Blythe Bessie in the milking shiel, ‡
   Says—I'll be wed, come o't what will :
Out spake a dame in wrinkled eild—§
   O' gude advisement comes nae ill.

It's ye hae wooers mony ane,
   And lassie, ye're but young ye ken ;
Then wait a wee, and cannie wale ‖
   A routhie butt, a routhie ben ; ¶
There's Johnie o' the Buskie-glen,
   Fu' is his barn, fu' is his byre ;
Tak this frae me, my bonie hen,
   It's plenty beets ** the luver's fire.

For Johnie o' the Buskie-glen,
   I dinna care a single flie ;
He lo'es sae weel his craps and kye,
   He has nae love to spare for me ;
But blythe's the blink o' Robie's e'e,
   And weel I wat he lo'es me dear :
Ae blink o' him I wad na gie
   For Buskie-glen and a' his gear.

O thoughtless lassie, life's a faught ;
   The canniest gate, the strife is sair ;
But ay fu'-han't is fechtin best, ††
   A hungry care's an unco care :

---

* clover.   † sheltered spot.   ‡ out-house for keeping milk.
§ old age.   ‖ select.   ¶ a well-provided house out and in.
** sustains.   †† It is best to fight with a full-hand.

But some will spend and some will spare,
 An' wilfu' folk maun hae their will;
Syne as ye brew, my maiden fair,
 Keep mind that ye maun drink the yill.

O gear will buy me rigs o' land,
 And gear will buy me sheep and kye;
But the tender heart o' leesome loove,
 The gowd and siller canna buy;
We may be poor—Robie and I—
 Light is the burden luve lays on;
Content and loove brings peace and joy—
 What mair hae Queens upon a throne?

[The poet has here very successfully adorned his favourite sentiments in love-matters, and finely contrasted the generous ardour of the young country-lass with the prudent, yet affectionate counsels of her experienced adviser.]

BESSY AND HER SPINNIN WHEEL.

O LEEZE * me on my spinnin-wheel,
And leeze me on my rock and reel;
Frae tap to tae that cleeds me bien, †
And haps me biel ‡ and warm at e'en,
I'll set me down and sing and spin,
While laigh descends the simmer sun,
Blest wi' content, and milk and meal,
O leeze me on my spinnin-wheel.

On ilka hand the burnies trot,
And meet below my theekit § cot;
The scented birk and hawthorn white,
Across the pool their arms unite,
Alike to screen the birdie's nest,
And little fishes' caller rest;

---

* commend me to.   † warm.   ‡ comfortable.   § thatched.

The sun blinks kindly in the biel', *
Where blythe I turn my spinnin-wheel.

On lofty aiks the cushats † wail,
And Echo cons the doolfu' tale ;
The lintwhites ‡ in the hazel braes,
Delighted, rival ither's lays ;
The craik § amang the claver‖ hay,
The pairtrick whirrin ¶ o'er the ley,
The swallow jinkin round my shiel, **
Amuse me at my spinnin-wheel.

Wi' sma' to sell and less to buy,
Aboon distress, below envy,
O wha wad leave this humble state,
For a' the pride of a' the great ?
Amid their flairing, idle toys,
Amid their cumbrous, dinsome joys,
Can they the peace and pleasure feel
Of Bessie at her spinnin-wheel ?

[Comfort, contentment, and industry combined, is here the poet's theme ;
and never was the subject treated with more felicity of expression in
descriptive song.]

FRAGMENTS OF SONG.

No cold approach, no altered mien,
　　Just what would make suspicion start ;
No pause the dire extremes between,
　　He made me blest—and broke my heart.

[These lines were inserted by Burns to complete the closing stanza of a
song by Miss Cranstoun, who became the second wife of Professor Dugald
Stewart, on 26th July 1790. The title of her song is " The tears I shed
must ever fall."]

| * sheltered cot. | † wild-pigeons. | ‡ linnets. | § corncraik. |
| ‖ clover. | ¶ partridge fluttering. | | ** cottage. |

LOVE FOR LOVE.

ITHERS seek they ken na what,
Features, carriage, and a' that ;
Gie me loove in her I court,
Loove to loove maks a' the sport.

Let loove sparkle in her e'e ;
Let her lo'e nae man but me ;
That's the tocher gude I prize,
There the luver's treasure lies.

[Burns has inserted these lines of his own to form the middle portion of a song in the Tea Table Miscellany, called "Jocky fou and Jenny fain," which Johnson has transplanted into the *Museum*]

FRAGMENT ON MARIA.

How gracefully Maria leads the dance !
She's life itself : I never saw a foot
So nimble and so elegant.   It speaks,
And the sweet whispering Poetry it makes
Shames the musician.

Adriano, or, The first of June.

[This elegant little fragment appears, in the poet's holograph, on the back of a MS. copy of the "Lament of Mary Queen of Scots" that apparently had been presented by the author to a lately acquired friend, Mrs Maria Riddell of Woodley Park, near Dumfries, wife of Mr Walter Riddell, a younger brother of Captain Riddell of Glenriddell.

The poet seems to have been introduced to this fascinating lady about the time he came to reside with his family in Dumfries.   Her mansion stood about four miles to the south of Dumfries.   She was as yet under twenty years of age, although a mother, and having a taste for literature and natural history, she delighted in the society of men of talent.   The vivid genius of Burns soon attracted her attention, and he became a frequent visitor at Woodley Park.]

SAW YE BONIE LESLEY.

O SAW ye bonie Lesley,
  As she gaed o'er the Border?
She's gane, like Alexander,
  To spread her conquests farther.

To see her is to love her,
  And love but her for ever;
For Nature made her what she is,
  And never made anither!

Thou art a queen, fair Lesley,
  Thy subjects, we before thee;
Thou art divine, fair Lesley,
  The hearts o' men adore thee.

The deil he could na scaith thee,
  Or aught that wad belang thee;
He'd look into thy bonie face,
  And say—'I canna wrang thee!'

The Powers aboon will tent thee,
  Misfortune sha'na steer thee;
Thou'rt like themsel' sae lovely,
  That ill they'll ne'er let near thee.

Return again, fair Lesley,
  Return to Caledonie!
That we may brag we hae a lass
  There's nane again sae bonie.

[The poet communicated the above to his friend and correspondent, Mrs Dunlop, in a letter dated "Annan Water-foot, 22nd August 1792." He wrote thus: "Do you know that I am almost in love with an acquaintance of yours? Almost! said I—I am in love, souce over head and ears, deep as the most unfathomable abyss of the boundless ocean!

"But let me do justice to the sacred purity of my attachment. The heart-struck awe, the distant humble approach, the delight we should have in gazing upon and listening to a messenger of Heaven, appearing in all the unspotted purity of his celestial home, among the coarse, polluted, far in-

ferior sons of men, to deliver to them tidings that make their hearts swim in joy, and their imaginations soar in transport—such, so delighting, and so pure, were the emotions of my soul on meeting the other day with Miss Lesley Baillie, your neighbour at Mayfield. Mr B., with his two daughters, accompanied by Mr H. of G., passing through Dumfries a few days ago, on their way to England, did me the honour of calling on me ; on which I took my horse—though, God knows, I could ill spare the time—and accompanied them fourteen or fifteen miles, and dined and spent the day with them. Twas about nine, I think, that I left them, and riding home, I composed the following ballad, of which you will probably think you have a dear bargain, as it will cost you another groat of postage. You must know that there is an old ballad beginning with :—

    ' My bonie Lizzie Baillie, I'll rowe thee in my plaidie,'

so I parodied it as follows, which is literally the first copy."

I'LL MEET THEE ON THE LEA RIG.

WHEN o'er the hill the e'ening star
   Tells bughtin time is near, my jo,
And owsen frae the furrow'd field
   Return sae dowf and weary O ;
Down by the burn, where birken buds
   Wi' dew are hangin' clear, my jo,
I'll meet thee on the lea-rig,
   My ain kind Dearie O.

At midnight hour, in mirkest glen,
   I'd rove, and ne'er be eerie O,
If thro' that glen I gaed to thee,
   My ain kind Dearie O ;
Altho' the night were ne'er sae wild,
   And I were ne'er sae weary O,
I'll meet thee on the lea-rig,
   My ain kind Dearie O.

The hunter lo'es the morning sun;
   To rouse the mountain deer, my jo ;
At noon the fisher takes the glen
   Adown the burn to steer, my jo :

Gie me the hour o' gloamin grey,
    It maks my heart sae cheery O,
To meet thee on the lea-rig,
    My ain kind Dearie O.

[This song, produced in October 1792, was the first that Burns supplied
for Thomson's Collection. That gentleman had sent him a list of eleven
songs for which he wished to substitute others by Burns, who, in sending
that which forms the text, remarked—"Let me tell you that you are too
fastidious in your ideas of songs and ballads: the songs you specify have
all, but one, the faults you remark in them; but who shall rise and say,
'Go to, I will make a better.' On reading over the *Lea-Rig*, I immediately
set about trying my hand on it, and after all, I could make nothing more
of it than the following, which, Heaven knows, is poor enough."]

MY WIFE'S A WINSOME WEE THING.

Ayr—" My Wife's a Wanton Wee Thing."

Chorus—She is a winsome wee thing,
        She is a handsome wee thing,
        She is a lo'esome wee thing,
            This dear wee wife o' mine.

    I NEVER saw a fairer,
    I never lo'ed a dearer,
    And neist my heart I'll wear her,
        For fear my jewel tine,
        She is a winsome, &c.

    The warld's wrack we share o't;
    The warstle and the care o't;
    Wi' her I'll blythely bear it,
        And think my lot divine.
        She is a winsome, &c.

[In communicating those unpretending, yet very pleasing and natural
words, to Thomson, Burns remarked—"If a few lines, smooth and pretty,
can be adapted to the tune, it is all you can expect. These were made
extempore to it; and though, on further study, I might give you something
more profound, yet it might not suit the light-horse gallop of the air so well
as this random clink."]

HIGHLAND MARY.

Tune—" Katherine Ogie."

YE banks and braes and streams around
   The castle o' Montgomery !
Green be your woods, and fair your flowers,
   Your waters never drumlie :
There Simmer first unfald her robes,
   And there the langest tarry ;
For there I took the last Farewell
   O' my sweet Highland Mary.

How sweetly bloom'd the gay, green birk,
   How rich the hawthorn's blossom,
As underneath their fragrant shade,
   I clasp'd her to my bosom !
The golden Hours on angel wings,
   Flew o'er me and my Dearie ;
For dear to me, as light and life,
   Was my sweet Highland Mary.

Wi' mony a vow, and lock'd embrace,
   Our parting was fu' tender ;
And, pledging aft to meet again,
   We tore oursels asunder ;
But oh ! fell Death's untimely frost,
   That nipt my Flower sae early !
Now green's the sod, and cauld's the clay.
   That wraps my Highland Mary !

O pale, pale now, those rosy lips,
   I aft hae kiss'd sae fondly !
And clos'd for ay, the sparkling glance
   That dwalt on me sae kindly !

And mouldering now in silent dust,
  That heart that lo'ed me dearly !
But still within my bosom's core
  Shall live my Highland Mary.

[In sending this to Thomson on 14th November 1792, the bard wrote
thus :—"The foregoing song pleases myself, I think it is in my happiest
manner; you will see at first glance that it suits the air. The subject of
the song is one of the most interesting passages of my youthful days; and
I own that I would be much flattered to see the verses set to an air which
would insure celebrity. Perhaps, after all, 'tis the still glowing prejudice
of my heart that throws a borrowed lustre over the merits of the
composition."]

THE RIGHTS OF WOMAN.

AN OCCASIONAL ADDRESS

SPOKEN BY MISS FONTENELLE ON HER BENEFIT NIGHT, NOVEMBER 26, 1792.

WHILE Europe's eye is fix'd on mighty things,
The fate of empires and the fall of kings ;
While quacks of State must each produce his plan,
And even children lisp the Rights of Man ;
Amid this mighty fuss just let me mention,
The Rights of Woman merit some attention.

First, in the sexes' intermix'd connection,
One sacred Right of Woman is *protection.*—
The tender flower that lifts its head, elate,
Helpless, must fall before the blasts of fate,
Sunk on the earth, defac'd its lovely form,
Unless your shelter ward th' impending storm.

Our second Right—but needless here is caution,
To keep that right inviolate's the fashion ;
Each man of sense has it so full before him,
He'd die before he'd wrong it—'tis *decorum.*—

There was, indeed, in far less polish'd days,
A time, when rough rude man had naughty ways;
Would swagger, swear, get drunk, kick up a riot,
Nay even thus invade a lady's quiet.
Now, thank our stars! these Gothic times are fled;
Now, well-bred men—and you are all well-bred—
Most justly think (and we are much the gainers)
Such conduct neither spirit, wit, nor manners.
For Right the third, our last, our best, our dearest,
That right to fluttering female hearts the nearest;
Which even the Rights of Kings, in low prostration,
Most humbly own—'tis dear, dear *admiration!*
In that blest sphere alone we live and move;
There taste that life of life—immortal love.
Smiles, glances, sighs, tears, fits, flirtations, airs;
'Gainst such an host what flinty savage dares,
When awful Beauty joins with all her charms—
Who is so rash as rise in rebel arms?

But truce with kings, and truce with constitutions,
With bloody armaments and revolutions;
Let Majesty your first attention summon,
Ah! ca! ira! THE MAJESTY OF WOMAN!

[In sending this production the Poet thus wrote:—'To you, madam, on our humble Dumfries boards, I have been more indebted for entertainment than ever I was in prouder theatres. Your charms as a woman would insure applause to the most indifferent actress, and your theatrical talents would ensure admiration to the plainest figure."]

EPIGRAM ON SEEING MISS FONTENELLE IN A FAVOURITE CHARACTER.

SWEET naïveté of feature,
  Simple, wild, enchanting elf,
Not to thee, but thanks to Nature,
  Thou art acting but thyself.

Wert thou awkward, stiff, affected,
　Spurning Nature, torturing art ;
Loves and Graces all rejected,
　Then indeed thou'd'st act a part.

[The poet added in prose—"This, madam, is not the unmeaning or
insidious compliment of the frivolous or interested : I pay it from the same
honest impulse that the sublime of Nature excites my admiration or her
beauties give me delight."]

EXTEMPORE ON SOME COMMEMORATIONS
OF THOMSON.

Dost thou not rise, indignant shade,
　And smile wi' spurning scorn,
When they wha wad hae starved thy life,
　Thy senseless turf adorn ?

Helpless, alane, thou clamb the brae,
　Wi' meikle honest toil,
And claught th' unfading garland there—
　Thy sair-won, rightful spoil.

And wear it there ! and call aloud
　This axiom undoubted—
Would thou hae Nobles' patronage ?
　First learn to live without it !

To whom hae much, more shall be given,
　Is every Great man's faith ;
But he, the helpless, needful wretch,
　Shall lose the mite he hath.

[This was first published in the *Edinburgh Gazetteer* in December 1792,
and the poet enclosed a copy of it to Mr Graham of Fintry.]

AULD ROB MORRIS.

THERE'S Auld Rob Morris that wons in yon glen,
He's the King o' gude fellows, and wale o' auld men ;
He has gowd in his coffers, he has owsen and kine,
And ae bonie lass, his dautie and mine.

She's fresh as the morning, the fairest in May ;
She's sweet as the ev'ning amang the new hay ;
As blythe and as artless as the lambs on the lea,
And dear to my heart as the light to my e'e.

But oh ! she's an Heiress, auld Robin's a laird,
And my daddie has nought but a cot-house and yard ;
A wooer like me maunna hope to come speed,
The wounds I must hide that will soon be my dead.

The day comes to me, but delight brings me nane ;
The night comes to me, but my rest it is gane ;
I wander my lane like a night-troubled ghaist,
And I sigh as my heart it wad burst in my breast.

O had she but been of a lower degree,
I then might hae hop'd she wad smil'd upon me !
O how past descriving had then been my bliss,
As now my distraction nae words can express.

DUNCAN GRAY.

DUNCAN GRAY cam' here to woo,
    Ha, ha, the wooing o't,
On blythe Yule-night when we were fou,
    Ha, ha, the wooing o't,
Maggie coost her head fu' high,
Look'd asklent and unco skeigh,
Gart poor Duncan stand abeigh ;
    Ha, ha, the wooing o't.

Duncan fleech'd* and Duncan pray'd ;
    Ha, ha, the wooing o't,
Meg was deaf as Ailsa craig,
    Ha, ha, the wooing o't :
Duncan sigh'd baith out and in,
Grat † his e'en baith bleer't ‡ an' blin',
Spak o' lowpin o'er a linn ;
    Ha, ha, the wooing o't.

Time and Chance are but a tide,
    Ha, ha, the wooing o't,
Slighted love is sair to bide,
Ha, ha, the wooing o't :
Shall I like a fool, quoth he,
For a haughty hizzie die ?
She may gae to—France for me !
    Ha, ha, the wooing o't.

How it comes let doctors tell,
    Ha, ha, the wooing o't ;
Meg grew sick, as he grew hale,
    Ha, ha, the wooing o't.
Something in her bosom wrings,
For relief a sigh she brings :
And oh ! her een they spak sic things !
    Ha, ha, the wooing o't.

Duncan was a lad o' grace,
    Ha, ha, the wooing o't :
Maggie's was a piteous case,
    Ha, ha, the wooing o't :
Duncan could na be her death,
Swelling Pity smoor'd his wrath ;
Now they're crouse and canty baith,
    Ha, ha, the wooing o't.

---

* supplicated.   † cried.   ‡ red and inflamed.

[Few of Burns's songs acquired a more rapid popularity than this; it is so thoroughly pointed and natural throughout; and the melody is so familiar to everybody that the very children learned the language of the ballad. "Spak o' lowpin o'er a linn," wrote the Hon. Andrew Erskine to the poet, after perusing the song, "is a line of itself that should make you immortal."]

HERE'S A HEALTH TO THEM THAT'S AWA.

HERE'S a health to them that's awa,
  Here's a health to them that's awa ;
And wha winna wish gude luck to our cause,
  May never gude luck be their fa' !
It's gude to be merry and wise,
  It's gude to be honest and true ;
It's gude to support Caledonia's cause,
  And bide by the buff and the blue.

Here's a health to them that's awa,
  Here's a health to them that's awa,
Here's a health to Charlie the chief o' the clan,
  Altho' that his band be but sma' ! [1]
May Liberty meet wi' success !
  May Prudence protect her frae evil !
May tyrants and tyranny tine i' the mist,
  And wander their way to the devil !

Here's a health to them that's awa,
  Here's a health to them that's awa ;
Here's a health to Tammie, the Norlan' laddie,
  That lives at the lug o' the law [2]
Here's freedom to them that wad read,
  Here's freedom to them that would write,

---

[1] Charles James Fox. The *buff and blue* was the Whig livery.
[2] Hon. Thos. Erskine, afterwards Lord Erskine.

There's nane ever fear'd that the truth should be heard,
    But they whom the truth would indite.[1]

  Here's a health to them that's awa,
    An' here's to them that's awa !
Here's to Maitland and Wycombe, let wha does na like 'em
    Be built in a hole in the wa,[2]
Here's timmer that's red at the heart,
    Here's fruit that is sound at the core ;
And may he that wad turn the buff and blue coat
    Be turn'd to the back o' the door.

  Here's a health to them that's awa,
    Here's a health to them that's awa ;
Here's chieftain M'Leod, a chieftain worth gowd,
    Tho' bred amang mountains o' snaw,[3]
Here's friends on baith sides o' the firth,
    And friends on baith sides o' the Tweed ;
And wha wad betray old Albion's right,
    May they never eat of her bread !

[This noble, patriotic effusion was composed about the close of 1792, and forwarded to the Edinburgh Gazetteer for publication.

Captain Wm. Johnstone, the proprietor of the Gazetteer, was imprisoned by the Government party on February 16th, 1793, under a treasonable charge. Burns became a subscriber to that paper on 18th November 1792. In his letter, he says : " I have just read your prospectus. If you go on in your paper with the same spirit, it will, beyond all comparison, be the first composition of the kind in Europe .... Go on, sir ! Lay bare with un-daunted heart and steady hand that horrid mass of corruption called politics and state-craft. Dare to draw in their native colours those 'calm-thinking villains whom no faith can fire,' whatever be the shibboleth of their pretended party."]

---

[1] The word has been explained by Chambers as the Scots word "indict," to accuse, as by a public prosecutor. On the other hand, we prefer the common English meaning—to dictate or prescribe dogmas which must be accepted as truth.

[2] Maitland and Wycombe were two distinguished Liberals of the day. This verse is not in Cromek's copy, and first appeared in the Kilmarnock edition, 1871.

[3] M'Leod of Dunvegan, Isle of Skye, M P. for the county of Inverness, a distinguished Reformer.

A TIPPLING BALLAD

ON THE DUKE OF BRUNSWICK'S BREAKING UP HIS
CAMP, AND THE DEFEAT OF THE AUSTRIANS, BY
DUMOURIER, NOV. 1792.

WHEN Princes and Prelates,
And hot-headed zealots,
A' Europe had set in a low, a low,
The poor man lies down,
Nor envies a crown,
And comforts himself as he dow, as he dow,
And comforts himself as he dow.

The black-headed eagle,
As keen as a beagle,
He hunted o'er height and o'er howe, o'er howe,
In the braes o' Gemappe,
He fell in a trap,
E'en let him come out as he dow, dow, dow,
E'en let him come out as he dow.

                *   *   *

But truce with commotions,
And new-fangled notions,
A bumper, I trust you'll allow;
Here's George our good king,
And Charlotte his queen,
And lang may they ring as they dow, dow, dow,
And lang may they ring as they dow.

[In a letter addressed by the bard to Mr Graham of Fintry on 5th
January 1793 reference is thus made to this ballad :—"As to France, I was
her enthusiastic votary in the beginning of the business. But when she
came to show her old avidity for conquest, in annexing Savoy, &c., to her
dominions and invading the rights of Holland, I altered my sentiments. A
tippling ballad, which I made on the Prince of Brunswick's breaking up
his camp, and sung one convivial evening, I shall likewise send you,
sealed up."]

A.D. 1793.

IN Politics if thou would'st mix,
  And mean thy fortunes be;
Bear this in mind, be deaf and blind,
  Let great folk hear and see.

[The original of this epigram was inscribed on one of the window-panes of the Globe Inn, Dumfries. On 6th December 1792, the poet had thus written to his Ayrshire correspondent, Mrs Dunlop :—"We in this country here have many alarms of the Reforming or rather the Republican spirit of *your* part of the kingdom. Indeed we are a good deal in commotion ourselves. For me, I am a placeman, you know; a very humble one indeed, Heaven knows, but still so much as to gag me. What my private sentiments are, you will find out without an interpreter." He transcribed for her perusal his recently composed *Address* on "The Rights of Women," and closed his letter thus :—"I shall soon have the honour of receiving your criticisms in person at Dunlop."

Burns accordingly visited Ayrshire in December, and spent four days with Mrs Dunlop. He also sojourned a night or two with his friends in the vale of Afton, and at Sanquhar. During his absence at this period "some envious, malicious devil raised a little demur concerning his political principles." Such is his own account in a letter addressed to Mrs Dunlop on 31st December, which he concludes thus :—"I have set henceforth, a seal on my lips as to these unlucky politics; although to you I must breathe my sentiments." In his letter to Mr Erskine of Mar, in April following, he expressly states that but for the kind intercession of Mr Graham of Fintry with the Board of Excise, he would have been deprived of his office. He also added these words, which so well illustrate the satirical lines which form the present text :—"One of our supervisors-general, a Mr Corbet, was instructed to enquire on the spot, and to document me—that my business was to act, *not to think*; and that, whatever might be men and measures, it was for me to be silent and obedient."

So early as on 5th January 1793, his mind was so far relieved concerning this "political blast, which threatened his welfare," as to enable him to give Mrs Dunlop this assurance :—"Although the Board had made me the subject of their animadversions, yet I have the pleasure of informing you that all is set to rights in that quarter." Not altogether "to rights" we suspect; for to Mr Erskine he appended the following qualification; "only I understand that all hopes of my getting officially forward are blasted."]

POORTITH CAULD AND RESTLESS LOVE.

Tune—"Cauld Kail in Aberdeen."

O POORTITH* cauld, and restless love,
   Ye wrack my peace between ye ;
Yet poortith a' I could forgive,
   An' 'twere na for my Jeanie.

Chorus—O why should Fate sic pleasure have,
        Life's dearest bands untwining?
       Or why sae sweet a flower as love
        Depend on Fortune's shining?

The warld's wealth, when I think on,
   It's pride and a' the lave o't ;
O fie on silly coward man,
   That he should be the slave o't !
     O why, &c.

Her e'en, sae bonie blue betray
   How she repays my passion ;
But prudence is her o'erword † ay,
   She talks o' rank and fashion.
     O why, &c.

O wha can prudence think upon,
   And sic a lassie by him?
O wha can prudence think upon,
   And sae in love as I am?
     O why, &c.

How blest the simple cotter's fate !
   He woo's his artless dearie ;

---

* poverty.   † burden of her talk.

The silly bogles, wealth and state,
    Can never make him eeric.*
        O why, &c.

[This fine song, produced early in January 1793, was prompted by the charms of Jean Lorimer. Her father, as we have seen, was a farmer and publican at *Kemmis Ha'*, on Nithside, about two miles below Ellisland, who for some time bore the reputation of being in affluent circumstances. He was, however, a practised smuggler of the exciseable commodities he dealt in, and ultimately became a bankrupt.

Chambers gives what he terms the story of "Chloris" (the poetical name by which Burns addressed this flaxen-haired syren). He tells us that Miss Lorimer in March 1793, while yet under eighteen years old, contracted a hasty run-away marriage with a young wild-rake farmer from the county of Cumberland, who had taken the farm of Barnhill, near Moffat. He adds that the pair had not been many weeks united, when her husband (Whelpdale, by name) was forced by his debts to leave Scotland and abandon his wife.

Burns's note to the song "Craigieburn Wood" styles her "Miss Lorimer, afterwards a Mrs Whelpdale;" so that the date assigned by Mr Chambers for her marriage may be correct; but there exists the most convincing proof that she was the heroine of the present song, composed two months prior to her so-called marriage. And moreover, in the month of April following, the poet tells Thomson that he has vowed to make a song to the tune of *Cauld Kail* on the lady he attempted to celebrate in the words "O Poortith Cauld." This he accordingly performed in August thereafter.]

BRAW LADS O' GALLA WATER.

Braw, braw lads on Yarrow-braes,
    They rove amang the blooming heather;
But Yarrow braes, nor Ettrick shaws
    Can match the lads o' Galla Water.

But there is ane, a secret ane,
    Aboon them a' I loe him better;
And I'll be his, and he'll be mine,
    The bonie lad o' Galla Water.

---
* dismayed.

Altho' his daddie was nae laird,
    And tho' I hae na meikle tocher,
Yet rich in kindest, truest love,
    We'll tent our flocks by Galla Water.

It ne'er was wealth, it ne'er was wealth,
    That coft contentment, peace, or pleasure :
The bands and bliss o' mutual love,
    O that's the chiefest warld's treasure.

[This favourite lyric was composed in the beginning of January 1793.
The author became acquainted with the pastoral districts therein referred
to, in course of his Border tour in May 1787.

    The ancient song, which was supplanted by Burns's version of "Gala
Water," possessed a certain kind of merit, as the following specimen will
shew :—

   Chorus—Braw, braw lads o' Gala Water,
     Bonie lads o' Gala Water ;
     Louden lads will ne'er compare
     Wi' the braw lads o' Gala Water.

Tho' barley rigs are fair to see,
    Flocks o' sheep are meikle better ;
And oats will shake on a windy day,
    When the lambs will play by Gala Water,
        Braw, braw lads, &c.

Louden lads are black wi' reek,
    Tevi'dale lads are little better :
But let them a' say what they will,
    The gree gaes ay down Gala Water,
        Braw, braw lads, &c.

There's Blindilee, and Torwoodlee,
    And Galashiels that rides the water ;
But young Ha'tree, he bears the gree
    Of a' the Pringles o' Gala Water,
        Braw, braw lads, &c.

What the tourist by the Waverley route now beholds as the extensive
manufacturing town of Galashiels was, in the days referred to in the old
song, only a few straggling thatched houses planted on the Selkirk side of
the water, inhabited by hand-loom weavers, wool-dressers, and dysters.
The Laird of Gala Hill, or "Gudeman of Galashiels" as he was termed,
was, in the time of Mary Queen of Scots, a stubborn papist, who was frequently under the discipline of the Reforming authorities. His surname

was Pringle, which was also the name of all the neighbouring lairds
mentioned in the closing stanza of the ancient song; and it still is the prevailing surname of the natives of Galashiels.]

SONNET WRITTEN ON THE AUTHOR'S BIRTHDAY,

ON HEARING A THRUSH SING IN HIS MORNING WALK.

"I made the following sonnet the other day, which has been so fortunate
as to obtain the approbation of no ordinary judge—our friend Syme."—
Letter to Alexander Cunningham, February 20*th,* 1793.

SING on, sweet thrush, upon the leafless bough,
   Sing on, sweet bird, I listen to thy strain,
   See aged Winter, 'mid his surly reign,
At thy blythe carol, clears his furrowed brow.

So in lone Poverty's dominion drear,
   Sits meek Content with light, unanxious heart;
   Welcomes the rapid moments, bids them part,
Nor asks if they bring ought to hope or fear.

I thank thee, Author of this opening day!
   Thou whose bright sun now gilds yon orient skies!
   Riches denied, thy boon was purer joys—
What wealth could never give nor take away!

Yet come, thou child of poverty and care,
The mite high Heav'n bestow'd, that mite with thee I'll
   share.

[Amid the surging of the political emotions of that period, Burns, like
the sagacious *John o' Badenyon,* "tuned his pipe and pleased himsel'"
with a song or a sonnet. In the letter which is partly quoted in our heading, he asks his correspondent, "Are you deeply engaged in the mazes of

the 'law, the mysteries of love, or in the profound wisdom of modern politics?—Curse on the word which ended the period!

"*Quere.* What is Politics? *Answer.* Politics is a science wherewith, by means of nefarious cunning and hypocritical pretence, we govern civil politics for the emolument of ourselves and our adherents.

"*Quere.* What is a Minister? *Answer.* A minister is an unprincipled fellow who, by the influence of hereditary or acquired wealth—by superior abilities, or by a lucky conjuncture of circumstances, obtains a principal place in the administration of the affairs of government.

"*Quere.* What is a Patriot? *Answer.* A patriot is an individual exactly of the same description as a minister, only *out of place.*"

In the copy of this sonnet enclosed to Cunningham, now lying before us, there is not the slightest variation from that printed by Currie.]

LORD GREGORY.

O MIRK, mirk is this midnight hour,
    And loud the tempest's roar;
A waefu' wanderer seeks thy tower,
    Lord Gregory, ope thy door.
An' exile frae her father's ha',
    And a' for sake o' thee;
At least some pity on me shaw,
    If love it may na be.

Lord Gregory, mind'st thou not the grove
    By bonie Irwine side,
Where first I own'd that virgin love
    I lang, lang had denied.
How aften didst thou pledge and vow,
    Thou wad for ay be mine!
And my fond heart, itsel' sae true,
    It ne'er mistrusted thine.

Hard is thy heart, Lord Gregory,
    And flinty is thy breast:
Thou bolt of Heaven that flashest by,
    O, wilt thou bring me rest!

Ye mustering thunders from above,
  Your willing victim see ;
But spare and pardon my fause Love,
  His wrangs to Heaven and me.

[This pathetic ballad (founded on the ancient one called "The Lass of Lochryan") was transmitted to Thomson on 26th January 1793. The copy we print from, which shews a few delicate variations, is a touching manuscript of the bard, written at Brow, on 7th July 1796, exactly fourteen days before his death. His Edinburgh friend, Alexander Cunningham, had requested to be favoured with a copy of "Lord Gregory," and accordingly the obliging poet made an effort to transcribe it in that melancholy letter which Currie first gave to the public—" Alas, my friend, I fear the voice of the bard will soon be heard among you no more. . . . You actually would not know me if you saw me. Pale, emaciated, and so feeble as occasionally to need help from my chair, my spirits fled—fled ! . . . What way, in the name of thrift, shall I maintain myself, and keep a horse in country quarters, with a wife and five children at home, on £50?"

It will be remembered that the ballad in the text was a favourite one with the author. When he visited Lord Selkirk at St Mary's Isle in July 1793, in company with Mr Syme—that gentleman, in his well-written narrative of the tour, says: "Urbani, the Italian, sung us many Scottish songs accompanied with instrumental music. The two young ladies of Selkirk sung also. We had the old song of Lord Gregory, which I asked for to have an opportunity of calling on Burns to recite *his* ballad to that tune. He did recite it, and such was the effect, that a dead silence ensued. It was such a silence as a mind of feeling naturally preserves, when touched with that enthusiasm which banishes every other thought but the comtemplation of the sympathy produced. Burns's *Lord Gregory* is in my opinion a most beautiful and affecting ballad. The most fastidious critic may perhaps say some of the sentiments and imagery are of too elevated a kind for such a style of composition, for instance, ' Thou bolt of heaven that flashest by,' and 'ye mustering thunders,' &c., but this is a cold-blooded objection, which will be *said* rather than *felt.*"]

WANDERING WILLIE.

First Version.

HERE awa, there awa, wandering Willie,
  Now tired with wandering, haud awa hame ;
Come to my bosom, my ae only dearie,
  And tell me thou bring'st me my Willie the same.

Loud blew the cauld winter winds at our parting ;
　It was na the blast brought the tear in my e'e :
Now welcome the Simmer, and welcome my Willie,
　The Simmer to Nature, my Willie to me.

Ye hurricanes rest in the cave o' your slumbers,
　O how your wild horrors a lover alarms !
Awaken ye breezes, row gently ye billows,
　And waft my dear laddie ance mair to my arms.
But if he's forgotten his faithfullest Nannie,
　O still flow between us, thou wide roaring main ;
May I never see it, may I never trow it,
　But, dying, believe that my Willie's my ain !

[This fine lyric was sent to Thomson in March 1793, with the remark :—
" I leave it to you, my dear sir, to determine whether the above, or the old
' Thro' the lang muir ' be the best."

There has been a good deal of variegated surmise regarding the heroineship of this effusion, some contending for Clarinda, and others for Mrs
Walter Riddell. We consider that there is not the slightest ground for
connecting the name of the latter with it, and are content to hold that the
old song of Wandering Willie, recorded in Herd's second volume, p. 140,
was quite sufficient in itself to suggest the lines in the text to the muse of
Burns. We here annex the original words :

　　　Here awa, there awa, here awa, Willie,
　　　　Here awa, there awa, here awa hame ;
　　　Lang have I sought thee, dear I have bought thee,
　　　　Now I hae gotten my Willie again.

　　　Thro' the lang muir I have follow'd my Willie,
　　　　Thro' the lang muir I have follow'd him hame ;
　　　Whatever betide us, nought shall divide us ;
　　　　Love now rewards all my sorrow and pain.

　　　Here awa, there awa, here awa Willie,
　　　　Here awa, there awa, here awa hame,
　　　Come love, believe me, nothing can grieve me,
　　　　Ilka thing pleases while Willie's at hame.]

WANDERING WILLIE.

Revised Version.

HERE awa, there awa, wandering Willie,
  Here awa, there awa, haud awa hame ;
Come to my bosom, my ain only dearie,
  Tell me thou bring'st me my Willie the same.
Winter winds blew loud and cauld at our parting,
  Fears for my Willie brought tears to my e'e,
Welcome now Simmer, and welcome my Willie,
  The Simmer to Nature, my Willie to me.

Rest, ye wild storms, in the cave of your slumbers,
  How your dread howling a lover alarms !
Wauken ye breezes, row gently ye billows,
  And waft my dear laddie ance mair to my arms.
But oh, if he's faithless, and minds na his Nannie,
  Flow still between us, thou wide roaring main !
May I never see it, may I never trow it,
  But, dying, believe that my Willie's my ain.

OPEN THE DOOR TO ME, OH.

IRISH SONG ALTERED BY BURNS.

OH, open the door, some pity to shew,
  Oh, open the door to me, oh,
Tho' thou hast been false, I'll ever prove true,
  Oh, open the door to me, oh.

Cauld is the blast upon my pale cheek,
  But caulder thy love for me, oh :
The frost that freezes the life at my heart,
  Is nought to my pains frae thee, oh.

The wan Moon is setting behind the white wave,
    And Time is setting with me, oh :
False friends, false love, farewell! for mair
    I'll ne'er trouble them, nor thee, oh.

She has open'd the door, she has open'd it wide,
    She sees the pale corse on the plain, oh :
" My true love !" she cried, and sank down by his side,
    Never to rise again, oh.

[Carlyle refers to one of the couplets of this song thus :—"We see that in this man there was the gentleness, the trembling pity of a woman, with the deep earnestness, the force and passionate ardour of a hero. Tears lie in him, and consuming fire ; as lightning lurks in the drops of the summer cloud. . . . It is needless to multiply examples of his graphic power and clearness of sight. One trait of the finest sort we select from multitudes of such among his songs. It gives, in a single line, to the saddest feeling, the saddest environment and local habitation :

    " The wan Moon is setting behind the white wave,
      And Time is setting with me, O ;
    False friends, false love, farewell ! for mair
    I'll ne'er trouble them nor thee, O."]

LOVELY YOUNG JESSIE.

TRUE hearted was he, the sad swain o' the Yarrow,
    And fair are the maids on the banks of the Ayr ;
But by the sweet side o' the Nith's winding river,
    Are lovers as faithful, and maidens as fair :
To equal young JESSIE seek Scotland all over ;
    To equal young JESSIE you seek it in vain,
Grace, beauty, and elegance fetter her lover,
    And maidenly modesty fixes the chain.

Fresh is the rose in the gay, dewy morning,
    And sweet is the lily, at evening close ;
But in the fair presence o' lovely young JESSIE,
    Unseen is the lily, unheeded the rose.

Love sits in her smile, a wizard ensnaring;
   Enthron'd in her een he delivers his law :
And still to her charms SHE alone is a stranger;
   Her modest demeanor's the jewel of a'.

[Thomson received this contribution in March 1793, with a note from the author, thus :—"I send a song on a celebrated toast in this country to suit the tune *Bonie Dundee*." The lady was Jessie Staig, second daughter of the Provost of Dumfries, who afterwards married Major William Miller, one of the sons of the poet's former landlord. About eighteen months after this song was composed, Burns made her the subject of a complimentary Epigram, on her recovery from fever. Alas! after a very brief married life she sunk into a decline, and was laid in Dumfries Church-yard to sleep after life's fitful fever, in March 1801, at the untimely age of twenty-six.]

MEG O' THE MILL.

O KEN ye what Meg o' the Mill has gotten,
An ken ye what Meg o' the Mill has gotten?
She's gotten a coof* wi' a claute† o' siller,
And broken the heart o' the barley Miller.

The Miller was strappin,‡ the Miller was ruddy;
A heart like a lord, and a hue like a lady;
The laird was a widdifu',§ bleerit‖ knurl;¶
She's left the gude fellow, and taen the churl.

The Miller he hecht** her a heart leal and loving,
The laird did address her wi' matter mair moving,
A fine pacing-horse wi' a clear chained bridle,
A whip by her side, and a bonie side-saddle.

O wae on the siller, it is sae prevailin',
And wae on the love that is fixed on a mailen!
A tocher's nae word in a true lover's parl,
But gie me my love, and a fig for the warl!

---

* silly person.   † hoard.   ‡ tall and powerful.   § twisted.
‖ dim-visaged.   ¶ dwarfed, but strong.   ** offered.

[The poet, in reply to some of Thomson's objections to this song, thus wrote :—"My song, 'Ken ye what Meg o' the Mill has gotten?' pleases me so much, that I cannot try my hand at another song to the same air; so I shall not attempt it. I know you will laugh at this; but ilka man wears his belt his ain gate." About the same time Burns forwarded to Johnson a very humorous song bearing the same title, to which we will next introduce the reader.]

MEG O' THE MILL.

Another Version

O KEN ye what Meg o' the Mill has gotten,
An' ken ye what Meg o' the Mill has gotten?
A braw new naig wi' the tail o' a rottan,
And that's what Meg o' the Mill has gotten.

O ken ye what Meg o' the Mill loes dearly,
An' ken ye what Meg o' the Mill loes dearly?
A dram o' gude strunt * in a morning early,
And that's what Meg o' the Mill loes dearly.

O ken ye how Meg o' the Mill was married,
An' ken ye how Meg o' the Mill was married?
The priest he was oxter'd,† the clark he was carried,
And that's how Meg o' the Mill was married.

O ken ye how Meg o' the Mill was bedded,
An ken ye how Meg o' the Mill was bedded?
The groom gat sae fu', he fell awald‡ beside it,
And that's how Meg o' the Mill was bedded.

[This song presents as graphic a picture of real life as Teniers ever painted.]

---

* strong liquor.   † held up by an assistant at each arm-pit.
‡ doubled up helpless.

THE SOLDIER'S RETURN.

Air—"The Mill, mill, O."

WHEN wild war's deadly blast was blawn,
　And gentle peace returning,
Wi' mony a sweet babe fatherless,
　And mony a widow mourning ;
I left the lines and tented field,
　Where lang I'd been a lodger,
My humble knapsack a' my wealth,
　A poor and honest sodger.

A leal, light heart was in my breast,
　My hand unstain'd wi' plunder ;
And for fair Scotia, hame again,
　I cheery on did wander :
I thought upon the banks o' Coil,
　I thought upon my Nancy,
I thought upon the witching smile
　That caught my youthful fancy.

At length I reach'd the bonie glen,
　Where early life I sported ;
I pass'd the mill and trysting thorn,
　Where Nancy aft I courted :
Wha spied I but my ain dear maid,
　Down by her mother's dwelling !
And turn'd me round to hide the flood
　That in my e'en was swelling.

Wi' alter'd voice, quoth I, Sweet lass,
　Sweet as yon hawthorn's blossom,
O ! happy, happy may he be,
　That's dearest to thy bosom :
My purse is light, I've far to gang,
　And fain would be thy lodger ;

I've serv'd my king and country lang—
　Take pity on a sodger.

Sae wistfully she gaz'd on me,
　And lovelier was than ever ;
Quo' she, A sodger ance I lo'ed,
　Forget him shall I never :
Our humble cot, and hamely fare,
　Ye freely shall partake it ;
That gallant badge—the dear cockade,
　Ye're welcome for the sake o't.

She gaz'd—she redden'd like a rose—
　Syne pale like ony lily ;
She sank within my arms, and cried,
　Art thou my ain dear Willie ?
By Him who made yon sun and sky !
　By whom true love's regarded,
I am the man ; and thus may still
　True lovers be rewarded !

The wars are o'er, and I'm come hame,
　And find thee still true-hearted ;
Tho' poor in gear, we're rich in love,
　And mair we'se ne'er be parted.
Quo' she, My grandsire left me gowd,
　A mailen plenish'd fairly ;
And come, my faithfu' sodger lad,
　Thou'rt welcome to it dearly !

For gold the merchant ploughs the main,
　The farmer ploughs the manor ;
But glory is the sodger's prize,
　The sodger's wealth is honor :
The brave poor sodger ne'er despise,
　Nor count him as a stranger ;

III.   F

Remember he's his country stay,
    In day and hour of danger.

[This charming ballad, destined to become so widely popular, was sent to
Thomson early in April 1793, without a remark from the author, so far as
appears in the preserved correspondence.]

Uersicles, A.D. 1793.

THE TRUE LOYAL NATIVES.

" At this period of our poet's life, when private animosity was made the
ground of private quarrel, the following foolish verses were sent as an attack
on Burns and his friends for their political opinions.

THE LOYAL NATIVES' VERSES.

" Ye Sons of Sedition, give ear to my song,
    Let Syme, Burns, and Maxwell pervade every throng,
    With Cracken the attorney and Mundell the quack,
    Send Willie, the monger, to hell with a smack.

" These lines having been handed over the table to Burns, at a convivial
meeting, he instantly indorsed the subjoined reply."—*Reliques*, p. 168.

Ye true " Loyal Natives " attend to my song,
In uproar and riot rejoice the night long ;
From Envy and Hatred your core is exempt,
But where is your shield from the darts of Contempt !

[The " Loyal Native Club " of the Burgh of Dumfries was formed on 18th
January 1793, "for preserving the Peace, Liberty, and Property, and for
supporting the Laws and Constitution of the Country." The president of
the Association was Commissary Goldie ; and Mr Francis Sprott, town-clerk,
acted as its secretary.

ON COMMISSARY GOLDIE'S BRAINS.

LORD, to account who dares thee call,
    Or e'er dispute thy pleasure ?
Else why, within so thick a wall,
    Enclose so poor a treasure ?

[This sarcasm displays the poet's manner of throwing " the darts of contempt " on the whole core of *Loyal Natives.*—" When the Head is sick, the
whole body is full of trouble."]

LINES INSCRIBED IN A LADY'S POCKET ALMANAC.

GRANT me, indulgent Heaven, that I may live,
To see the miscreants feel the pains they give ;
Deal Freedom's sacred treasures free as air,
Till Slave and Despot be but things that were.

THANKSGIVING FOR A NATIONAL VICTORY.

YE hypocrites ! are these your pranks ?
To murder men, and give God thanks !
Desist, for shame !—proceed no further,
God wont accept your thanks for MURTHER !

LINES ON THE COMMEMORATION OF RODNEY'S VICTORY.

INSTEAD of a song, boys, I'll give you a toast ;
Here's to the memory of those we have lost !—
That we *lost*, did I say?—nay, by Heav'n, that we *found;*
For their fame it will last while the world goes round.
The next in succession I'll give you 's THE KING !
Whoe'er would betray him, on high may he swing !
And here's the grand fabric, the free CONSTITUTION,
As built on the base of our great Revolution !
And longer with Politics not to be cramm'd,
Be ANARCHY curs'd, and be TYRANNY damn'd !
And who would to LIBERTY e'er prove disloyal,
May his son be a hangman—and himself his first trial !

[Admiral Rodney's great victory over the French fleet, off Dominica, in the West Indies, was so far back as April 12, 1782, and the Admiral, who was created a Peer in consequence, died in 1792. It was the custom in loyal Dumfries and elsewhere to commemorate that victory year after year, and Burns did not shrink to join in such manifestations, whatever were his real opinions regarding aggressive warfare.]

KIRK AND STATE EXCISEMEN.

YE men of wit and wealth, why all this sneering
'Gainst poor Excisemen?   Give the cause a hearing:
What are your Landlord's rent-rolls?—taxing ledgers!
What   Premiers?—what   ev'n   Monarchs?—mighty
    Gaugers!
Nay, what are Priests? (those seeming godly wise-men,)
What are they, pray, but Spiritual Excisemen!

THE RAPTURES OF FOLLY.

THOU greybeard, old Wisdom! may boast of thy treasures;
  Give me with old Folly to live;
I grant thee thy calm-blooded, time-settled pleasures,
  But Folly has raptures to give.

[The first of these Epigrams was inscribed by the poet on a window at the King's Arms Tavern, Dumfries; and the latter was similarly inscribed on a window of the Globe Tavern there. They speak for their own parentage, and tell their own story.]

EXTEMPORE REPLY TO AN INVITATION.

THE King's most humble servant, I
  Can scarcely spare a minute;
But I'll be wi' you by an' by;
  Or else the Deil's be in it.

[The above answer to an invitation was written extempore on a leaf torn from his Excise-book.]

GRACE AFTER MEAT.

L.—D, we thank, and thee adore,
  For temporal gifts we little merit;
At present we will ask no more—
  Let *William Hislop* give the spirit.

GRACE BEFORE AND AFTER MEAT.

O LORD, when hunger pinches sore,
    Do thou stand us in stead,
And send us, from thy bounteous store,
    A tup or wether head !   Amen.

O LORD, since we have feasted thus,
    Which we so little merit,
Let Meg now take away the flesh,
    And Jock bring in the spirit !   Amen.

[These "Graces" appear to have been emitted extemporaneously at the
poet's favourite "howff"—the Globe Tavern, of which Wm. Hislop was
landlord.]

IMPROMPTU ON GENERAL DUMOURIER'S DESERTION FROM THE FRENCH REPUBLICAN ARMY.

YOU'RE welcome to Despots, Dumourier ;
You're welcome to Despots, Dumourier :
    How does Dampiere do ?
    Aye, and Bournonville too ?
Why did they not come along with you, Dumourier ?

I will fight France with you, Dumourier ;
I will fight France with you, Dumourier ;
    I will fight France with you,
    I will take my chance with you
By my soul, I'll dance with you, Dumourier.

Then let us fight about, Dumourier ;
Then let us fight about, Dumourier ;

Then let us fight about,
Till Freedom's spark be out,
Then we'll be d—d, no doubt, Dumourier

[Dumourier, after achieving important triumphs as a General in the army
of the French Republic, somewhat unexpectedly veered round in favour of
the interests of Monarchy, and was only prevented by fortuitous circumstances from betraying his troops into the enemy's hands. Dampiere and
Bournonville, referred to in the opening stanzas, were respectively a brother
General and an emissary of the Convention, whom he had calculated on per-
suading to follow his example ; but in this he was disappointed. Dumourier
deserted and made his escape from France, on 5th April 1793.]

THE LAST TIME I CAME O'ER THE MOOR.

THE last time I came o'er the moor,
    And left Maria's dwelling,
What throes, what tortures passing cure,
    Were in my bosom swelling :
Condemn'd to drag a hopeless chain,
    And yet in secret languish ;
To feel a fire in every vein,
    Yet dare not speak my anguish.

The wretch of love unseen, unknown,
    I fain my crime would cover :
The bursting sigh, th' unweeting groan,
    Betray the guilty lover.
I know my doom must be despair,
    Thou wilt nor canst relieve me ;
But oh, Maria, hear my prayer,
    For Pity's sake, forgive me !

The music of thy tongue I heard,
    Nor wist while it enslav'd me ;
I saw thine eyes, yet nothing fear'd,
    Till fear no more had sav'd me:

The unwary sailor thus, aghast,
  The wheeling torrent viewing,
'Mid circling horrors yields at last
  To overwhelming ruin.

[This finely expressed but rather daring appeal in lyrical form to Mrs
Walter Riddell, was forwarded to George Thomson in April 1793.
  Chambers remarks thus of the present song :—"The sentiments are not
pleasing. They hint at a discreditable passion, in which no pure mind could
possibly sympathize ; therefore they must be held as unfitted for song. It
can scarcely be doubted that they were suggested by some roving sensations
of the bard towards the too-witching Mrs Riddell; though it is equally
probable that these bore no great proportion to the mere *métier* of the artist
aiming at a certain literary effect."]

BLYTHE HAE I BEEN ON YON HILL.

BLYTHE hae I been on yon hill,
  As the lambs before me ;
Careless ilka thought and free,
  As the breeze flew o'er me ;
Now nae langer sport and play,
  Mirth or sang can please me ;
LESLEY is sae fair and coy,
  Care and anguish seize me.

Heavy, heavy is the task,
  Hopeless love declaring ;
Trembling, I dow nocht but glow'r,
  Sighing, dumb despairing !
If she winna ease the thraws
  In my bosom swelling,
Underneath the grass-green sod,
  Soon maun be my dwelling.

[The name " Lesley " will lead the reader to understand that Miss Lesley
Baillie, already referred to in connection with the song, "O saw ye bonie
Lesley," is also the subject of these tender verses, which flow so exquisitely
to the melody. Of this young lady and her sister Burns had thus written

in July 1788:—"I declare one day I had the honour of dining at Mr Baillie's, I was almost in the predicament of the children of Israel, when they could not look on Moses' face for the glory that shone in it when he descended from mount Horeb."

LOGAN BRAES.

"25th June 1793.—Have you ever, my dear sir, felt your bosom ready to burst with indignation, on reading of, or seeing how, the mighty villains who divide kingdom against kingdom, desolate provinces, and lay nations waste, out of the wantonness of ambition, or often from still more ignoble passions? In a mood of this kind to-day, I recollected the air of *Logan Water*, and it occurred to me that its querulous melody probably had its origin from the plaintive indignation of some swelling, suffering heart, fired at the tyrannic strides of some Public Destroyer, and overwhelmed with private distress—the consequence of a country's ruin.

"If I have done anything at all like justice to my feelings, the following song, composed in three-quarters of an hour's lucubrations in my elbow-chair, ought to have some merit."—(Letter to Thomson.)

O LOGAN, sweetly didst thou glide,
That day I was my Willie's bride,
And years sin syne hae o'er us run,
Like Logan to the simmer sun :
But now thy flowery banks appear
Like drumlie Winter, dark and drear,
While my dear lad maun face his faes,
Far, far frae me and Logan braes.

Again the merry month of May
Has made our hills and vallies gay ;
The birds rejoice in leafy bowers,
The bees hum round the breathing flowers ;
Blythe Morning lifts his rosy eye,
And Evening's tears are tears o' joy :
My soul, delightless a' surveys,
While Willie's far frae Logan braes.

Within yon milk-white hawthorn bush,
Amang her nestlings sits the thrush ;

Her faithfu' mate will share her toil,
Or wi' his song her cares beguile ;
But I wi' my sweet nurslings here,
Nae mate to help, nae mate to cheer,
Pass widow'd nights and joyless days,
While Willie's far frae Logan braes.

O wae be to you, Men o' State,
That brethren rouse in deadly hate !
As ye make mony a fond heart mourn,
Sae may it on your heads return !
How can your flinty hearts enjoy
The widow's tear, the orphan's cry ?
But soon may peace bring happy days,
And Willie hame to Logan braes !

O WERE MY LOVE YON LILAC FAIR.

Air—" Hughie Graham."

O WERE my love yon Lilac fair,
    Wi' purple blossoms to the Spring,
And I, a bird to shelter there,
    When wearied on my little wing !
How I wad mourn when it was torn
    By Autumn wild, and Winter rude !
But I wad sing on wanton wing,
    When youthfu' May its bloom renew'd.

O gin my love were yon red rose,
    That grows upon the castle wa' ;
And I mysel a drap o' dew,
    Into her bonie breast to fa' !
O there, beyond expression blest,
    I'd feast on beauty a' the night ;

Seal'd on her silk-saft faulds to rest,
   Till fley'd awa' by Phœbus' light !

[Only the first double-stanza of this production is by Burns. In June
1793 he forwarded the song to Thomson, asking him if he was acquainted
with the closing eight lines, which had been published as an old fragment in
Herd's collection. The poet observed thus :—"The thought in these lines
is inexpressibly beautiful, and, so far as I know, quite original. It is too
short for a song, else I would forswear you altogether except you gave it a
place. I have often tried to eke a stanza to it, but in vain."]

BONIE JEAN.—A BALLAD.

To its ain tune.

THERE was a lass, and she was fair,
   At kirk and market to be seen ;
When a' our fairest maids were met,
   The fairest maid was bonie Jean.

And ay she wrought her mammie's wark,
   And ay she sang sae merrilie ;
The blythest bird upon the bush
   Had ne'er a lighter heart than she.

But hawks will rob the tender joys
   That bless the little lintwhite's nest ;
And frost will blight the fairest flowers,
   And love will break the soundest rest.

Young Robie was the brawest lad,
   The flower and pride of a' the glen ;
And he had owsen, sheep, and kye,
   And wanton naigies nine or ten.

He gaed wi' Jeanie to the tryste,
   He danc'd wi' Jeanie on the down ;
And, lang ere witless Jeanie wist,
   Her heart was tint, her peace was stown !

As in the bosom of the stream,
    The moon-beam dwells at dewy e'en ;
So trembling, pure, was tender love
    Within the breast of bonie Jean.

And now she works her mammie's wark,
    And ay she sighs wi' care and pain ;
Ye wist na what her ail might be,
    Or what wad make her weel again.

But did na Jeanie's heart loup light,
    And did na joy blink in her e'e ;
As Robie tauld a tale o' love :
    Ae e'enin on the lily lea ?

The sun was sinking in the west,
    The birds sang sweet in ilka grove ;
His cheek to hers he fondly laid,
    And whisper'd thus his tale o' love :

" O Jeanie fair, I lo'e thee dear ;
    O canst thou think to fancy me,
Or wilt thou leave thy mammie's cot,
    And learn to tent the farms wi' me ?

" At barn or byre thou shalt na drudge,
    Or naething else to trouble thee ;
But stray amang the heather-bells,
    And tent the waving corn wi' me."

Now what could artless Jeanie do ?
    She had nae will to say him na :
At length she blush'd a sweet consent,
    And love was ay between them twa.

[The heroine of this ballad was Miss Jean M'Murdo, who was afterwards
married to a Mr Crawford. Her sister Phillis, who was a celebrated beauty,
became the wife of Mr Norman Lockhart of Carnwath. Their brother
Archibald became a Lieut.-Colonel, and died in 1829, aged fifty-four; and the

sons of the latter were—1. Col. John M'Murdo of the Scottish Borderers;
2. Admiral Archibald M'Murdo of Cargenholm; and 3. Col. William Montague M'Murdo, son-in-law of Sir Charles Napier, the hero of Scinde,
whom he accompanied through his campaigns.]

LINES ON JOHN M'MURDO, ESQ.

BLEST be M'Murdo to his latest day!
No envious cloud o'ercast his evening ray;
No wrinkle, furrow'd by the hand of care,
Nor ever sorrow add one silver hair!
O may no son the father's honor stain,
Nor ever daughter give the mother pain!

[Mr M'Murdo was Chamberlain to the Duke of Queensberry. We have
not ascertained the date of his death.]

EPITAPH ON A LAP-DOG.

IN wood and wild, ye warbling throng,
   Your heavy loss deplore;
Now, half extinct your powers of song,
   Sweet "Echo" is no more.

Ye jarring, screeching things around,
   Scream your discordant joys;
Now, half your din of tuneless sound
   With "Echo" silent lies.

[Mr John Syme, of Ryedale, with whom the poet was in the closest
terms of intimacy throughout the Dumfries period of his life, contributed
a very lively account to Dr Currie, of a tour through Galloway that he had
with Burns for a week or two commencing on 27th July 1793. Arriving at
the house of Mr Gordon of Kenmore in the evening, the excursionists were
hospitably entertained there for three days. "Mrs Gordon's lap-dog *Echo*
was dead. She would have an epitaph for him. Several had been made.
Burns was asked for one. This was setting Hercules to his distaff. He
disliked the subject, but to please the lady, he would try." The above is
what he produced on the spot.]

EPIGRAMS AGAINST THE EARL OF GALLOWAY.

"From Gatehouse we went next day to Kirkcudbright, through a fine country. But I must tell you that Burns had got a pair of *jemmy* boots for the journey, which had got thoroughly wet, and then dried in such a manner that it was not possible to get them on again. The brawny poet tried force, and tore them to shreds. A whiffling vexation of this sort is more trying to the temper than a serious calamity. We were going to Saint Mary's Isle, the seat of the Earl of Selkirk, and the forlorn Burns was discomfited at the thought of his ruined boots. A sick stomach and a head-ache lent their aid, and the man of verse was quite *accablé.* I attempted to reason with him. Mercy on us, how he did fume and rage! Nothing could re-instate him in temper. I tried various expedients, and at last hit on one that succeeded. I shewed him the House of Garlies, across the bay of Wigton. Against the Earl of Galloway, with whom he was offended, he expectorated his spleen, and regained a most agreeable temper. He was in a most epigrammatic humour indeed!"—*John Syme's Narrative of the Tour.*

WHAT dost thou in that mansion fair?
　Flit, Galloway, and find
Some narrow, dirty, dungeon cave,
　The picture of thy mind.

No Stewart art thou, Galloway,
　The Stewarts all were brave;
Besides, the Stewarts were but fools,
　Not one of them a knave.

Bright ran thy line, O Galloway,
　Thro' many a far-famed sire!
So ran the far-famed Roman way,
　And ended in a mire.

On Mr Syme suggesting that the Earl would resent such pasquinades, if made public.

Spare me thy vengeance, Galloway!
　In quiet let me live:
I ask no kindness at thy hand,
　For thou hast none to give.

EPIGRAM ON THE LAIRD OF LAGGAN.

"He was in a most epigrammatic humour indeed! Having settled Lord Galloway, he afterwards fell on humbler game. There is one Morine whom he does not love. He had a passing blow at him."—*John Syme's Narrative.*

WHEN Morine, deceas'd, to the Devil went down,
'Twas nothing would serve him but Satan's own crown ;
" Thy fool's head," quoth Satan, " that crown shall wear
    never,
I grant thou'rt as wicked, but not quite so clever."

SONG.—PHILLIS THE FAIR.

Tune—" Robin Adair."

WHILE larks, with little wing, fann'd the pure air,
Tasting the breathing Spring, forth I did fare :
    Gay the sun's golden eye
    Peep'd o'er the mountains high ;
Such thy morn ! did I cry, Phillis the fair.

In each bird's careless song, glad I did share ;
While yon wild-flow'rs among, chance led me there !
    Sweet to the op'ning day,
    Rosebuds bent the dewy spray ;
Such thy bloom ! did I say, Phillis the fair.

Down in a shady walk, doves cooing were ;
Mark'd I the cruel hawk caught in a snare :
    So kind may fortune be,
    Such make his destiny,
He who would injure thee, Phillis the fair.

[The reader will perceive that the subject of the above was Miss Phillis M'Murdo, and that Stephen Clarke was the supposed singer.]

SONG.—HAD I A CAVE.

Tune—"Robin Adair."

" That crinkum-crankum tune *Robin Adair*, has run so in my head, and
I succeeded so ill in my last attempt, that I have ventured, in this morning's
walk, one essay more. You, my dear sir, will remember an unfortunate
part of our worthy friend Cunningham's story, which happened about three
years ago. That struck my fancy, and I endeavoured to do the idea
justice, as follows."

HAD I a cave on some wild distant shore,
Where the winds howl to the wave's dashing roar :
    There would I weep my woes,
    There seek my lost repose,
    Till grief my eyes should close,
        Ne'er to wake more !

Falsest of womankind, can'st thou declare
All thy fond, plighted vows fleeting as air !
    To thy new lover hie,
    Laugh o'er thy perjury ;
    Then in thy bosom try
        What peace is there !

[The poet's lyric success never went beyond this grand result, apparently
reached with so little effort—not in Scots verse, but pure English.

Such was the strength of Cunningham's craze for the object of his
blighted love that, long after being jilted, and long after he had married, he
was observed on many an evening stealthily to traverse for hours the
opposite side of Princes Street where she resided, in order that he might
catch a glimpse of her person. He would pause now and again opposite
her windows, and seem gratified even with a passing glance of her shadow
cast on the white screen by the light within—then he would burst into tears,
and wend his way slowly home by the most lonely path, absorbed in morbid
contemplation. He survived till 27th January 1812.

His perjured "Anna" had three daughters and one son to her husband,
Dr Dewar ; the son became an Advocate at the Scottish Bar, and her
second daughter Jessie was justly celebrated as the loveliest girl who, at
the period, adorned the Scottish metropolis. A clerk in the Royal Bank
went almost out of his wits through his passion for her, and annoyed her
with his addresses. The father of the young man was a woollen draper,
and she looked for some higher connection. At length, Kay the carica·

turist put an extinguisher on the poor pilgrim of love, by publishing an admirable likeness of the beautiful Jessie Dewar passing up the North Bridge followed by her imploring tormentor, whose likeness was equally perfect. A label from his mouth displayed the words, " If it were not for those d—d blankets I would have got her !" This fair inspirer afterwards married the Hon. and Rev. Mr Tournier of London.

In 1838, Robert Chambers thus wrote regarding the widow of Dr Dewar : —" One evening, a very few years ago, a friend of mine, visiting a musical family who resided in Princes Street nearly opposite St John's Chapel, chanced to request one of the young ladies to sing " Had I a cave," &c. She was about to comply, when it was recollected that the heroine of the lyric lived in the flat below, an aged widow, who might overhear it. For that reason the intention of singing the song was laid aside."]

SONG—BY ALLAN STREAM.

By Allan stream I chanc'd to rove,
   While Phebus sank beyond Benledi ;
The winds were whispering thro' the grove,
   The yellow corn was waving ready :
I listen'd to a lover's sang,
   An' thought on youthfu' pleasures mony ;
And ay the wild-wood echoes rang—
   " O, dearly do I lo'e thee, Annie !

" O, happy be the woodbine bower,
   Nae nightly bogle make it eerie ;
Nor ever sorrow stain the hour,
   The place and time I met my Dearie !
Her head upon my throbbing breast,
   She, sinking, said, ' I'm thine for ever !'
While mony a kiss the seal imprest—
   The sacred vow we ne'er should sever."

The haunt o' Spring's the primrose-brae,
   The summer joys the flocks to follow ;
How cheery thro' her short'ning day,
   Is Autumn in her weeds o' yellow ;

But can they melt the glowing heart,
Or chain the soul in speechless pleasure?
Or thro' each nerve the rapture dart,
Like meeting her, our bosom's treasure?

["Autumn is my propitious season, I make more verses in it than in all
the year else. God bless you!"—so wrote the exulting poet when he forwarded the above song to Thomson. *August 19th* was the date of the
letter which enclosed it. He had performed the Galloway Tour—had met
with Clarke at the *Globe*, where he discovered that "the Georgium Sidus
was out of tune." He had composed and forwarded "Phillis the fair"—
followed quickly by the immortal "Had I a cave." Then he sent the song
in the text; to be followed by "Whistle and I'll come to you my lad!"—
by "Phillis the Queen of the Fair"—after which, by the songs, "Come
let me take thee to my breast"—and "Meet me on the Warlock Knowe,"
—yet all the while performing his daily Excise routine thoroughly. What
a month of August indeed! A fitting prelude to "Bruce's March to
Bannockburn" with which he opened September.]

WHISTLE AND I'LL COME TO YOU, MY LAD.

Chorus—O WHISTLE an' I'll come to ye, my lad,
O whistle an' I'll come to ye, my lad,
Tho' father an' mother an' a' should gae mad,
O whistle an' I'll come to ye, my lad.

But warily tent when ye come to court me,
And come nae unless the back-yett be a-jee;
Syne up the back-style, and let naebody see,
And come as ye were na comin to me,
And come as ye were na comin to me.
O whistle an' I'll come, &c.

At kirk, or at market, whene'er ye meet me,
Gang by me as tho' that ye car'd na' a flie;
But steal me a blink o' your bonie black e'e,
Yet look as ye were na lookin to me,
Yet look as ye were na lookin to me.
O whistle an' I'll come, &c.

III.   G

Ay vow and protest that ye care na for me,
And whyles ye may lightly my beauty a-wee;
But court na anither tho' jokin ye be,
For fear that she wyle your fancy frae me,
For fear that she wyle your fancy frae me.
    O whistle and I'll come, &c.

[This song was inspired by the charms of Jean Lorimer, although Cunning·
ham and Motherwell held that Mrs Maria Riddell laid claim to be the heroine.
The author of the song ought to have known that matter best, and he
afterwards instructed Thomson to alter the closing line of the chorus to
"Thy Jeanie will venture wi' ye, my lad;" and he added—"In fact a fair
dame whom the Graces have attired in witchcraft, and whom the Loves
have armed with lightning—a Fair One, *herself the heroine of the song*,
insists on the amendment, and dispute her commands if you dare." This
latter order was issued on 5th August 1795, two years after the song was
composed, but recalled in February 1796, when he had evidently conceived
a disrelish to "Chloris" and her flaxen ringlets.]

PHILLIS THE QUEEN O' THE FAIR.

Another favourite air of mine is "The muckin o' Geordie's Byre." When
sung slow with expression, I wish that it had better poetry. That I have
endeavoured to supply as follows :—

ADOWN winding Nith I did wander,
    To mark the sweet flowers as they spring;
Adown winding Nith I did wander,
    Of Phillis to muse and to sing.

Chorus—Awa' wi' your Belles and your Beauties,
        They never wi' her can compare,
    Whaever has met wi' my Phillis,
        Has met wi' the queen o' the Fair.

The Daisy amus'd my fond fancy,
    So artless, so simple, so wild;
Thou emblem, said I, o' my Phillis—
    For she is Simplicity's child,
        Awa' wi' your Belles, &c.

The Rose-bud's the blush o' my charmer,
　　Her sweet balmy lip when 'tis prest :
How fair and how pure is the Lily !
　　But fairer and purer her breast,
　　　Awa' wi' your Belles, &c.

Yon knot of gay flowers in the arbour,
　　They ne'er wi' my Phillis can vie :
Her breath is the breath of the woodbine,
　　Its dew-drop o' diamond her eye,
　　　Awa' wi' your Belles, &c.

Her voice is the song o' the morning,
　　That wakes thro' the green-spreading grove,
When Phebus peeps over the mountains,
　　On music, and pleasure, and love.
　　　Awa' wi' your Belles, &c.

But, Beauty, how frail and how fleeting !
　　The bloom of a fine summer's day ;
While Worth in the mind o' my Phillis,
　　Will flourish without a decay.
　　　Awa' wi' your Belles, &c.

[Miss Philadelphia M'Murdo was the subject of this elegant song, and it was produced to gratify Mr Stephen Clarke, the musician.]

COME, LET ME TAKE THEE TO MY BREAST.

That tune, "Cauld Kail" is such a favourite of yours that I once more roved out yester evening for a gloamin-shot * at the Muses : when the Muse that presides o'er the shores of Nith, or rather, my old inspiring, dearest nymph, Coila, whispered me the following :—

COME, let me take thee to my breast,
　　And pledge we ne'er shall sunder ;
And I shall spurn, as vilest dust,
　　The world's wealth and grandeur :

---

* Gloamin—twilight.　A beautiful Saxon word which ought to be adopted in England.　A " gloamin-shot," a twilight interview with.—*Currie.*

And do I hear my Jeanie own
  That equal transports move her?
I ask for dearest life alone,
  That I may live to love her.

Thus, in my arms, wi' a' her charms,
  I clasp my countless treasure;
I'll seek nae mair o' Heav'n to share,
  Than sic a moment's pleasure:
And by thy e'en sae bonie blue,
  I swear I'm thine for ever!
And on thy lips I seal my vow,
  And break it shall I never.

[The inspirer of the song was Jean Lorimer.
Some of our readers may be disposed to conjecture that Mrs Burns was
the "Jeanie" of this song, as well as of "Poortith cauld," and of "Whistle
and I'll come to you;" but the references to the blue eyes of the charmer,
prove that he did not in these effusions sing of his black-eyed spouse.
          "Her een sae bonie blue betray
          How she repays my passion."]

DAINTY DAVIE.

Now rosy May comes in wi' flowers,
To deck her gay, green-spreading bowers;
And now comes in the happy hours,
  To wander wi' my Davie.

Chorus—Meet me on the warlock knowe,
          Dainty Davie, Dainty Davie;
        There I'll spend the day wi' you,
          My ain dear Dainty Davie.

The crystal waters round us fa',
  The merry birds are lovers a',
The scented breezes round us blaw,
  A wandering wi' my Davie.
    Meet me on, &c.

As purple morning starts the hare,
To steal upon her early fare,
Then thro' the dews I will repair,
  To meet my faithfu' Davie.
    Meet me on, &c.

When day, expiring in the west,
The curtain draws o' Nature's rest,
I flee to his arms I loe the best,
  And that's my ain dear Davie.
    Meet me on, &c.

[On the same day that the poet had posted to Thomson the preceding song, to the tune "Cauld Kail," he despatched the one in the text, with these remarks—"I have written you already by to-day's post (28th Aug. 1793), where I hinted of a song of mine (O were I on Parnassus Hill) which might suit *Dainty Davie.* I have been looking over another, and a better song of mine in the *Museum,* which I have altered as follows, and which I am persuaded will please you. The words "Dainty Davie" glide so sweetly in the air, that, to a Scots ear, any song to it, without Davie being the hero, would have a lame effect.

"The chorus, you know, is to the low part of the tune. In the *Museum* they have drawled out the tune to twelve lines of poetry, which is nonsense Four lines of song, and four of chorus, is the way."]

ROBERT BRUCE'S MARCH TO BANNOCK-BURN.

To its ain tune.

"Independently of my enthusiasm as a Scotsman, I have rarely met with anything in history which interests my feelings as a man, equal with the story of Bannockburn. On the one hand, a cruel, but able usurper, leading on the finest army in Europe, to extinguish the last spark of freedom among a greatly-daring and greatly-injured people; on the other hand, the desperate relics of a gallant nation devoting themselves to rescue their bleeding country or perish with her. Liberty! thou art a prize truly and indeed invaluable, for never canst thou be too dearly bought!"—*Burns to Lord Buchan,* 12th Jan. 1794.

SCOTS, wha hae wi' WALLACE bled,
Scots, wham BRUCE has aften led,
Welcome to your gory bed,
                Or to Victorie!

Now's the day, and now's the hour ;
See the front o' battle lour ;
See approach proud EDWARD'S power--
         Chains and Slaverie !

Wha will be a traitor knave?
Wha can fill a coward's grave ?
Wha sae base as be a Slave?
         Let him turn and flee !
Wha, for Scotland's King and Law,
Freedom's sword will strongly draw,
FREE-MAN stand, or FREE-MAN fa',
         Let him on wi' me !

By Oppression's woes and pains !
By your Sons in servile chains !
We will drain our dearest veins,
         But they *shall* be free !
Lay the proud Usurpers low !
Tyrants fall in every foe !
LIBERTY'S in every blow !—
         Let us Do—or Die ! ! !

So may God ever defend the cause of Truth and
Liberty, as He did that day ! Amen !—*R. B.*

[This appears to have been posted to Thomson on 1st Sept. 1793. Burns
thus wrote :—" My Dear Sir,—You know that my pretentions to musical
taste are merely a few of nature's instincts, untaught or untutored by art.
For this reason, many musical compositions, particularly where much of the
merit lies in counterpoint, however they may transport and ravish the ears
of you connoisseurs, affect my simple lug no otherwise than merely as
melodious *Din*. On the other hand, by way of amends, I am delighted with
many little melodies which the learned musician despises as silly and insipid.
I do not know whether the old air, ' Hey tutti taitie,' may rank among this
number ; but well I know that, with Fraser's hautboy, it has often filled my
eyes with tears. There is a tradition, which I have met with in many
places in Scotland—that it was Robert Bruce's March at the battle of
Bannockburn. This thought in my yesternight's evening-walk, warmed me

to a pitch of enthusiasm on the theme of Liberty and Independence which
I threw into a kind of Scots Ode, fitted to the air, that one might suppose
to be the gallant royal Scot's address to his heroic followers on that eventful
morning."

By the kindness of Frederick Locker, Esq., author of "London Lyrics,"
&c., who is in possession of our poet's first draft of this famous ode, undoubtedly penned on 31st August 1793, immediately after the "evening
walk" above referred to, we are enabled to furnish the following verbatim
copy of Burns's earliest conception of this heroic effusion. As might be
expected, that MS. shews several readings which he was enabled marvel-
lously to improve after enjoying the refreshment of balmy sleep—Nature's
"sweet restorer."]

ROBERT BRUCE'S MARCH TO BANNOCKBURN.

Tune—"Hey tutti taitie."

Scots, wha hae wi' WALLACE bled,
Scots, wham BRUCE has aften led,
Welcome to your gory bed,
          Or to Victorie.

Now's the day, and now's the hour,
See approach proud Edward's power ;
Sharply maun we bide the stoure—
          Either they, or we.

Wha will be a traitor knave ?
Wha can fill a coward's grave ?
Wha sae base as be a slave ?
          Let him turn and flie !

Wha for Scotland's KING, and LAW,
Freedom's sword will strongly draw,
Free-man stand, or Free-man fa',
          Let him follow me !

Do you hear your children cry—
"Were we born in chains to lie ?"
No ! Come Death, or Liberty !
          Yes, they shall be free !

Lay the proud Usurpers low !
Tyrants fall in every foe !
Liberty's in every blow !
          Let us Do—or Die ! ! !

BEHOLD THE HOUR, THE BOAT ARRIVE.

Version Second.

BEHOLD the hour, the boat arrive ;
　　Thou goest, the darling of my heart ;
Sever'd from thee, can I survive,
　　But Fate has will'd and we must part.
I'll often greet the surging swell,
　　Yon distant Isle will often hail :
" E'en here I took the last farewell ;
　　There, latest mark'd her vanish'd sail."

Along the solitary shore,
　　While flitting sea-fowl round me cry,
Across the rolling, dashing roar,
　　I'll westward turn my wistful eye :
" Happy, thou Indian grove," I'll say,
　　" Where now my Nancy's path may be !
While thro' thy sweets she loves to stray,
　　O tell me, does she muse on me ! "

[This is a somewhat altered version of the same song which the poet
enclosed to Clarinda on 27th December 1791.]

DOWN THE BURN, DAVIE.

As down the burn they took their way,
　　And thro' the flowery dale ;
His cheek to hers he aft did lay,
　　And love was ay the tale :
With " Mary, when shall we return,
　　Sic pleasure to renew ? "
Quoth Mary—" Love, I like the burn,
　　And ay shall follow you."

[This was forwarded to Thomson in September 1793, as a closing double
stanza to supersede some rather indelicate verses of a well-known old song
by Robert Crawford. The lines in the text appeared in Thomson's third

volume, 1802, in connection with Crawford's song; but Burns's alteration was subsequently withdrawn to make way for two very puerile double stanzas by Thomson himself, who considered that our bard "did not bring the song to the desirable conclusion *here* given to it."

For the delectation of the reader, we append Thomson's improvement on Burns.

"As down the burn they took their way, he told his tender tale,
  Where all the opening sweets of May adorn'd the flowery dale.
' Not May in all her maiden pride is half sae sweet as thee ;
  O say thou'lt be my ain dear bride? thou'rt a' the warld to me !'

' Tho' Sandy ca's me sweet and fair, and boasts his sheep and kine ;
  In vain he seeks me late and air, my heart is only thine !'
' Oh ! rapturous sounds ! my first, best Love, come take my plighted hand ;
  My faith and troth I'll fondly prove, in Wedlock's holy band.' "

Popular tradition has assigned to David Rizzio the venerable old air, "Down the Burn, Davie." The old-fashioned people about Edinburgh point out the very "Burn" in a sequestered dell near "Little France," in the vicinity of Craigmillar Castle, as that which Queen Mary directed her "Davie-love" to go down and she would follow.]

THOU HAST LEFT ME EVER, JAMIE.

Tune—" Fee him, father, fee him."

THOU hast left me ever, Jamie,
  Thou hast left me ever ;
Thou hast left me ever, Jamie,
  Thou hast left me ever :
Aften hast thou vow'd that Death
  Only should us sever ;
Now thou'st left thy lass for ay—
  I maun see thee never, Jamie,
  I'll see thee never.

Thou hast me forsaken, Jamie,
  Thou hast me forsaken ;
Thou hast me forsaken, Jamie,
  Thou hast me forsaken ;

Than canst love another jo,
 While my heart is breaking ;
Soon my weary een I'll close,
 Never mair to waken, Jamie,
 Never mair to waken !

[This song was forwarded to Thomson in September 1793, with these observations:—" I enclose you Fraser's set of this tune. When he plays it slow, in fact he makes it the language of despair.[1] I shall here give you two stanzas in that style, merely to try if it will be any improvement. Were it possible, in singing, to give it half the pathos which Fraser gives it in playing, it would make an admirably pathetic song. I do not give these verses for any merit they have. I composed them at the time in which ' Patie Allan's mother died—*that was about the back o' midnight,*' and by the lee-side of a bowl of punch, which had overset every mortal in company except the *hautbois* and the Muse."]

WHERE ARE THE JOYS I HAE MET?

Tune—" Saw ye my father."

WHERE are the joys I hae met in the morning,
 That danc'd to the lark's early sang?
Where is the peace that awaited my wand'ring,
 At e'ening the wild-woods amang?

Nae mair a winding the course o' yon river,
 And marking sweet flowerets sae fair,
Nae mair I trace the light footsteps o' Pleasure,
 But Sorrow and sad-sighing Care.

Is it that Summer's forsaken our vallies,
 And grim, surly Winter is near?
No, no, the bees humming round the gay roses
 Proclaim it the pride o' the year.

---

[1] " I well recollect, about the year 1824, hearing Fraser play the air on his benefit night, in the Edinburgh Theatre, ' in the manner in which he had played it to Burns.' It was listened to with breathless attention, as if the house had felt it to be a medium of communion with the spirit of the departed bard."—*Chambers,* 1852.

Fain wad I hide what I fear to discover,
　Yet lang, lang, too well hae I known ;
A' that has caused the wreck in my bosom,
　Is Jenny, fair Jenny alone.

Time cannot aid me, my griefs are immortal,
　Not Hope dare a comfort bestow :
Come then, enamor'd and fond of my anguish,
　Enjoyment I'll seek in my woe.

[The " Jenny " of this song is simply the artist's favourite model, placed
with her face in shadow. The words of the old ballad, "Saw ye my
father," are very poetical, although the subject is somewhat objectionable ;
and accordingly these verses of Burns have not had the effect of banishing
from "Love's shining circle," the "Bonie Grey Cock"—another title
by which the ballad is known. The melody is very exquisite.]

DELUDED SWAIN, THE PLEASURE.

Tune—"The Collier's Dochter."

DELUDED swain, the pleasure
　The fickle Fair can give thee,
Is but a fairy treasure,
　Thy hopes will soon deceive thee :
The billows on the ocean,
　The breezes idly roaming,
The cloud's uncertain motion,
　They are but types of Woman.

O art thou not asham'd
　To doat upon a feature ?
If Man thou wouldst be nam'd
　Despise the silly creature.
Go, find an honest fellow,
　Good claret set before thee
Hold on till thou art mellow,
　And then to bed in glory !

[This clever Bacchanal, furnished to Thomson in September 1793, is an
improvement on an old English song.]

THINE AM I, MY FAITHFUL FAIR.

Tune— "The Quaker's Wife."

THINE am I, my faithful Fair,
  Thine, my lovely Nancy;
Ev'ry pulse along my veins,
  Ev'ry roving fancy.
To thy bosom lay my heart,
  There to throb and languish;
Tho' despair had wrung its core,
  That would heal its anguish.

Take away those rosy lips,
  Rich with balmy treasure;
Turn away thine eyes of love,
  Lest I die with pleasure!
What is life when wanting Love?
  Night without a morning:
Love's the cloudless summer sun,
  Nature gay adorning.

ON MRS RIDDELL'S BIRTHDAY.

4TH NOVEMBER 1793.

OLD WINTER, with his frosty beard,
Thus once to Jove his prayer preferred:
" What have I done of all the year,
To bear this hated doom severe?
My cheerless suns no pleasure know;
Night's horrid car drags dreary slow;
My dismal months no joys are crowning,
But spleeny English hanging, drowning.

" Now Jove, for once be mighty civil,
To counterbalance all this evil ;
Give me, and I've no more to say,
Give me Maria's natal day !
That brilliant gift shall so enrich me,
Spring, Summer, Autumn, cannot match me."
" 'Tis done ! " says Jove ; so ends my story,
And Winter once rejoiced in glory.

MY SPOUSE NANCY.

Tune—" My Jo Janet."

" HUSBAND, husband, cease your strife,
　　Nor longer idly rave, Sir ;
Tho' I am your wedded wife
　　Yet I am not your slave, Sir."
" One of two must still obey,
　　Nancy, Nancy ;
Is it Man or Woman, say,
　　My spouse Nancy ? "

" If 'tis still the lordly word,
　　Service and obedience ;
I'll desert my sov'reign lord,
　　And so, good bye, allegiance ! "
" Sad will I be, so bereft,
　　Nancy, Nancy ;
Yet I'll try to make a shift,
　　My spouse Nancy."

" My poor heart, then break it must,
　　My last hour I am near it :
When you lay me in the dust,
　　Think how you will bear it."

" I will hope and trust in Heaven,
Nancy, Nancy ;
Strength to bear it will be given,
My spouse Nancy."

" Well, Sir, from the silent dead,
Still I'll try to daunt you ;
Ever round your midnight bed
Horrid sprites shall haunt you !"
" I'll wed another like my dear
Nancy, Nancy ;
Then all hell will fly for fear,
My spouse Nancy."

[This witty dramatic song has been very popular from the day it was first
given to the public. The poet's working sketches of some of the stanzas
are in the British Museum, where the second verse is thus varied :—

' If the word is still obey !
Always love and fear you ;
I will take myself away,
And never more come near you.'
Sad will I be, &c.

The closing stanza thus begins—

' Well, ev'n from the silent dead,
Sir, I'll try to daunt you,' &c.]

ADDRESS,

SPOKEN BY MISS FONTENELLE ON HER BENEFIT NIGHT, DECEMBER 4TH, 1793, AT THE THEATRE, DUMFRIES.

STILL anxious to secure your partial favor,
And not less anxious, sure, this night than ever,
A Prologue, Epilogue, or some such matter,
'Twould vamp my bill, said I, if nothing better ;
So sought a poet, roosted near the skies,
Told him I came to feast my curious eyes ;

Said, nothing like his works was ever printed ;
And last, my prologue-business slily hinted.
" Ma'am, let me tell you," quoth my man of rhymes,
" I know your bent—these are no laughing times :
Can you—but, Miss, I own I have my fears—
Dissolve in pause, and sentimental tears ;
With laden sighs, and solemn-rounded sentence,
Rouse from his sluggish slumbers, fell Repentance ;
Paint Vengeance as he takes his horrid stand,
Waving on high the desolating brand,
Calling the storms to bear him o'er a guilty land ? "

I could no more—askance the creature eyeing,
D'ye think, said I, this face was made for crying?
I'll laugh, that's poz—nay more, the world shall know it ;
And so, your servant ! gloomy Master Poet !

　　Firm as my creed, Sirs, 'tis my fix'd belief,
That Misery's another word for Grief :
I also think—so may I be a bride !
That so much laughter, so much life enjoy'd.

Thou man of crazy care and ceaseless sigh,
Still under bleak Misfortune's blasting eye ;
Doom'd to that sorest task of man alive—
To make three guineas do the work of five :
Laugh in Misfortune's face—the beldam witch !
Say, you'll be merry, tho' you can't be rich.

Thou other man of care, the wretch in love,
Who long with jiltish arts and airs hast strove ;
Who, as the boughs all temptingly project,
Measur'st in desperate thought—a rope—thy neck—
Or, where the beetling cliff o'erhangs the deep,
Peerest to meditate the healing leap :
Would'st thou be cur'd, thou silly, moping elf?
Laugh at her follies—laugh e'en at thyself :

Learn to despise those frowns now so terrific,
And love a kinder—that's your grand specific.

To sum up all, be merry, I advise ;
And as we're merry, may we still be wise.

[This second Address written by the Bard for his favourite actress, Miss
Fontenelle, has been preserved to the public through the accident of its
having been communicated in a letter from Burns to Mrs Dunlop.]

COMPLIMENTARY EPIGRAM ON
MARIA RIDDELL.

" PRAISE Woman still," his lordship roars,
   " Deserv'd or not, no matter !"
But thee, whom all my soul adores,
   Ev'n Flattery cannot flatter :
MARIA, all my thought and dream,
   Inspires my vocal shell ;
The more I praise my lovely theme,
   The more the truth I tell.

[This trifle, a copy of which is inscribed on the back of the poet's first
draft of " Scots wha hae," &c., was bought at the sale of Burns's manu-
scripts which belonged to the late Mr Pickering. An indorsation explains
that some one, in presence of Mrs Riddell, informed the poet that Lord
Buchan, in an argument, vociferated that " Women must be always flattered
grossly, or not praised at all." Whereupon Burns pencilled these lines on
a slip of paper which he handed to the lady. We suspect that our poet was
here only establishing, instead of seeking to rebut, his lordship's argument.
In November 1793, Mrs Riddell, who was then living alone at Woodley
Park during her husband's absence in the West Indies, seems frequently to
have enjoyed the society of Burns by meeting him at her private box in the
Theatre, if she could not, in the circumstances, gratify her sociable nature
by having him as her guest at home. It appears, however, that in course
of December, Mr Riddell returned to this country, and (as Chambers has
remarked) " it was but natural at such a time, that he should wish to have
his friends about him, and the ever-brilliant bard amongst the number.
But unfortunately, at his board the wine flowed in such profusion that his
guests were apt to be deprived of reason and memory alike."
The incident which at length caused a quarrel between Burns and the
Riddells of Woodley Park, has not been very distinctly recorded ; but it

scems that early in the year 1794, at one of the Bacchanalian meetings
referred to by Chambers, he and the other gentlemen at Riddell's flowing
board (probably the result of a concerted frolic) suddenly invaded, like
a herd of Satyrs, the drawing-room, where Mrs Riddell and the lady-guests
were enjoying themselves, and a sort of miniature "rape of the Sabines'
was suddenly enacted.   Burns seized and saluted Mrs Riddell, while the
others secured each a lady in like manner, and kissed her.   This outrage,
as might be expected, gave great offence, and next morning Burns addressed
the remorseful apology to Mrs Riddell, written "from the regions of Hell,
amid the horrors of the d——d," which is found in his printed correspondence.]

REMORSEFUL APOLOGY.

THE friend whom, wild from Wisdom's way,
   The fumes of wine infuriate send,
(Not moony madness more astray)
   Who but deplores that hapless friend?

Mine was th' insensate frenzied part,
   Ah ! why should I such scenes outlive?
Scenes so abhorrent to my heart !—
   'Tis thine to pity and forgive.

[It is not very certain to whom these lines were addressed, although we
suspect they were addressed to Mrs Riddell.

Chambers tells us that these pleading lines were addressed to Mr Riddell,
the husband of the lady whom he had so rudely treated, as explained in our
last note ; but in his letter to the lady herself, he wrote in a very different
strain, thus :—"To the men of the company I make no apology. Your
husband, who insisted on my drinking more than I chose, has no right to
blame me ; and the other gentlemen were partakers of my guilt."

The breach did not, for several weeks after the incident, assume a very
hopeless aspect, but by and by, through the insidious whisperings of back-
biters and slanderers, the current of friendship was arrested, and wounded
pride soon obtained such a mastery over the spirit of Burns, that he at
length considered himself not the sinner, but the *sinned against.*]

WILT THOU BE MY DEARIE?

Tune—"The Sutor's Dochter."

WILT thou be my Dearie?
When Sorrow wrings thy gentle heart,
O wilt thou let me cheer thee !
By the treasure of my soul,
That's the love I bear thee :
I swear and vow that only thou
Shall ever be my Dearie !
Only thou, I swear and vow,
Shall ever be my Dearie !

Lassie, say thou lo'es me ;
Or, if thou wilt na be my ain,
O say na thou'lt refuse me !
If it winna, canna be,
Thou for thine may choose me,
Let me, lassie, quickly die,
Still trusting that thou lo'es me !
Lassie, let me quickly die,
Still trusting that thou lo'es me !

[This is one of the most remarkable of all Burns's lyrics, and one in which
he specially prided himself. We cannot resist coming to the conclusion
that Maria Riddell was its intended heroine. The first mention we have of
it is in the poet's letter to Alexander Cunningham, dated 3rd March 1794,
thus :—"*Apropos*, do you know the much admired Highland air, called
'The Sutor's Dochter?' It is a first-rate favourite of mine, and I have
written what I reckon one of my best songs to it. I will send it to you as
it was sung, with great applause in some fashionable circles, by Major
Robertson of Lude, who was here with his corps."

The correspondence of the poet, prior to the close of 1793, contains repeated reference to the "lobster-coated puppies" who associated with Mrs
Riddell at that period; and the lady's grandson, Mr Arthur de Noe
Walker, has now in his possession the poet's holograph copy of this song
which he presented to Mrs Riddell, along with "The last time I came o'er
the muir."]

A FIDDLER IN THE NORTH.

Tune—"The King o' France he rade a race."

AMANG the trees, where humming bees,
    At buds and flowers were hinging, O,
Auld Caledon drew out her drone,
    And to her pipe was singing, O :
'Twas Pibroch, Sang, Strathspeys and Reels,
    She dirl'd them aff fu' clearly, O ;
When there cam' a yell o' foreign squeels,
    That dang her tapsalteerie, O.

Their capon craws an' queer "ha, ha's,"
    They made our lugs grow eerie, O ;
The hungry bike did scrape and fyke,
    Till we were wae and weary, O :
But a royal ghaist, wha ance was cas'd,
    A prisoner, aughteen year awa',
He fir'd a Fiddler in the North,
    That dang them tapsalteerie, O.

[It appears probable from the terms of one of the poet's letters, that Neil
Gow paid a visit to Dumfries about this period, and had several meetings
with Burns; and it seems reasonable to infer that the present production
was one of the results of those interviews. The poet thus wrote to his
correspondent :—" I was much obliged to you for making me acquainted
with Gow. He is a modest, intelligent, worthy fellow, besides his being a
man of genius in his way. I have spent many happy hours with him in the
short while he has been here." The "royal ghaist" referred to is King
James I. of Scotland, who was kept a prisoner in England for eighteen years.]

THE MINSTREL AT LINCLUDEN.

As I stood by yon roofless tower,
    Where the wa'flow'r scents the dewy air,
Where the houlet mourns in her ivy bower,
    And tells the midnight moon her care.

Chorus—A lassie all alone, was making her moan,
　　　　Lamenting our lads beyond the sea ;
　　　In the bluidy wars they fa', and our honor's
　　　　　gane an' a',
　　　　And broken-hearted we maun die.

The winds were laid, the air was still,
　　The stars they shot along the sky ;
The tod was howling on the hill,
　　And the distant-echoing glens reply.
　　　A lassie all alone, &c.

The burn, adown its hazelly path,
　　Was rushing by the ruin'd wa',
Hasting to join the sweeping Nith,
　　Whase roarings seem'd to rise and fa'.
　　　A lassie all alone, &c.

The cauld blae North was streaming forth
　　Her lights, wi' hissing, eerie din,
Athort the lift they start and shift,
　　Like Fortune's favors, tint as win'.
　　　A lassie all alone, &c.

Now, looking over frith and fauld,
　　Her horn the pale-faced Cynthia rear'd,
When lo ! in form of Minstrel auld,
　　A stern and stalwart ghaist appear'd.
　　　A lassie all alone, &c.

And frae his harp sic strains did flow,
　　Might rous'd the slumbering Dead to hear ;
But oh, it was a tale of woe,
　　As ever met a Briton's ear !
　　　A lassie all alone, &c.

He sang wi' joy his former day,
He, weeping, wail'd his latter times ;
But what he said—it was nae play,
I winna ventur't in my rhymes.
A lassie all alone, &c.

[The above is the poet's first version of a sublime lyric, which he ultimately left on record under the title, "A Vision," in which some changes
are made in the text, and the chorus is excluded. Our country was at that
period at war with the French Republic—a war which Burns bitterly
deplored, although circumstances compelled him to set "a seal on his lips
as to those unlucky politics." He had been nearly forced into a duel by "an
epauletted puppy," who took mortal offence at a toast which the witty poet
proposed in his presence—"May our success in the present war be equal to
the justice of our cause." He had quarrelled with the Riddells, and according to his own account, his "soul was tossed on a sea of troubles, without
one friendly star to guide her course." On 25th Feb. 1794, he informed his
Edinburgh friend Cunningham, that for two months back he had not been
able to lift a pen. "My constitution and frame," he added, "were *ab
origine* blasted with a deep, incurable taint of hypochondria, which poisons
my existence. Of late, a number of domestic vexations, and some pecuniary
share in the ruin of these cursed times—losses which, though trifling, were
yet what I could ill bear—have so irritated me, that my feelings at times
could only be envied by a reprobate spirit listening to the sentence that
dooms it to perdition."

The main pillar which the poet depended on to bear up his soul amid
such a wreck of misfortune and misery was "a certain noble, stubborn
something in man, known by the names of Courage, Fortitude, Magnanimity." Accordingly, about this period (such was the recollection of the
poet's eldest son) he passed most of his musing hours amid the Lincluden
ruins. These occupy a romantic situation on a piece of rising ground in the
angle at the junction of the Cluden water with the Nith, at a short distance
above Dumfries. "Such," says Chambers, "is the locality of this grand
and thrilling ode, in which he hints (for more than a hint could not be
ventured upon) his sense of the degradation of the ancient manly spirit of
his country under the conservative terrors of the passing era."]

A VISION.

As I stood by yon roofless tower,
Where the wa'flower scents the dewy air,
Where the howlet mourns in her ivy bower,
And tells the midnight moon her care.

The winds were laid, the air was still,
    The stars they shot alang the sky ;
The fox was howling on the hill,
    And the distant echoing glens reply.

The stream, adown its hazelly path,
    Was rushing by the ruin'd wa's,
To join yon river on the Strath,
    Whase distant roaring swells and fa's.

The cauld blae North was streaming forth
    Her lights, wi' hissing, eerie din ;
Athwart the lift they start and shift,
    Like Fortune's favors, tint as win.

By heedless chance I turn'd my eyes,
    And, by the moonbeam, shook to see
A stern and stalwart ghaist arise,
    Attir'd as Minstrels wont to be.

Had I statue been o' stane,
    His daring look had daunted me ;
And on his bonnet grav'd was plain,
    The sacred posy—" LIBERTIE !"

And frae his harp sic strains did flow,
    Might rous'd the slumb'ring Dead to hear ;
But oh, it was a tale of woe,
    As ever met a Briton's ear !

He sang wi' joy his former day,
    He, weeping, wailed his latter times ;
But what he said—it was nae play,
    I winna ventur't in my rhymes.

[Dr Currie thus remarks concerning these verses :—" Though this poem has a political bias, yet it may be presumed that no reader of taste, whatever his opinions may be, would forgive its being omitted. Our poet's prudence suppressed the song of ' LIBERTIE,' perhaps fortunately for his reputation. It may be questioned whether, even in the resources of his genius, a strain of poetry could have been found worthy of the grandeur and solemnity of this preparation."]

A RED, RED ROSE.

My Luve is like a red, red rose,
   That's newly sprung in June :
My Luve is like the melodie,
   That's sweetly play'd in tune.

As fair art thou, my bonie lass,
   So deep in luve am I ;
And I will luve thee still, my Dear,
   Till a' the seas gang dry.

Till a' the seas gang dry, my Dear,
   And the rocks melt wi' the sun ;
And I will luve thee still, my Dear,
   While the sands o' life shall run.

And fare-thee-well, my only Luve !
   And fare-thee-well, a while !
And I will come again, my Luve,
   Tho' 'twere ten thousand mile !

[This little Love-chant has been a universal favourite since it was first
given to the world. It is one of those lyrics, in imitation of the old minstrels,
which called forth the commendations of Hazlitt in his critical remarks
on Burns's poetry.]

RESISTLESS KING OF LOVE.

YOUNG JAMIE, pride of a' the plain,
Sae gallant and sae gay a swain,
Thro' a' our lasses he did rove,
And reign'd resistless King of Love.

But now, wi' sighs and starting tears,
He strays amang the woods and breers ;
Or in the glens and rocky caves,
His sad complaining dowie raves :—

" I wha sae late did range and rove,
And chang'd with every moon my love,
I little thought the time was near,
Repentance I should buy sae dear.

" The slighted maids my torments see,
And laugh at a' the pangs I dree ;
While she, my cruel, scornful Fair,
Forbids me e'er to see her mair."

[An examination of the words suggests that this song may have been one of those pastorals which the poet composed with a view to conciliate the temper, and melt the coldness of Maria Riddell, whose lyrical tastes were very Arcadian. After the quarrel between that pair of Platonic lovers, to which we have referred, the chronology of Chambers brings us too suddenly into the gall of bitterness, and even disregard of decency which affected the wounded spirit of Burns after the failure of his conciliatory overtures. The prose correspondence betwixt them plainly exhibits a kind of diplomatic coquettishness, whose issue might be either reconciliation or open rupture. Unfortunately, the policy of Mrs Riddell led her to overstretch the *haut-en-bas rigour* by which she meant to depress and discipline her offending lover; and that roused the "stubborn something in his bosom" which impelled him to adopt the position of an injured man, in whom meekness would be pusillanimity, and revenge the noblest of virtues.]

THE FLOWERY BANKS OF CREE.

HERE is the glen, and here the bower
    All underneath the birchen shade ;
The village-bell has told the hour,
    O what can stay my lovely maid ?

'Tis not Maria's whispering call ;
    'Tis but the balmy-breathing gale,
Mixt with some warbler's dying fall,
    The dewy star of eve to hail.

It is Maria's voice I hear ;
    So calls the woodlark in the grove.
His little, faithful mate to cheer ;
    At once 'tis music and 'tis love.

And art thou come ! and art thou true !
O welcome dear to love and me !
And let us all our vows renew,
Along the flowery banks of Cree.

[This song appears to have been composed with the same purpose as that immediately preceding. The poet forwarded it to Thomson in April 1794, with directions to set it to an air called "The Banks of Cree," composed by Lady Elizabeth Heron of Heron. He had sent Thomson no verses since the month of December preceding, and now he wrote, " For six or seven months I shall be quite in song, as you shall see by and by."

Meanwhile the original breach between Burns and his intimate friends at Woodley Park became wide, in spite of all his efforts at reconciliation, and oy way of accounting for it Chambers blames "the tittle-tattle of injudicious friends." The poet became at length so deeply incensed against the once admired Maria and her husband that he stooped to express his rancour in strains truly unworthy of him ; and these we must now proceed to give.]

MONODY

ON A LADY FAMED FOR HER CAPRICE.

"Tell me what you think of the following Monody. The subject of it is a woman of fashion in this country, with whom at one period I was well acquainted. By some scandalous conduct to me, and two or three other gentlemen here as well as me, she steered so far to the north of my good opinion, that I have made her the theme of some ill-natured things. The epigram appended struck me the other day as I passed her carriage."— *Burns to Mrs M'Lehose,* 1794.

How cold is that bosom which folly once fired,
    How pale is that cheek where the rouge lately glisten'd ;
How silent that tongue which the echoes oft tired,
    How dull is that ear which to flatt'ry so listen'd !

If sorrow and anguish *their* exit await,
    From friendship and dearest affection remov'd ;
How doubly severer, Maria, thy fate,
    Thou diedst unwept, as thou livedst unlov'd.

Loves, Graces, and Virtues, I call not on you ;
    So shy, grave, and distant, ye shed not a tear :

But come, all ye offspring of Folly so true,
  And flowers let us cull for Maria's cold bier.

We'll search through the garden for each silly flower,
  We'll roam thro' the forest for each idle weed ;
But chiefly the nettle, so typical, shower,
  For none e'er approach'd her but rued the rash deed.

We'll sculpture the marble, we'll measure the lay ;
  Here Vanity strums on her idiot lyre ;
There keen Indignation shall dart on his prey,
  Which spurning Contempt shall redeem from his ire.

THE EPITAPH.

HERE lies, now a prey to insulting neglect,
  What once was a butterfly, gay in life's beam :
Want only of wisdom denied her respect,
  Want only of goodness denied her esteem.

PINNED TO MRS WALTER RIDDELL'S CARRIAGE.

IF you rattle along like your Mistress's tongue,
  Your speed will outrival the dart ;
But a fly for your load, you'll break down on the road,
  If your stuff be as rotten's her heart.

EPITAPH FOR MR WALTER RIDDELL.

SIC a reptile was Wat, sic a miscreant slave,
That the worms ev'n d—d him when laid in his grave ;
'In his flesh there's a famine,' a starved reptile cries,
'And his heart is rank poison !' another replies.

[The foregoing productions, all very characteristic of their author, must
be left to speak for themselves. Chambers truly remarks that "to have
given expression to such sentiments regarding a female, even though a

positive wrong had been inflicted, would have been totally indefensible;
and still more astounding is it to find, that the bard could think of exhibiting
such effusions to another female. Strange that the generous heart which
never failed to have ruth on human woe, which felt even for 'the ourie
cattle and the silly sheep,' which glowed with patriotic fire, and disdained
everything like a sordid or shabby action, should have been capable of
condescending to expressions of coarse and rancorous feelings against a
woman, and one who had shewn him many kindnesses." In Dr Currie's
edition, the name of the victim is sympathisingly changed from *Maria* to
"Eliza."]

EPISTLE FROM ESOPUS TO MARIA.

" Well! divines may say of it what they please; but *execration* is to the
mind what phlebotomy is to the body; the vital sluices of both are wonder-
fully relieved by their respective evacuations."—*Letter to Peter Hill.*

From those drear solitudes and frowsy cells,
Where Infamy with sad Repentance dwells;
Where turnkeys make the jealous portal fast,
And deal from iron hands the spare repast;
Where truant 'prentices, yet young in sin,
Blush at the curious stranger peeping in;
Where strumpets, relics of the drunken roar,
Resolve to drink, nay half—to whore no more;
Where tiny thieves not destin'd yet to swing,
Beat hemp for others, riper for the string:
From these dire scenes my wretched lines I date,
To tell Maria her Esopus' fate.

"Alas! I feel I am no actor here!"
'Tis real hangmen real scourges bear!
Prepare, Maria, for a horrid tale
Will turn thy very rouge to deadly pale;
Will make thy hair, tho' erst from gipsy poll'd,
By barber woven, and by barber sold,
Though twisted smooth with Harry's nicest care,
Like hoary bristles to erect and stare.

The hero of the mimic scene, no more
I start in Hamlet, in Othello roar;
Or, haughty Chieftain, 'mid the din of arms,
In Highland bonnet, woo Malvina's charms;
While sans-culottes stoop up the mountain high,
And steal from me Maria's prying eye.
Blest Highland bonnet! once my proudest dress,
Now prouder still, Maria's temples press;
I see her wave thy towering plumes afar,
And call each coxcomb to the wordy war:
I see her face the first of Ireland's sons,
And even out-Irish his Hibernian bronze;
The crafty Colonel leaves the tartan'd lines,
For other wars, where he a hero shines:
The hopeful youth, in Scottish senate bred,
Who owns a Bushby's heart without the head,
Comes 'mid a string of coxcombs, to display
That *veni, vidi, vici*, is his way:
The shrinking Bard adown the alley skulks,
And dreads a meeting worse than Woolwich hulks;
Though there, his heresies in Church and State
Might well award him Muir and Palmer's fate:
Still she undaunted reels and rattles on,
And dares the public like a noontide sun.
What scandal called Maria's jaunty stagger
The ricket reeling of a crooked swagger?
Whose spleen (e'en worse than Burns's venom, when
He dips in gall unmix'd his eager pen,
And pours his vengeance in the burning line,)—
Who christen'd thus Maria's lyre-divine
The idiot strum of Vanity bemus'd,
And even th' abuse of Poesy abus'd?—
Who called her verse a Parish Workhouse, made
For motley foundling Fancies, stolen or strayed?

A Workhouse! ah, that sound awakes my woes,
And pillows on the thorn my rack'd repose!

In durance vile here must I wake and weep,
And all my frowsy couch in sorrow steep ;
That straw where many a rogue has lain of yore,
And vermin'd gipsies litter'd heretofore.

Why, Lonsdale, thus thy wrath on vagrants pour?
Must earth no rascal save thyself endure?
Must thou alone in guilt immortal swell,
And make a vast monopoly of hell?
Thou know'st the Virtues cannot hate thee worse ;
The Vices also, must they club their curse?
Or must no tiny sin to others fall,
Because thy guilt's supreme enough for all?

Maria, send me too thy griefs and cares ;
In all of thee sure thy Esopus shares.
As thou at all mankind the flag unfurls,
Who on my fair one Satire's vengeance hurls—
Who calls thee, pert, affected, vain coquette,
A wit in folly, and a fool in wit !
Who says that fool alone is not thy due,
And quotes thy treacheries to prove it true !

Our force united on thy foes we'll turn,
And dare the war with all of woman born :
For who can write and speak as thou and I?
My periods that decyphering defy,
And thy still matchless tongue that conquers all reply!

[The peculiar plan of this final poetical attack on the Maria whom its author had so recently worshipped, was explained in a communication made by a well-informed correspondent of the *Kendal Mercury*, so recently as in July 1852.

A dramatic company, headed by Mr James Williamson, an actor of considerable merit, occasionally performed in the little theatre behind the George Inn of Dumfries. About the close of 1793, Williamson, like Burns, was frequently admitted into the charmed circle at Woodley Park. In the following Spring, after the fatal quarrel, the poet happened to hear of a most extraordinary adventure having befallen Williamson and his associates while performing at Whitehaven. The Earl of Lonsdale, a local despot whose ill-fame was not unknown to Burns, had committed the whole company to prison as vagrants. Seizing on this incident, Burns conceived the idea of the foregoing epistle (formed on the model of "Eloisa to Abelard,") as being penned by Williamson under the name "Esopus," in prison at Whitehaven, to the lady whose society he had recently enjoyed.

A principal cause of the deep-rooted umbrage which Burns conceived against the accomplished Maria, lay in the fact that through her capricious displeasure, he lost the cherished friendship of the Laird of Carse and his lady; for they sided with their relatives at Woodley Park in this affair. Mrs Walter Riddell had the indiscretion to repeat to her brother-in-law some jocular remarks which Burns had made on the peculiarities of Capt. Riddell; and this little instance of womanly spleen the poet resented more than her unforgiving attitude towards himself, inasmuch as he was thereby deprived of the esteem of those ancient friends whom he had really reverenced.]

EPITAPH ON A NOTED COXCOMB,

CAPT. WM. RODDICK, OF CORBISTON.

LIGHT lay the earth on Billy's breast,
    His chicken heart so tender;
But build a castle on his head,
    His *scull* will prop it under.

ON CAPT. LASCELLES.

WHEN Lascelles thought fit from this world to depart,
Some friends warmly thought of embalming his heart;
A bystander whispers—"Pray don't make so much o't,
The subject is poison, no reptile will touch it."

ON WM. GRAHAM, ESQ. OF MOSSKNOWE.

"STOP thief!" dame Nature call'd to Death,
    As Willy drew his latest breath;
How shall I make a fool again?
    My choicest model thou hast ta'en.

ON JOHN BUSHBY, ESQ., TINWALD DOWNS.

Here lies John Bushby—*honest man,*
Cheat him, Devil—if you can !

[The preceding four Epigrams are among the list of those sent by Burns
to Creech, in May 1795; and they are also recorded in the author's handwriting, in the Glenriddell volume of his poetry, now in the Liverpool
Athenæum.]

SONNET ON THE DEATH OF ROBERT RIDDELL,

OF GLENRIDDELL AND FRIARS' CARSE.

No more, ye warblers of the wood ! no more ;
    Nor pour your descant grating on my soul ;
    Thou young-eyed Spring ! gay in thy verdant stole,
More welcome were to me grim Winter's wildest roar.

How can ye charm, ye flowers, with all your dyes?
    Ye blow upon the sod that wraps my friend !
    How can I to the tuneful strain attend ?
That strain flows round the untimely tomb where Riddell
        lies.

Yes, pour, ye warblers ! pour the notes of woe,
    And soothe the Virtues weeping o'er his bier :
    The man of worth—and hath not left his peer !
Is in his "narrow house," for ever darkly low.

Thee, Spring ! again with joy shall others greet ;
Me, memory of my loss will only meet.

[Somewhat unexpectedly, the Laird of Carse died on 21st April 1794,
unreconciled to Burns, who remembering only his worth and former kindness, immediately conceived this elegiac sonnet. The recollection of this
magnanimous act of Burns must have touched Maria Riddell's mind with
some compunctuous force, when she performed a kindred act, little more
than two years thereafter, for their author, also laid in his last sleep.]

THE LOVELY LASS O' INVERNESS.

THE lovely lass o' Inverness,
   Nae joy nor pleasure can she see ;
For, e'en to morn she cries "alas !"
   And ay the saut tear blin's her e'e.

" Drumossie moor, Drumossie day—
   A waefu' day it was to me !
For there I lost my father dear,
   My father dear, and brethren three.

" Their winding-sheet the bluidy clay,
   Their graves are growin green to see ;
And by them lies the dearest lad
   That ever blest a woman's e'e !

" Now wae to thee, thou cruel lord,
   A bluidy man I trow thou be ;
For mony a heart thou has made sair,
   That ne'er did wrang to thine or thee !"

[The kindly Spring wakened up the chords of song within the bosom of our Minstrel, and bestirring himself to produce lyrics for the pages of Johnson and Thomson, he was gradually diverted from the morbid desire to write lampoons and personal satire.]

CHARLIE, HE'S MY DARLING.

'TWAS on a Monday morning,
   Right early in the year,
That Charlie came to our town,
   The young Chevalier.

Chorus—An' Charlie, he's my darling,
   My darling, my darling,
   Charlie, he's my darling,
   The young Chevalier.

As he was walking up the street,
　The city for to view,
O there he spied a bonie lass
　The window looking through,
　　　An' Charlie, &c.

Sae light's he jumped up the stair,
　And tirl'd at the pin ;
And wha sae ready as hersel'
　To let the laddie in !
　　　An' Charlie, &c.

He set his Jenny on his knee,
　All in his Highland dress ;
For brawly well he ken'd the way
　To please a bonie lass,
　　　An Charlie, &c.

It's up yon heathery mountain,
　An' down yon scroggie glen,
We daur na gang a milking,
　For Charlie and his men,
　　　An' Charlie, &c.

BANNOCKS O' BEAR MEAL.

Chorus—Bannocks o' bear meal,
　　　Bannocks o' barley,
　　　Here's to the Highlandman's
　　　Bannocks o' barley !

WHA, in a brulyie, will
　First cry "a parley"?
Never the lads wi' the
　Bannocks o' barley,
　　　Bannocks o' bear meal, &c

Wha, in his wae days,
 Were loyal to Charlie?
Wha but the lads wi' the
 Bannocks o' barley !
  Bannocks o' bear meal, &c.

THE HIGHLAND BALOU.

HEE balou, my sweet wee Donald,
Picture o' the great Clanronald ;
Brawlie kens our wanton Chief
Wha gat my young Highland thief.

Leeze me on thy bonie craigie,
An' thou live, thou'll steal a naigie,
Travel the country thro' and thro',
And bring hame a Carlisle cow.

Thro' the Lawlands, o'er the Border,
Weel, my babie, may thou furder !
Harry the louns o' the laigh Countrie,
Syne to the Highlands hame to me.

THE HIGHLAND WIDOW'S LAMENT.

OH I am come to the low Countrie,
 Ochon, Ochon, Ochrie !
Without a penny in my purse,
 To buy a meal to me.

It was na sae in the Highland hills,
 Ochon, Ochon, Ochrie !
Nae woman in the Country wide,
 Sae happy was as me.

For then I had a score o' kye,
  Ochon, Ochon, Ochrie !
Feeding on yon hill sae high,
  And giving milk to me.

And there I had three score o' yowes,
  Ochon, Ochon, Ochrie !
Skipping on yon bonie knowes,
  And casting woo to me.

I was the happiest of a' the Clan,
  Sair, sair may I repine ;
For Donald was the brawest man,
  And Donald he was mine.

Till Charlie Stewart cam at last,
  Sae far to set us free ;
My Donald's arm was wanted then,
  For Scotland and for me.

Their waefu' fate what need I tell,
  Right to the wrang did yield ;
My Donald and his Country fell,
  Upon Culloden field.

Ochon ! O Donald, oh !
  Ochon, Ochon, Ochrie !
Nae woman in the warld wide,
  Sae wretched now as me.

IT WAS A' FOR OUR RIGHTFU' KING.

It was a' for our rightfu' King
  We left fair Scotland's strand ;
It was a' for our rightfu' King
  We e'er saw Irish land, my dear,
    We e'er saw Irish land.

Now a' is done that men can do,
  And a' is done in vain ;
My Love and Native Land fareweel,
  For I maun cross the main, my dear,
  For I maun cross the main.

He turn'd him right and round about,
  Upon the Irish shore ;
And gae his bridle reins a shake,
  With adieu for evermore, my dear,
  And adieu for evermore.

The soger frae the wars returns,
  The sailor frae the main ;
But I hae parted frae my Love,
  Never to meet again, my dear,
  Never to meet again.

When day is gane, and night is come,
  And a' folk bound to sleep ;
I think on him that's far awa,
  The lee-lang night and weep, my dear,
  The lee-lang night and weep.

[We are informed, both by Lockhart and by Kirkpatrick Sharpe, that Sir Walter Scott never tired of hearing this admirable ballad sung by his daughter. Mr Sharpe has pointed to a very poor stall-ballad, called "Molly Stuart," consisting of eleven verses of disconnected doggerel, in which occurs, "like a jewel in a swine's snout," the most picturesque stanza in the text—that beginning, "He turned him right and round about,"—but we have no doubt that the broadside referred to was printed after 1796.

Sir Walter, under the impression that the stanza in question is ancient, has made very free use of it, first in "Rokeby" (1813), and then in Elspeth's Ballad, in "The Antiquary" (1816). In the former, as part of the fine song, "A weary lot is thine, fair maid," he thus introduces the verse :—

  " He turn'd his charger as he spake.
    Upon the river shore,
  He gave his bridle reins a shake,
    Said, 'Adieu for evermore, my love,
    And adieu for evermore.' "]

ODE FOR GENERAL WASHINGTON'S BIRTHDAY.

"I am just going to trouble your critical patience with the first sketch of a stanza I have been framing as I passed along the road. The subject is LIBERTY: you know, my honoured friend, how dear the theme is to me. I design it as an irregular Ode for General Washington's birthday."—*Letter to Mrs Dunlop, 25th June* 1794.

No Spartan tube, no Attic shell,
  No lyre Æolian I awake ;
'Tis liberty's bold note I swell,
  Thy harp, Columbia, let me take !
See gathering thousands, while I sing,
A broken chain exulting bring,
  And dash it in a tyrant's face,
  And dare him to his very beard,
  And tell him he no more is feared—
  No more the despot of Columbia's race !
A tyrant's proudest insults brav'd,
They shout—a People freed ! They hail an Empire saved.

Where is man's godlike form?
  Where is that brow erect and bold—
  That eye that can unmov'd behold
The wildest rage, the loudest storm
That e'er created fury dared to raise?
Avaunt ! thou caitiff, servile, base,
That tremblest at a despot's nod,
Yet, crouching under the iron rod,
  Canst laud the hand that struck th' insulting blow !
Art thou of man's Imperial line ?
Dost boast that countenance divine?
  Each skulking feature answers, No !

But come, ye sons of Liberty,
Columbia's offspring, brave as free,
In danger's hour still flaming in the van,
Ye know, and dare maintain, the Royalty of Man!

Alfred! on thy starry throne,
    Surrounded by the tuneful choir,
    The bards that erst have struck the patriot lyre,
    And rous'd the freeborn Briton's soul of fire,
No more thy England own!
Dare injured nations form the great design,
    To make detested tyrants bleed?
    Thy England execrates the glorious deed!
    Beneath her hostile banners waving,
    Every pang of honour braving,
England in thunder calls, "The tyrant's cause is mine!"
That hour accurst how did the fiends rejoice
And hell, thro' all her confines, raise the exulting voice,
That hour which saw the generous English name
Linkt with such damned deeds of everlasting shame!

Thee, Caledonia! thy wild heaths among,
Fam'd for the martial deed, the heaven-taught song,
    To thee I turn with swimming eyes;
Where is that soul of Freedom fled?
Immingled with the mighty dead,
    Beneath that hallow'd turf where Wallace lies!
Hear it not, WALLACE! in thy bed of death.
    Ye babbling winds! in silence sweep,
    Disturb not ye the hero's sleep,
Nor give the coward secret breath!
Is this the ancient Caledonian form,
Firm as the rock, resistless as the storm?
Show me that eye which shot immortal hate,
    Blasting the despot's proudest bearing;
Show me that arm which, nerv'd with thundering fate,

Crush'd Usurpation's boldest daring !—
Dark-quench'd as yonder sinking star,
No more that glance lightens afar ;
That palsied arm no more whirls on the waste of war.

[Dr Josiah Walker, who had been introduced to Burns in 1787, and who
in 1811 published anonymously a memoir of him, visited the poet at
Dumfries in October 1794 (not 1795, as he has in error set down). He says,
"I called upon him early in the forenoon, and found him in a small house
of one story. He was sitting on a window-seat with the doors open, the
family arrangements going on in his presence, and altogether without that
appearance of snugness and seclusion which a student requires. After conversing with him for some time, he proposed a walk, and promised to
conduct me through some of his favourite haunts. We accordingly quitted
the town, and wandered a considerable way up the beautiful banks of the
Nith. Here he gave me an account of his latest productions, and repeated
some satirical ballads which he had composed to favour one of the candidates
at the last borough election. These I thought inferior to his other pieces,
though they had some lines in which vigour compensated for coarseness.
He repeated also his fragment of an ' Ode to Liberty' (the closing portion of
the poem in the text), with marked and peculiar energy, and shewed a disposition—which, however, was easily repressed—to throw out political
remarks, of the same nature with those for which he had been reprehended.
On finishing our walk, he passed some time with me at the inn, and I left
him early in the evening."]

INSCRIPTION TO MISS GRAHAM OF FINTRY.

"I have presented a copy of your book of songs to the daughter of a much-
valued and much-honoured friend of mine—Mr Graham of Fintry. I wrote
on the blank side of the title page, the following address to the young
lady."—*Letter to George Thomson, July* 1794.

HERE, where the Scottish Muse immortal lives,
    In sacred strains and tuneful numbers joined,
Accept the gift ; though humble he who gives,
    Rich is the tribute of the grateful mind.

So may no ruffled feeling in thy breast,
    Discordant, jar thy bosom-chords among ;
But Peace attune thy gentle soul to rest,
    Or Love ecstatic wake his seraph song,

Or Pity's notes, in luxury of tears,
    As modest Want the tale of woe reveals ;
While conscious Virtue all the strains endears,
    And heaven-born Piety her sanction seals.

ON THE SEAS AND FAR AWAY.

Tune—"O'er the hills and far away."

How can my poor heart be glad,
When absent from my sailor lad ;
How can I the thought forego—
He's on the seas to meet the foe?
Let me wander, let me rove,
Still my heart is with my love ;
Nightly dreams, and thoughts by day,
Are with him that's far away.

Chorus.—On the seas and far away,
        On stormy seas and far away ;
        Nightly dreams and thoughts by day,
        Are ay with him that's far away.

When in summer noon I faint,
As weary flocks around me pant,
Haply in this scorching sun,
My sailor's thund'ring at his gun ;
Bullets, spare my only joy !
Bullets, spare my darling boy !
Fate, do with me what you may,
Spare but him that's far away.
    On the seas and far away,
    On stormy seas and far away ;
    Fate, do with me what you may,
    Spare but him that's far away.

At the starless, midnight hour
When Winter rules with boundless power
As the storms the forests tear,
And thunders rend the howling air,
Listening to the doubling roar,
Surging on the rocky shore,
All I can—I weep and pray
For his weal that's far away.
 On the seas and far away,
 On stormy seas and far away :
 All I can—I weep and pray,
 For his weal that's far away.

Peace, thy olive wand extend,
And bid wild War his ravage end,
Man with brother Man to meet,
And as a brother kindly greet ;
Then may heav'n with prosperous gales,
Fill my sailor's welcome sails ;
To my arms their charge convey,
My dear lad that's far away.
 On the seas and far away,
 On stormy seas and far away ;
 To my arms their charge convey,
 My dear lad that's far away.

[This effusion, sent to Thomson on 30th August 1794, is introduced with the following passage :—"The last evening as I was straying out and thinking of ' O'er the Hills and far away,' I spun the following stanzas for it ; but whether my spinning will deserve to be laid up in stores, like the precious thread of the silkworm, or brushed to the devil, like the vile manufacture of the spider, I leave, my dear Sir, to your usual candid criticism. I was pleased with several lines in it at first, but I own that now it appears rather a flimsy business."]

CA' THE YOWES TO THE KNOWES.

SECOND VERSION.

Chorus.—Ca' the yowes to the knowes,
    Ca' them where the heather grows,
    Ca' them where the burnie rowes,
      My bonie Dearie.

HARK the mavis' e'ening sang,
Sounding Clouden's woods amang ;
'hen a-faulding let us gang,
    My bonie Dearie.
      Ca' the yowes, &c.

We'll gae down by Clouden side,*
Thro' the hazles, spreading wide,
O'er the waves that sweetly glide,
    To the moon sae clearly.
      Ca' the yowes, &c.

Yonder Clouden's silent towers,†
Where, at moonshine's midnight hours,
O'er the dewy bending flowers,
    Fairies dance sae cheery.
      Ca' the yowes, &c.

Ghaist nor bogle shalt thou fear,
Thou'rt to Love and Heav'n sae dear,
Nocht of ill may come thee near ;
    My bonie Dearie.
      Ca' the yowes, &c.

---

* A little river so called, near Dumfries.—*R. B.*
† An old ruin in a sweet situation at the confluence of the Clouden and
the Nith.—*R. B.*

Fair and lovely as thou art,
Thou hast stown my very heart ;
I can die—but canna part,
  My bonie Dearie.
    Ca' the yowes, &c.

[In sending this to Thomson in September 1794, the poet thus wrote :—
"I am flattered at your adopting 'Ca' the yowes,' as it was owing to me
that it ever saw the light. About seven years ago, I was well acquainted
with a worthy little fellow of a clergyman, a Mr Clunie, who sang it charm-
ingly ; and, at my request, Mr Clarke took it down from his singing. When
I gave it to Johnson, I added some stanzas to the song and mended others,
but still it will not do for you. In a solitary stroll which I took to-day, I
tried my hand on a few pastoral lines, following up the idea of the old
chorus, which I would preserve."]

SHE SAYS SHE LOES ME BEST OF A'.

Tune—"Oonagh's Waterfall."

SAE flaxen were her ringlets,
  Her eyebrows of a darker hue,
Bewitchingly o'er-arching
  Twa laughing e'en o' lovely blue ;
Her smiling, sae wyling,
  Wad make a wretch forget his woe ;
What pleasure, what treasure,
  Unto these rosy lips to grow !
Such was my Chloris' bonie face,
  When first that bonie face I saw ;
And ay my Chloris' dearest charm—
  She says, she lo'es me best of a'.

Like harmony her motion,
  Her pretty ancle is a spy,

Betraying fair proportion,
　　Wad make a saint forget the sky :
Sae warming, sae charming,
　　Her fautless form and gracefu' air ;
Ilk feature—auld Nature
　　Declar'd that she could do nae mair :
Hers are the willing chains o' love,
　　By conquering Beauty's sovereign law ;
And still my Chloris' dearest charm—
　　She says, she lo'es me best of a'.

Let others love the city,
　　And gaudy show, at sunny noon ;
Gie me the lonely valley,
　　The dewy eve and rising moon,
Fair beaming, and streaming,
　　Her silver light the boughs amang ;
While falling, recalling,
　　The amorous thrush concludes his sang :
There, dearest Chloris, wilt thou rove,
　　By wimpling burn and leafy shaw,
And hear my vows o' truth and love,
　　And say, thou lo'es me best of a'.

[This gushing effusion, sent to Thomson in September 1794, is ushered in
with the following remarks :—" Do you know, my dear Sir, a blackguard
Irish song called 'Oonagh's Waterfall'? Our friend Cunningham sings it
delightfully. The air is charming, and I have often regretted the want of
decent verses to it. It is too much, at least for *my* humble rustic Muse, to
expect that every effort of hers must have merit; still, I think that it is
better to have mediocre verses to a favourite air than none at all. On this
principle I have all along proceeded in the 'Scots Musical Museum ;' and
as that publication is at its last volume, I intend the following song to the
air above mentioned, for that work."

　　Thomson in reply said :—" *She says she lo'es me best of a'* is one of the
pleasantest table-songs I have seen, and henceforth shall be mine when the
song is going round."]

TO DR MAXWELL,

ON MISS JESSY STAIG'S RECOVERY.

MAXWELL, if here you merit crave,
   That merit I deny ;
You save fair Jessie from the grave !—
   An Angel could not die !

[In September 1794, the poet closed one of his letters to Thomson by in-
troducing this Epigram thus :—" How do you like the following epigram,
which I wrote the other day on a lovely young girl's recovery from a fever?
Dr Maxwell—the identical Maxwell whom Burke mentioned in the House
of Commons, was the physician who seemingly saved her from the grave."
The reader will understand that Miss Jessy Staig was the heroine of the
song, " Lovely Young Jessie."]

TO THE BEAUTIFUL MISS ELIZA J——N,
ON HER PRINCIPLES OF LIBERTY AND EQUALITY.

How, Liberty ! girl, can it be by thee nam'd?
Equality too ! hussey, art not asham'd?
Free and Equal indeed, while mankind thou enchainest,
And over their hearts a proud Despot so reignest.

[This is one of the scraps sent by the author to Mr Creech on 30th May
1795. We are unable to point out who the lady was.]

ON CHLORIS

REQUESTING ME TO GIVE HER A SPRIG OF BLOSSOMED
THORN.

FROM the white-blossom'd sloe my dear Chloris requested
   A sprig, her fair breast to adorn :
No, by Heavens ! I exclaim'd, let me perish, if ever
   I plant in that bosom a thorn !

[These lines are included among the seventeen Epigrams forwarded
by the poet to Mr Creech in May 1795. Charles Dibdin added a

stanza, to make the song of reasonable length. The added stanza is as follows:—

> " When I shewed her the ring and implor'd her to marry,
> She blush'd like the dawning of morn :
> Yes, I will l she replied, if you'll promise, dear Harry,
> No rival shall laugh me to scorn."]

ON SEEING MRS KEMBLE IN YARICO.

KEMBLE, thou cur'st my unbelief
Of Moses and his rod ;
At Yarico's sweet note of grief
The rock with tears had flow'd.

[This lady was the wife of Stephen Kemble, " the Fat," who played Falstaff without stuffing. Her maiden name was Satchell. Boaden is enthusiastic in her praise. (See his Life of Mrs Siddons, p. 214, Vol. I.) " From many fair eyes now shut have we seen her *Ophelia* draw tears in the mad scene : she was a delicious *Juliet*, and an altogether incomparable *Yarico*."—*Blackwood's Magazine*, 1832. This epigram is one of the seventeen sent to Creech. Mrs Kemble made her first appearance in Dumfries, in the Opera of " Inkle and Yarico," in October 1794.]

EPIGRAM ON A COUNTRY LAIRD,

NOT QUITE SO WISE AS SOLOMON.

BLESS Jesus Christ, O Cardoness,
With grateful, lifted eyes,
Who taught that not the soul alone,
But *body* too shall rise ;
For had He said " the soul alone
From death I will deliver,"
Alas, alas ! O Cardoness,
Then hadst thou lain for ever.

[Mr David Maxwell of Cardoness was the gentleman thus satirized ; but we are not aware what personal ground of offence he had given to our poet. A daughter of this gentleman became the second wife of Wm. Cunninghame, Esq., of Enterkine, whose first wife, a daughter of Mrs Stewart of Afton Lodge, died in 1809.]

ON BEING SHEWN A BEAUTIFUL COUNTRY SEAT

BELONGING TO THE SAME LAIRD.

WE grant they're thine, those beauties all,
   So lovely in our eye;
Keep them, thou eunuch, Cardoness,
   For others to enjoy !

[This also occurs among the "poetic clinches" sent by Burns to Creech
in May 1795. The satirist here compares to a eunuch possessed of a beautiful
mistress, the landowner who has not the soul to enjoy his own beautiful
estate. This Laird ranked higher in the opinion of some others than in that
of Burns. In 1804 he was made a Baronet. He survived to 1825.]

ON HEARING IT ASSERTED FALSEHOOD

IS EXPRESSED IN THE REV. DR BABINGTON'S VERY LOOKS.

THAT there is a falsehood in his looks,
   I must and will deny :
They tell their Master is a knave,
   And sure they do not lie.

[This very severe thing is recorded by Burns himself in the Glenriddell
volume now at Liverpool; and it was also one of the trifles sent to Creech
in May 1795.]

ON A SUICIDE.

EARTH'D up, here lies an imp o' hell,
   Planted by Satan's dibble ;
Poor silly wretch, he's damned himsel',
   To save the Lord the trouble.

ON A SWEARING COXCOMB.

HERE cursing, swearing Burton lies,
A buck, a beau, or " Dem my eyes !"
Who in his life did little good,
And his last words were, "Dem my blood !"

ON AN INNKEEPER NICKNAMED 'THE MARQUIS.'

HERE lies a mock Marquis, whose titles were shamm'd,
If ever he rise, it will be to be damn'd.

ON ANDREW TURNER.

IN se'enteen hunder 'n forty-nine,
The deil gat stuff to mak a swine,
　　An' coost it in a corner ;
But wilily he chang'd his plan,
An' shap'd it something like a man,
　　An' ca'd it Andrew Turner.

[These four epigrams we have classed together, as requiring little comment, and as exhausting the trifles of that kind attributed to Burns which we deem worthy of being reproduced here. Cunningham tells a circumstantial story of the first of these, which we can scarcely credit; for we think the kindly poet would have bestowed a tear of pity rather than waste his satire on such a forlorn wretch.

Andrew Turner, the hero of the last of them, was a " haveril," who had the vanity to ask Burns to make an epigram on him : 1749 was the year of Andrew's birth.]

PRETTY PEG.

As I gaed up by yon gate-end,
　　When day was waxin weary,
Wha did I meet come down the street,
　　But pretty Peg, my dearie !

Her air sae sweet, an' shape complete,
    Wi' nae proportion wanting,
The Queen of Love did never move
    Wi' motion mair enchanting.

Wi' linkèd hands we took the sands,
    Adown yon winding river ;
Oh, that sweet hour and shady bower,
    Forget it shall I never !

[These stanzas were first published in the Edinburgh Magazine for 1818

ESTEEM FOR CHLORIS.

AH, Chloris, since it may not be,
    That thou of love wilt hear ;
If from the lover thou maun flee,
    Yet let the *friend* be dear.

Altho' I love my Chloris, mair
    Than ever tongue could tell ;
My passion I will ne'er declare—
    I'll say, I wish thee well.

Tho' a' my daily care thou art,
    And a' my nightly dream,
I'll hide the struggle in my heart,
    And say it is esteem.

[There is considerable elegance in these lines, reminding one of the poet's
manner in his earlier lines to Clarinda.]

SAW YOU MY DEAR, MY PHILLY.

Tune—" When she cam' ben she bobbet."

O SAW ye my Dear, my Philly?
O saw ye my Dear, my Philly,
She's down i' the grove, she's wi' a new Love,
    She winna come hame to her Willy.

What says she my Dear, my Philly?
What says she my Dear, my Philly?
She lets thee to wit she has thee forgot,
 And for ever disowns thee, her Willy.

O had I ne'er seen thee, my Philly!
O had I ne'er seen thee, my Philly!
As light as the air, and fause as thou's fair,
 Thou's broken the heart o' thy Willy.

HOW LANG AND DREARY IS THE NIGHT.

Tune—" Cauld Kail in Aberdeen."

How lang and dreary is the night
 When I am frae my Dearie;
I restless lie frae e'en to morn
 Tho' I were ne'er sae weary.

Chorus.—For oh, her lanely nights are lang!
 And oh, her dreams are eerie;
 And oh, her widow'd heart is sair,
 That's absent frae her Dearie!

When I think on the lightsome days
 I spent wi' thee, my Dearie;
And now what seas between us roar,
 How can I be but eerie?
 For oh, &c.

How slow ye move, ye heavy hours;
 The joyless day how dreary:
It was na sae—ye glinted by,
 When I was wi' my Dearie!
 For oh, &c.

[The reader will see that this song is merely a new adaptation, without
being an improvement, of a fine song already given. This alteration was
made in order to carry out the poet's vow to have a song in honour of

Chloris to suit the air " Cauld Kail," and Thomson, who declined setting
to that tune two former songs written expressly for it, appears to have been
satisfied with this.   Burns says in his next letter, " I am happy that I have
at last pleased you with verses to your right hand tune *Cauld Kail.*"]

INCONSTANCY IN LOVE.

Tune—" Duncan Gray."

LET not Woman e'er complain
  Of inconstancy in love ;
Let not Woman e'er complain
  Fickle Man is apt to rove :
Look abroad thro' Nature's range,
Nature's mighty Law is change,
Ladies, would it not seem strange
  Man should then a monster prove !

Mark the winds, and mark the skies,
  Ocean's ebb, and ocean's flow,
Sun and moon but set to rise,
  Round and round the seasons go.
Why then ask of silly Man
To oppose great nature's plan ?
We'll be constant while we can—
  You can be no more you know.

[This song, sent on 19th October 1794, as English words for the tune
" Duncan Gray," was produced at a time when the Muse of Burns was
more than usually active. He gives Chloris the credit of this ; but at the
same time shows that the sentiments of the song in the text are the prevailing ones in his own practice. Poor Clarinda is nowhere now! He recom-
mends Thomson to adapt one of her songs, " Talk not of love, it gives me
pain," to the air—" My lodging is on the cold ground." His words are,
" There is a song in the *Museum* by a *ci-devant* goddess of mine, which I
think not unworthy of that air."   Chambers makes the following philosophical observations on this matter, which are too valuable to lose sight of :—
" It was right, even in these poetico-Platonic affairs, to be ' off with the old
love before he was on with the new.' Yet it was only four months before
that Burns had addressed Mrs M'Lehose as ' My ever dearest Clarinda!'

A letter of simple friendship was then too cold to be attempted. O Woman-kind! think of that when you are addressed otherwise than in the language of sober common-sense! So lately as June, 'my ever dearest,' and now only ' a *ci-devant* goddess!'"]

THE LOVER'S MORNING SALUTE TO HIS MISTRESS.

Tune—"Deil tak the wars."

SLEEP'ST thou, or wak'st thou, fairest creature?
  Rosy morn now lifts his eye,
Numbering ilka bud which Nature
    Waters wi' the tears o' joy.
    Now, to the streaming fountain,
    Or up the heathy mountain,
The hart, hind, and roe, freely, wildly-wanton stray;
    In twining hazel bowers,
    Its lay the linnet pours,
    The laverock to the sky
    Ascends, wi' sangs o' joy?
While the sun and thou arise to bless the day.

Phœbus gilding the brow of morning,
  Banishes ilk darksome shade,
Nature, gladdening and adorning;
    Such to me my lovely maid.
    When frae my Chloris parted,
    Sad, cheerless, broken-hearted,
The night's gloomy shades, cloudy, dark, o'ercast my sky:
    But when she charms my sight,
    In pride of Beauty's light—
    When thro' my very heart
    Her burning glories dart;
'Tis then—'tis then I wake to life and joy!

[This song was transmitted with the three preceding effusions on 19th October 1794, and thus he concluded his communication : "Since the above, I have been out in the country taking dinner with a friend, where I met with the lady whom I mentioned in the second page of this odds-and-ends of a letter. As usual, I got into song; and in returning home composed the following." He afterwards transcribed the song with some variations, and added—" I could easily throw this into an English mould ; but, to my taste, in the simple and tender of the Pastoral song, a sprinkling of the old Scots has an inimitable effect. The air, if I understand the expression of it properly, is the very native language of Simplicity, Tenderness and Love."]

THE WINTER OF LIFE.

BUT lately seen in gladsome green,
  The woods rejoic'd the day,
Thro' gentle showers, the laughing flowers
  In double pride were gay :
But now our joys are fled
  On winter blasts awa' ;
Yet maiden May, in rich array,
  Again shall bring them a'.

But my white pow, nae kindly thowe
  Shall melt the snaws of Age ;
My trunk of eild,* but buss or beild,†
  Sinks in Time's wintry rage.
Oh, Age has weary days,
  And nights o' sleepless pain :
Thou golden time o' Youthfu' prime,
  Why comes thou not again !

[It seems very evident that the vigour of the poet's constitution, before the close of 1794, began to give way under the tear and wear of disappointed hopes, and the effects of his occasional imprudent course of life. We can scarcely believe that the brawny farmer and exciseman had exhibited these symptoms so early as the autumn of 1791, as conceived by the late Sir Egerton Brydges in his imaginary interview with Burns at Ellisland at that period, in the following language :—" His great Beauty was his manly strength, and his energy and elevation of thought and feeling. I perceived in Burns's cheek the symptoms of an energy which had been pushed too

---

* decayed trunk.   † without bush or shelter.

far ; and he had this feeling himself, for every now and then, he spoke of
the grave as soon about to close over him."

The first hint we find in his correspondence of the constitutional decline
referred to is in his letter to Mrs Dunlop—25th June 1794—where he says :
" To tell you that I have been in poor health will not be excuse enough for
neglecting your correspondence, though it is true.   I am afraid that I am
about to suffer for the follies of my youth.   My medical friends threaten me
with a flying gout ; but I trust they are mistaken."   The reader may
remember the poet's words to Thomson, in May 1796, when he was
approaching his exit from the stage of life—" I have now reason to believe
that my complaint is a flying gout, a sad business !"   On 25th December
of this year (1794), in writing to Mrs Dunlop, he thus again reverts to his
consciousness of physical decay—" I already begin to feel the rigid fibre
and stiffening joints of old age coming fast o'er my frame."   These feelings
are freely depicted in the little song which forms our text, irresistibly
recalling his prophetic words of warning, delivered to his youthful compeers
in 1786, when the speaker was in the flush of youth and hope :—

> "Ye tiny elves that guiltless sport,
>   Like linnets in the bush,
> Ye little know the ills ye court,
>   When manhood is your wish !
> The losses, the crosses, that active man engage,
> The fears all, the tears all, of dim declining Age !"]

BEHOLD, MY LOVE, HOW GREEN THE GROVES.

Tune—" My lodging is on the cold ground."

November 1794.—On my visit the other day to my fair Chloris (that is
the poetic name of the lovely goddess of my inspiration), she suggested
an idea which, on my return from the visit, I wrought into the following
song :

> BEHOLD, my love, how green the groves,[1]
>   The primrose banks how fair ;
> The balmy gales awake the flowers,
>   And wave thy flowing hair.[2]

---

[1] In the MS. this reads, " My Chloris, mark how green," &c., but in Feb.
1796, the poet sanctioned the change thus :—" In my by-past songs I dislike
one thing—the name of Chloris."

[2] The change from " flaxen " to *flowing hair*, is also thus sanctioned by
Burns in the same letter to Thomson (Feb. 1796): " I have more amend-

The lav'rock shuns the palace gay,
    And o'er the cottage sings :
For Nature smiles as sweet, I ween,
    To Shepherds as to Kings.

Let minstrels sweep the skilfu' string,
    In lordly lighted ha' :
The Shepherd stops his simple reed,
    Blythe in the birken shaw.

The Princely revel may survey
    Our rustic dance wi' scorn ;
But are their hearts as light as ours,
    Beneath the milk-white thorn !

The shepherd, in the flowery glen ;
    In shepherd's phrase, will woo :
The courtier tells a finer tale,
    But is his heart as true !

These wild-wood flowers I've pu'd, to deck
    That spotless breast o' thine :
The courtiers' gems may witness love,
    But, 'tis na love like mine.

[" How do you like the simplicity and tenderness of this pastoral? I
think it pretty well. I like you for entering so candidly and so kindly into
the story of 'ma chère amie." Conjugal love is a passion which I deeply
feel and highly venerate; but somehow it does not make such a figure in
poesy as that other species of the passion, ' where love is liberty, and nature
law' Musically speaking, the first is an instrument of which the gamut is
scanty and confined, but the tones inexpressibly sweet, while the last has
powers equal to all the intellectual modulation of the human soul."]

---

ments to propose. What you once mentioned of ' flaxen locks ' is just : they
cannot enter into an elegant description of beauty. Of this also again—
God bless you.—*R. B.*"

THE CHARMING MONTH OF MAY.

SONG, ALTERED FROM AN OLD ENGLISH ONE.

IT was the charming month of May,
When all the flow'rs were fresh and gay,
One morning, by the break of day,
   The youthful, charming Chloe—
From peaceful slumber she arose,
Girt on her mantle and her hose,
And o'er the flow'ry mead she goes—
   The youthful, charming Chloe—

Chorus—Lovely was she by the dawn,
    Youthful Chloe, charming Chloe,
   Tripping o'er the pearly lawn,
    The youthful, charming Chloe.

The feather'd people you might see
Perch'd all around on every tree,
In notes of sweetest melody
   They hail the charming Chloe;
Till, painting gay the eastern skies,
The glorious sun began to rise,
Outrival'd by the radiant eyes
   Of youthful, charming Chloe.
    Lovely was she, &c.

["You may think meanly of this," wrote the poet to Thomson in transmitting it, along with the preceding song, and that which follows, "but take a look at the bombast original, and you will be surprised that I have made so much of it." The name "Chloe" will suggest to the reader that it is a diminutive of "Chloris," and also probably that occasional meetings between the poet and her took place at sunrise. It is more likely that, after a moonlight rove adown by Clouden side, the sun might overtake the lovers on their way home. The "bombast original" of the present song is to be found in the "Tea Table Miscellany."]

LASSIE WI' THE LINT-WHITE LOCKS

Tune—" Rothiemurchie's Rant."

Chorus—Lassie wi' the lint-white locks,
Bonie lassie, artless lassie,
Wilt thou wi' me tent the flocks,
Wilt thou be my Dearie, O ?

Now Nature cleeds the flowery lea,
And a' is young and sweet like thee,
O wilt thou share its joys wi' me,
And say thou'lt be my Dearie, O.
Lassie wi' the, &c.

The primrose bank, the wimpling burn,
The cuckoo on the milk-white thorn,
The wanton lambs at early morn,
Shall welcome thee, my Dearie, O.
Lassie wi' the, &c.

And when the welcome simmer shower
Has cheer'd ilk drooping little flower,
We'll to the breathing woodbine-bower,
At sultry noon, my Dearie, O.
Lassie wi' the, &c.

When Cynthia lights, wi' silver ray,
The weary shearer's hameward way,
Thro' yellow waving fields we'll stray,
And talk o' love, my Dearie, O.
Lass wi' the, &c.

And when the howling wintry blast
Disturbs my Lassie's midnight rest,
Enclaspèd to my faithfu' breast,
I'll comfort thee, my Dearie, O.
Lassie wi' the, &c.

[The poet, in transmitting this fine effusion, thus wrote regarding it :—
" This piece has at least the merit of a regular pastoral : the vernal morn,

the summer noon, the autumnal evening, and the winter night are regularly rounded."

Cunningham has the following interesting note attached to this song :— "Those acquainted with the Poet's life and habits of study, will perceive much of both in the sweet song, ' Lassie wi' the lint-white locks.' Dumfries is a small town; a few steps carried Burns to green lanes, daisied brae-sides, and quiet stream banks. Men returning from labour were sure to meet him 'all under the light of the moon,' sauntering forth as if he had no aim; his hands behind his back, his hat turned up a little behind by the shortness of his neck, and noting all, yet seeming to note nothing. Those who got near enough to him without being seen, might hear him humming some old Scots air, and fitting verses to it—the scene and the season supplying the imagery, and the Jeans, the Nancies, and Phillises of his admiration, furnishing bright eyes, white hands, and waving tresses, as the turn of the song required."]

DIALOGUE SONG.—PHILLY AND WILLY.

Tune—"The Sow's tail to Geordie."

He.   O Philly, happy be that day,
      When roving thro' the gather'd hay,
      My youthfu' heart was stown away,
        And by thy charms, my Philly.

She. O Willy, ay I bless the grove
      Where first I own'd my maiden love,
      Whilst thou did pledge the Powers above,
        To be my ain dear Willie.

Both. For a' the joys that gowd can gie,
        I dinna care a single flie;
        The { lad / lass } I love's the { lad / lass } for me,
        And that's my ain dear { Willy. / Philly. }

He.   As songsters of the early year,
      Are ilka day mair sweet to hear,
      So ilka day to me mair dear
        And charming is my Philly.

She. As on the brier the budding rose,
　　Still richer breathes and fairer blows,
　　So in my tender bosom grows
　　　　The love I bear my Willie.
Both. For a' the joys, &c.

He. The milder sun and bluer sky
　　That crown my harvest cares wi' joy,
　　Were ne'er sae welcome to my eye
　　　　As is a sight o' Philly.
She. The little swallow's wanton wing,
　　Tho' wafting o'er the flowery Spring,
　　Did ne'er to me sic tidings bring,
　　　　As meeting o' my Willy,
Both. For a' the joys, &c.

He. The bee that thro' the sunny hour
　　Sips nectar in the op'ning flower,
　　Compar'd wi' my delight is poor,
　　　　Upon the lips o' Philly.
She. The woodbine in the dewy weet,
　　When ev'ning shades in silence meet,
　　Is nocht sae fragrant or sae sweet
　　　　As is a kiss o' Willy.
Both. For a' the joys, &c.

He. Let fortune's wheel at random rin,
　　And fools may tyne, and knaves may win ;
　　My thoughts are a' bound up in ane,
　　　　And that's my ain dear Philly.
She. What's a' the joys that gowd can gie ?
　　I dinna care a single flie ;
　　The lad I love's the lad for me,
　　　　And that's my ain dear Willy.
Both. For a' the joys, &c.

[In communicating the above to Thomson, on 19th November 1794, the
bard thus wrote :—" This morning, though a keen blowing frost, in my walk

before breakfast I finished my duet which you were pleased to praise so much. (September 1794.) Whether I have uniformly succeeded I will not say; but here it is to you, though not half an hour old. Tell me honestly how you like it, and point out whatever you think faulty. I am much pleased with your idea of singing our songs in alternate stanzas, and regret that you did not hint it to me sooner. In those that remain, I shall have it in my eye "

In September the poet suggested the tune as a suitable one for Thomson's publication, and proposed to compose words for it in the dialogue form, the hero and heroine of which would be Mr and Mrs George Thomson. But their names, Geordie and Kirsty, being deemed too burlesque for sentiment, the song was completed as it appears in the text, and Thomson has given it a place in his collection. The title of the melody, however, being offensive to the refinement of Mr Thomson, is genteelly styled, in his publication, " A Jacobite Air."]

CONTENTED WI' LITTLE AND CANTIE WI' MAIR.

CONTENTED wi' little, and cantie * wi' mair,
Whene'er I forgather wi' Sorrow and Care,
I gie them a skelp † as they're creepin alang,
Wi' a cog o' gude swats ‡ and an auld Scottish sang.
    Chorus—Contented wi' little, &c.

I whyles § claw ‖ the elbow o' troublesome thought ;
But Man is a soger, and Life is a faught ;
My mirth and gude humour are coin in my pouch,
And my Freedom's my Lairdship nae monarch dare touch.
    Contented wi' little, &c.

A towmond ¶ o' trouble, should that be my fa', **
A night o' gude fellowship sowthers †† it a' :
When at the blythe end o' our journey at last,
Wha the deil ever thinks o' the road he has past ?
    Contented wi' little, &c.

* joyful.   † dash them aside.   ‡ ale.   ♮ at times.
‖ scratch.   ¶ twelvemonth.   ** fate.   †† solders.

Blind Chance, let her snapper and stoyte * on her way ;
Be't to me, be't frae me, e'en let the jade gae :
Come Ease, or come Travail, come Pleasure or Pain,
My warst word is : "Welcome, and welcome again !"
                    Contented wi' little, &c.

[This blythe song derives special interest from the fact that the poet,
while intimating to Thomson that some travelling artist had just executed
a very successful miniature likeness of him ("what I am at this moment"),
added—"I have some thoughts of suggesting to you to prefix a vignette
taken from it, to my song, 'Contented wi' little and cantie wi' mair,' in order
that the portrait of my face and the picture of my mind may go down the
stream of time together."]

FAREWELL THOU STREAM.

Air—"Nansie's to the greenwood gane."

FAREWELL, thou stream that winding flows
    Around Eliza's dwelling ;
O mem'ry ! spare the cruel throes
    Within my bosom swelling.
Condemn'd to drag a hopeless chain
    And yet in secret languish ;
To feel a fire in every vein,
    Nor dare disclose my anguish.

Love's veriest wretch, unseen, unknown,
    I fain my griefs would cover ;
The bursting sigh, th' unweeting groan,
    Betray the hapless lover.
I know thou doom'st me to despair,
    Nor wilt, nor canst relieve me ;
But, O Eliza, hear one prayer—
    For pity's sake forgive me !

---

* stumble and stagger.

The music of thy voice I heard,
   Nor wist while it enslav'd me !
I saw thine eyes, yet nothing fear'd,
   Till fears no more had sav'd me :
Th' unwary sailor thus, aghast
   The wheeling torrent viewing,
'Mid circling horrors sinks at last,
   In overwhelming ruin.

[This is merely an amended version of the song beginning, "The last time I came o'er the moor." Chambers observes that "the change most remarkable is the substitution of Eliza for Maria. The alienation of Mrs Riddell, and the poet's resentment against her, must have rendered the latter name no longer tolerable to him ; one can only wonder that, with his new and painful associations regarding that lady, he could endure the song itself, or propose laying it before the world."

CANST THOU LEAVE ME THUS, MY KATIE.

Tune—" Roy's Wife."

Chorus—Canst thou leave me thus, my Katie?
   Canst thou leave me thus, my Katie?
Well thou know'st my aching heart,
   And canst thou leave me thus, for pity?

Is this thy plighted, fond regard,
   Thus cruelly to part, my Katie?
Is this thy faithful swain's reward—
   An aching, broken heart, my Katie !
     Canst thou leave me, &c.

Farewell ! and ne'er such sorrows tear
   That fickle heart of thine, my Katie !
Thou mayest find those will love thee dear,
   But not a love like mine, my Katie.
     Canst thou leave me, &c.

[Burns sent the above to Thomson on 19th November 1794, as English verses to appear on the same page with Mrs Grant of Carron's song, "Roy's wife of Aldivalloch." Dr Currie, in form of a foot-note to the text, printed a composition of Mrs Walter Riddell, intended for singing to the same air, which reads like a reply to Burns's song. It was found among the poet's papers after his death, in the handwriting of the authoress, and Chambers accordingly correctly infers that our poet had sent Mrs Riddell a copy of the present song, as "a poetical expression of the more gentle feeling he was now beginning to entertain towards her." He conjectures that the injured lady, regarding that act "as a sort of olive-branch held out to her, received it in no unkindly spirit," and interchanged compliments by answering the song in the same strain and sending it to Burns.

MY NANIE'S AWA.

Tune—"There'll never be peace till Jamie comes hame."

Now in her green mantle blythe Nature arrays,
And listens the lambkins that bleat o'er her braes
While birds warble welcomes in ilka green shaw,
But to me it's delightless—my Nanie's awa.

The snawdrap and primrose our woodlands adorn,
And violets bathe in the weet o' the morn;
They pain my sad bosom, sae sweetly they blaw,
They mind me o' Nanie,—and Nanie's awa.

Thou lav'rock that springs frae the dews of the lawn,
The shepherd to warn o' the grey-breaking dawn,
And thou mellow mavis that hails the night-fa',
Give over for pity—my Nanie's awa.

Come Autumn, sae pensive, in yellow and grey,
And soothe me wi' tidings o' Nature's decay:
The dark, dreary Winter, and wild-driving snaw
Alane can delight me—now Nanie's awa.

[The post-mark of the letter which communicated this admired song to Thomson is of date December 9th, 1794, and the poet says: "I have just framed for you the following: how does it please you?" The grandson of Mrs M'Lehose, who endeavoured to appropriate, as compliments to his distinguished ancestress, every production of Burns in which the name of *Nancy* or *Nanie* occurs, distinctly states that the present song was com-

posed in the summer of 1792, during the absence of Clarinda in the West
Indies. Unfortunately the manuscript of it was never seen in the possession
of that lady or her representatives. This lyric certainly reads like an
appropriate sequel in the history of Burns's passion for Clarinda.

In January 1788, the following eloquent passage in one of Clarinda's
letters to Burns was justly admired by him; he said: "I shall certainly
steal it, and set it in some future production, and get immortal fame by it."
He did not forget the hint in his Elegy on Matthew Henderson; and it is
again adopted in the present song :—"Oh, let the scenes of Nature remind
you of Clarinda! In Winter, remember the dark shades of her fate—in
Summer, the warmth of her friendship—in Autumn her glowing wishes to
bestow plenty on all—and let Spring animate you with the hopes that your
friend may yet surmount the wintry blasts of life, and revive to taste a
spring-time of happiness. At all events, Sylvander, the storms of life will
quickly pass, and 'one unbounded Spring encircle all.' Love *there* is no
crime. I charge you to meet me there!"]

THE TEAR-DROP.

WAE is my heart, and the tear's in my e'e;
Lang, lang has Joy been a stranger to me:
Forsaken and friendless, my burden I bear,
And the sweet voice o' Pity ne'er sounds in my ear.

Love thou hast pleasures, and deep hae I luv'd;
Love, thou hast sorrows, and sair hae I pruv'd;
But this bruisèd heart that now bleeds in my breast,
I can feel by its throbbings, will soon be at rest.

Oh, if I were—where happy I hae been—
Down by yon stream, and yon bonie castle-green;
For there he is wand'ring and musing on me,
Wha wad soon dry the tear-drop that clings to my e'e.

[This pathetic little ballad is formed of Burns's very best material—indeed, he never excelled it. The stanza in Clarinda's *Ae fond Kiss* "Had
we never lov'd sae kindly," &c , which has been so highly commended as
"the alpha and omega of feeling," is nearly matched by the second verse
of the present text.]

FOR THE SAKE O' SOMEBODY.

My heart is sair—I dare na tell,
My heart is sair for Somebody;
I could wake a winter night
For the sake o' Somebody.
O-hon ! for Somebody !
O-hey ! for Somebody !
I could range the world around,
For the sake o' Somebody.

Ye Powers that smile on virtuous love,
O, sweetly smile on Somebody !
Frae ilka danger keep him free,
And send me safe my Somebody !
O-hon ! for Somebody !
O-hey ! for Somebody !
I wad do—what wad I not?
For the sake o' Somebody.

[The editor of Hamilton's "Select Songs of Scotland" (1848), thus wrote
regarding the present song :—" It shows how perfect was Burns's idea of
what was necessary to constitute a lasting and happy union between words
and music. We do not know a single song where the union is so happy.
The sentiment of the music becomes elevated or pathetic just at the proper
places, and seems as if no other medium of expression could ever by any
chance be dreamt of than that which our national poet chose for his fine love
words."]

A MAN'S A MAN FOR A' THAT.

Tune—" For a' that."

Is there for honest Poverty
That hings his head, an' a' that ;
The coward slave—we pass him by,
We dare be poor for a' that !

For a' that, an' a' that,
  Our toils obscure an' a' that,
The rank is but the guinea's stamp,
  The Man's the gowd for a' that.

What though on hamely fare we dine,
  Wear hoddin * grey, an' a' that ;
Gie fools their silks, and knaves their wine,
  A Man's a Man for a' that :
For a' that, an' a' that,
  Their tinsel show, an' a' that ;
The honest man, tho' e'er sae poor,
  Is king o' men for a' that.

Ye see yon birkie † ca'd "a lord,"
  Wha struts, an' stares, an' a' that ;
Tho' hundreds worship at his word,
  He's but a coof ‡ for a' that :
For a' that, an' a' that,
  His ribband, star, an' a' that ;
The man o' independent mind
  He looks an' laughs at a' that.

A prince can mak a belted knight,
  A marquis, duke, an' a' that ;
But an honest man's aboon his might,
  Gude faith, he mauna fa' § that !
For a' that, an' a' that,
  Their dignities an' a' that ;
The pith o' sense, an' pride o' worth,
  Are higher rank than a' that.

Then let us pray that come it may,
  (As come it will for a' that,)
That Sense and Worth, o'er a' the earth,
  Shall bear the gree,‖ an' a' that.

---

* cloth of coarse wool.   † forward fellow.   ‡ brainless person.
§ attempt.   ‖ pre-eminence.

For a' that, an' a' that,
    It's comin yet for a' that,
The Man to Man, the world o'er,
    Shall brothers be for a' that.

[This performance was produced on 1st January 1795, and is so characteristic of Burns, that of all the poems and songs he ever wrote, it could be
least spared from a collection of his works. Beranger of France, Goethe of
Germany, and indeed, people abroad of every nation, quote its generous
and powerful couplets whenever they speak of Burns. The French Revolution was now emerging from its bloody baptism. On 28th July preceding,
Robespierre, with his chief partisans, perished on the guillotine which they
had so freely and wantonly kept in perpetual motion. In October the
Jacobin Club had been suppressed, and the trials of Horne Tooke, of Hardy,
Thelwall, and others, for treason in this country, closely followed. The
sentiments therefore which are embodied in Burns's song found an echo in
many a British heart.]

CRAIGIEBURN WOOD.

SECOND VERSION.

SWEET fa's the eve on Craigieburn,
    And blythe awakes the morrow ;
But a' the pride o' Spring's return
    Can yield me nocht but sorrow.

I see the flowers and spreading trees,
    I hear the wild birds singing ;
But what a weary wight can please,
    And Care his bosom wringing !

Fain, fain would I my griefs impart,
    Yet dare na for your anger ;
But secret love will break my heart,
    If I conceal it langer.

If thou refuse to pity me,
    If thou shalt love another,

When yon green leaves fade frae the tree,
Around my grave they'll wither.

[This is little else than a smooth abridgement of the song of same title formerly given. These verses were forwarded to Thomson in the same letter that communicated "A man's a man for a' that." The poet was then engaged in the work of Supervisor of Excise, devolving on him in consesequence of the illness of Mr Findlater, his immediate superior officer, which extra employment seems to have lasted nearly four months.

About that period the poet thus wrote to one of his patrons, regarding his prospects of Excise advancement;—"I am on the supervisor's list, and as we come on by precedency, in two or three years I shall be at the head of that list, and be appointed of *course*. *Then*, a FRIEND might be of service to me in getting me into a place of the kingdom which I would like. A supervisor's income varies from about £120 to £200 a year; but the business is an incessant drudgery, and would be nearly a complete bar to every species of literary pursuit. The moment I am appointed supervisor, in the common routine, I may be nominated on the Collector's list; and this is always a business of purely political patronage. A collectorship varies much, from better than £200 to near £1000 a year. A life of literary leisure, with a decent competency, is the summit of my wishes." So it appears that even Burns amused himself at times with "building castles in the air."]

𝔙𝔢𝔯𝔰𝔦𝔠𝔩𝔢𝔰 of 1795.

THE SOLEMN LEAGUE AND COVENANT

THE Solemn League and Covenant
Now brings a smile, now brings a tear;
But sacred Freedom, too, was theirs:
If thou'rt a slave, indulge thy sneer.

[We believe that the public is indebted to Mr William M'Dowall, editor of the *Dumfries Standard*, for the discovery of these lines. The books in the public Library of which Burns was a member are now the property of the Dumfries and Maxwelltown Mechanics' Institution, and the poet had evidently borrowed the 13th vol. of Sir John Sinclair's Statistical Account of Scotland. Under the head "Balmaghie" a notice is given of several martyred Covenanters belonging to that parish, and the rude yet expressive lines engraved on their tombstones are quoted at length. The reverend clergyman who compiled the description, in referring to these rhymed inscriptions somewhat sneeringly observes that their authors "no doubt conceived they were making good poetry."

Burns administered a rebuke to the compiler by pencilling on the opposite margin the lines which form the text. They are not signed or initialed ; but the handwriting of the bard is unmistakable.]

COMPLIMENTS TO JOHN SYME OF RYEDALE.

LINES SENT WITH A PRESENT OF A DOZEN OF PORTER.

O HAD the malt thy strength of mind,
　　Or hops the flavour of thy wit,
'Twere drink for first of human kind,
　　A gift that ev'n for Syme were fit.

JERUSALEM TAVERN, DUMFRIES.

INSCRIPTION ON A GOBLET.

THERE'S Death in the cup, so beware !
　　Nay, more—there is danger in touching ;
But who can avoid the fell snare,
　　The man and his wine's so bewitching !

[This is said to have been inscribed by Burns on a crystal goblet in the house of Mr Syme, when pressed to stay and drink more.]

APOLOGY FOR DECLINING AN INVITATION TO DINE.

No more of your guests, be they titled or not,
　　And cookery the first in the nation ;
Who is proof to thy personal converse and wit,
　　Is proof to all other temptation.

[Dr Currie gives the date of this last Epigram to have been 17th December 1795, when Burns was in ill-health. Mr Syme had invited him to dine, and held out to him the temptation of the best company and the finest cookery. Mr John Syme was distributor of stamps in Dumfries, and had his office on the ground floor of the tenement in which Burns took up his residence on first coming to Dumfries. Being a man of literary tastes and accomplishments, the poet became very intimate with him, and frequently submitted his productions to the criticism of his friend. Chambers remarks that "Syme, like many other men of lively temperament, could not boast of historical accuracy in his narration of events. He most undoubtedly was carried away by his imagination in his statement regarding the composition of Bruce's Address to his troops. So also he appears to have been misled in a less agreeable, though equally picturesque story, about Burns having, in a moment of passion, drawn a sword-cane against him in his own house."

In 1829 Syme published some observations regarding Burns's personal appearance, and a portion of his picture we may here give :—" His eyes and lips—the first remarkable for fire, and the second for flexibility—formed at all times an index of his mind, and, as sunshine or shade predominated, you might have told, *à priori*, whether the company was to be favoured with a scintillation of wit, or a sentiment of benevolence, or a burst of fiery indignation. In his animated moments, and particularly when his anger was roused by instances of tergiversation, meanness or tyranny, they were actually like coals of living fire."]

EPITAPH FOR MR GABRIEL RICHARDSON.

HERE Brewer Gabriel's fire's extinct,
    And empty all his barrels :
He's blest—if, as he brew'd, he drink,
    In upright, honest morals.

[This gentleman was the principal brewer in Dumfries. He was provost of the burgh in 1802-1803. It appears that the eldest son of the poet and the eldest son of the brewer entered on the same day as pupils with Mr Gray, at the Grammar School. The provost's son became a great traveller and naturalist, and ultimately received the honour of knighthood. The above epigram was inscribed by the poet on a crystal goblet, which is still in possession of Lady Richardson.

We do not regard it as one of our poet's most successful efforts in that line. Its aim is intelligible enough ; but, through some defect of structure, its verbal obscurity is hopeless. The point turns on the homely proverb, "Just as ye brew, so shall ye drink."]

EPIGRAM ON MR JAMES GRACIE.

GRACIE, thou art a man of worth,
  O be thou Dean for ever!
May he be d—d to hell henceforth,
  Who fauts * thy weight or measure!

[The subject of this compliment was a respected banker in Dumfries and
Dean of Guild for the burgh. Among the last occasions on which Burns
used his pen was that of inscribing a note of thanks addressed to him, for
his kind offer to send a carriage to bring the dying bard from Brow to
Dumfries.]

INSCRIPTION AT FRIARS' CARSE HERMITAGE,

TO THE MEMORY OF ROBERT RIDDELL.

To RIDDELL, much lamented man,
  This ivied cot was dear;
Wand'rer, dost value matchless worth?
  This ivied cot revere.

[We are told that the first time Burns rode up Nithside after the death of
his friend of Friars' Carse, he dismounted and went into the hermitage, and
engraved these lines on one of its window-panes.]

BONIE PEG-A-RAMSAY.

CAULD is the e'enin blast
  O' Boreas o'er the pool,
An' dawin it is dreary,
  When birks are bare at Yule.

---

* challenges, or finds fault with.

Cauld blaws the e'enin blast,
  When bitter bites the frost,
And, in the mirk and dreary drift,
  The hills and glens are lost :

Ne'er sae murky blew the night
  That drifted o'er the hill,
But bonie Peg-a-Ramsay
  Gat grist to her mill.

[The title of this snatch of song is very ancient, as we may infer from its being quoted in "Twelfth Night," *Act* ii. *Scene* 3. Tom D'Urfey in his " Pills," gives a rude version of the old song.]

OVER SEA, OVER SHORE.

THERE was a bonie lass, and a bonie, bonie lass,
  And she loed her bonie laddie dear ;
Till War's loud alarms tore her laddie frae her arms,
  Wi' mony a sigh, and a tear.
Over sea, over shore, where the cannons loudly roar,
  He still was a stranger to fear ;
And nocht could him quail, or his bosom assail,
  But the bonie lass he loed sae dear.

[There is a nice touch of sentiment about this little song, especially when united to its music, which Stenhouse informs us is a favourite slow march]

WEE WILLIE GRAY.

WEE Willie Gray, and his leather wallet,
Peel a willow wand to be him boots and jacket ;
The rose upon the breer will be him trews an' doublet,
The rose upon the breer will be him trews an' doublet,

Wee Willie Gray, and his leather wallet,
Twice a lily-flower will be him sark and cravat ;

Feathers of a flee wad feather up his bonnet,
Feathers of a flee wad feather up his bonnet.

[This little Nursery chant was furnished by our poet to fit an old air called
"Wee Totum Fogg."]

O AY MY WIFE SHE DANG ME.

*Chorus—*O ay my wife she dang * me,
   An' aft my wife she bang'd † me,
  If ye gie a woman a' her will,
   Gude faith ! she'll soon o'er-gang ye.

ON peace an' rest my mind was bent,
  And, fool I was ! I married ;
But never honest man's intent
  Sae cursedly miscarried.
   O ay my wife, &c.

Some sairie ‡ comfort at the last,
  When a' thir days are done, man,
My "pains o' hell" on earth is past,
  I'm sure o' bliss aboon, man,
   O av my wife, &c.

[This is one of the very few bitter songs Burns has written against woman-
kind. In writing to his friend Alexander Cunningham shortly after his
marriage, he thus moralizes :—" I am a marrried man of older standing than
you, and shall give you my ideas of the happiness of the conjugal state,
(*En passant*—you know I am no Latinist, but is not "conjugal" derived
from *jugum*, a yoke ?) Well then ; the scale of good wifeship I divide into
ten parts :—Good-nature, 4 ; Good-sense, 2 ; Wit, 1 ; Personal charms, viz:—
a sweet face, eloquent eyes, fine limbs, graceful carriage, (I would add a
fine waist, too, but that is so soon spoilt, you know)—all these, 1 ; as for the
other qualities belonging to, or attending on, a wife, such as fortune, con-
nexions, education (I mean, more than the ordinary run), family, blood, &c.,
divide the two remaining degrees among them as you please. Only
remember that all these minor properties must be expressed by *fractions*,
for there is not any one of them, in my aforesaid scale, entitled to the
dignity of an *integer*."]

---

* discomfited.   † beat, knocked me about. ‡ poor, sorry.

GUDE ALE KEEPS THE HEART ABOON.

Chorus—O gude ale comes and gude ale goes ;
   Gude ale gars me sell my hose,
   Sell my hose, and pawn my shoon—
   Gude ale keeps my heart aboon !

I HAD sax owsen in a pleugh,
And they drew a' weel eneugh :
I sell'd them a' just ane by ane—
Gude ale keeps the heart aboon !
  O gude ale comes, &c.

Gude ale hauds me bare and busy,
Gars me moop wi' the servant hizzie,
Stand i' the stool when I hae dune—
Gude ale keeps the heart aboon !
  O gude ale comes, &c.

[The bulk of this song is by Burns, although a line here and there belongs to an older strain of even less delicacy. The closing verse has reference to the old ecclesiastical mode of punishing a certain class of offences by placing the culprit on a "cutty stool" before the congregation in church.]

O STEER HER UP AN' HAUD HER GAUN.

O STEER * her up, an' haud her gaun,†
  Her mither's at the mill, jo ;
 An' gin she winna tak a man,
  E'en let her tak her will, jo.
First shore ‡ her wi' a gentle kiss,
  And ca' anither gill, jo ;
An' gin she tak the thing amiss,
  E'en let her flyte § her fill, jo.

---

 * stir, rouse. † in motion. ‡ offer, entice. § scold.

O steer her up, an' be na blate, *
 An' gin she tak it ill, jo,
Then leave the lassie till her fate,
 And time nae longer spill, jo :
Ne'er break your heart for ae rebute,†
 But think upon it still, jo :
That gin the lassie winna do't,
 Ye'll find anither will, jo.

[Excepting the first four lines, which belong to an ancient song of same
title and subject, the song is by Burns.]

THE LASS O' ECCLEFECHAN.

Tune—"Jack o' Latin."

GAT ye me, O gat ye me,
 O gat ye me wi' naething ?
Rock an reel, and spinning wheel,
 A mickle quarter bason :
Bye attour, ‡ my Gutcher § has
 A heich house and a laich ane,
A' for bye my bonie sel,
 The toss‖ o' Ecclefechan.

O haud your tongue now, Lucky Lang,
 O haud your tongue and jauner ; ¶
I held the gate till you I met,
 Syne I began to wander :
I tint ** my whistle and my sang,
 I tint my peace and pleasure ;
But your green graff,†† now Lucky Lang,
 Wad airt ‡‡ me to my treasure.

[The supervising duties which devolved on Burns in consequence of
Findlater's illness, brought him in February 1795 to the village of Eccle-

---

* backward.   † rebuff, repulse. ‡ over and above.
§ goodsire, grandfather. ‖ toast. ¶ idle talk.
** lost.   †† turf, grave. ‡‡ direct.

fechan, in Annandale, where he was storm-stayed by a heavy fall of snow. In a letter which he penned to Thomson from the Inn, he described it as an "unfortunate, wicked little village," in which he was forced either to get drunk to forget his miseries, or to hang himself to get rid of them ; and so he added, "like a prudent man, of two evils I have chosen the least, and am very drunk at your service."]

O LET ME IN THIS AE NIGHT.

O LASSIE, are ye sleepin yet,
Or are ye waukin, I wad wit ?
For Love has bound me hand an' fit,
   And I would fain be in, jo.

> *Chorus*—O let me in this ae night,
>   This ae, ae, ae night ;
>   O let me in this ae night,
>   I'll no come back again, jo !

O hearst thou not the wind an' weet ?
Nae star blinks thro' the driving sleet ;
Tak pity on my weary feet,
   And shield me frae the rain, jo.
      O let me in, &c.

The bitter blast that round me blaws,
Unheeded howls, unheeded fa's ;
The cauldness o' thy heart's the cause
   Of a' my care and pine, jo.
      O let me in, &c.

HER ANSWER.

O tell na me o' wind an' rain,
Upbraid na me wi' cauld disdain,
Gae back the gate ye cam again,
   I winna let ye in, jo.

Chorus—I tell you now this ae night,
    This ae, ae, ae night ;
    And ance for a' this ae night,
    I winna let ye in, jo.

The snellest blast, at mirkest hours,
That round the pathless wand'rer pours
Is nocht to what poor she endures,
    That's trusted faithless man, jo.
        I tell you now, &c.

The sweetest flower that deck'd the mead,
Now trodden like the vilest weed—
Let simple maid the lesson read
    The weird may be her ain, jo.
        I tell you now, &c.

The bird that charm'd his summer day,
Is now the cruel Fowler's prey ;
Let witless, trusting, Woman say
    How aft her fate's the same, jo !
        I tell you now, &c.

[In August 1793, Burns had sent to Thomson a dressed-up version of the old song, "O let me in this ae night," usually found in the collections of last century ; but it did not give satisfaction. The present version was sent from Ecclefechan on February 9th, 1795.

In the MS. the poet suggests the following as an improvement on the closing verse ; but neither Thomson nor Currie adopted it :—

    The bird that charm'd his summer day,
    And now the cruel Fowler's prey—
    Let that to witless woman say,
      " The gratefu' heart of Man," jo !]

I'LL AY CA' IN BY YON TOWN.

Air—" I'll gang nae mair to yon toun."

Chorus—I'll ay ca' in by yon town,
    And by yon garden-green again ;
    I'll ay ca' in by yon town,
    And see my bonie Jean again.

There's nane shall ken, there's nane can guess
   What brings me back the gate again,
But she, my fairest faithfu' lass,
   And stow'nlins we sall meet again.
                  I'll ay ca' in, &c.

She'll wander by the aiken tree,
   When trystin time draws near again ;
And when her lovely form I see,
   O haith ! she's doubly dear again.
                  I'll ay ca' in, &c.

[This beautiful little lyric, supplied off-hand to Johnson, will perhaps be
more admired than the laboured version which follows. It may have been
inspired either by his own wife, or by Jean Lorimer ; most likely the latter,
for she was the author's favourite model at this period. He thus wrote from
Ecclefechan on 7th Feb. 1795, recommending Thomson to adopt the air :—
If you think it worthy of your attention, I have a fair dame in my eye, to
whom I would consecrate it. Try it with this doggrel, till I give you a
better :—

> *Chorus*—O wat ye wha's in yon town
>   Ye see the e'enin sun upon :
>   The dearest maid's in yon town,
>   That e'enin sun is shinin on.
>
> O sweet to me yon spreading tree,
>   Where Jeanie wanders aft her lane :
> The hawthorn flower that shades her bower,
>   O when shall I behold again !

[The expression " yon town," so frequently repeated, does not necessarily
apply to a town, or small city : a clump of cottages surrounding a country
mansion, or even a farm-steading is so denominated.
   The melody, in slowish time, flows finely with the words. It may interest
some readers to be told that the air was a marked favourite of King George
IV. Signor Girolamo Stabilini introduced it as a rondo with variations in
a Violin Concerto which was performed between the play and the after-
piece on the occasion of his Majesty attending the Theatre of Edinburgh
in 1822; and it was observed that the King drummed with his fingers to
the music while sitting in his box.]

O WAT YE WHA'S IN YON TOWN.

Tune—" I'll gang nae mair to yon town."

Chorus.—O wat ye wha's in yon town,
　　　Ye see the e'enin sun upon,
　　　The dearest maid's in yon town,
　　　That e'ening sun is shining on

Now haply down yon gay green shaw,
　　She wanders by yon spreading tree ;
How blest ye flowers that round her blaw,
　　Ye catch the glances o' her e'e !
　　　　　O wat ye wha's, &c.

How blest ye birds that round her sing,
　　And welcome in the blooming year ;
And doubly welcome be the Spring,
　　The season to my Jeanie dear.
　　　　　O wat ye wha's, &c.

The sun blinks blythe in yon town,
　　Among the broomy braes sae green :
But my delight in yon town,
　　And dearest pleasure, is my Jean.
　　　　　O wat ye wha's, &c.

Without my Fair, not a' the charms
　　O' Paradise could yield me joy ;
But give me Jeanie in my arms
　　And welcome Lapland's dreary sky !
　　　　　O wat ye wha's, &c.

My cave wad be a lover's bower,
　　Tho' raging Winter rent the air ;
And she a lovely little flower,
　. That I wad tent and shelter there.
　　　　　O wat ye wha's, &c.

O sweet is she in yon town,
   The sinkin Sun's gane down upon ;
A fairer than's in yon town,
   His setting beam ne'er shone upon.
          O wat ye wha's, &c.

If angry Fate is sworn my foe,
   And suff'ring I am doom'd to bear ;
I careless quit aught else below,
   But spare, O spare me Jeanie dear.
          O wat ye wha's, &c.

For while life's dearest blood is warm,
   Ae thought frae her shall ne'er depart,
And she, as fairest is her form,
   She has the truest, kindest heart.
          O wat ye wha's, &c.

[It was no unusual thing with Burns to shift the devotion of verse from one person to another. What was composed under the influence of Jean Lorimer's charms, could easily be made applicable to any other personage he might desire to compliment. Accordingly, by changing the name "Jeanie," to *Lucy*, he made these verses serve as a tributary offering to the wife of Richard A. Oswald, Esq. of Auchencruive, then residing in Dumfries. That gentleman had been about two years married to a celebrated beauty, Miss Lucy Johnston, daughter of Wynne Johnston, Esq. of Hilton, and it occurred to our poet that the family would be pleased with this dedication. In a letter to Mr John Syme, enclosing a copy of the song, he explains thus :—"I have endeavoured to do justice to what would be Mr Oswald's feelings, on seeing, in the scene I have drawn, the habitation of his Lucy. As I am a good deal pleased with the performance, I, in my first fervour, thought of sending it to Mrs Oswald, but on second thoughts, perhaps what I offer as the honest incense of genuine respect, might be construed into some modification or other of that servility which my soul abhors."]

Ballads on Mr Heron's Election, 1795.

" SIR,— I enclose you some copies of a couple of political ballads, one of which, I believe, you have never seen. Would to heaven I could make you master of as many votes in the Stewartry! In order to bring my humble efforts to bear with more effect on the foe, I have privately printed a good many copies of both ballads, and have sent them among friends all about the country."—*Letter to Mr Heron, of Kerroughtree.*

BALLAD FIRST.

WHOM will you send to London town,
  To Parliament and a' that?
Or wha in a' the country round
  The best deserves to fa' that?
    For a' that, and a' that,
    Thro' Galloway and a' that,
  Where is the Laird or belted Knight
    That best deserves to fa' that?

Wha sees Kerroughtree's open yett,
  (And wha is't never saw that?)
Wha ever wi' Kerroughtree met,
  And has a doubt of a' that?
    For a' that, and a' that,
    Here's Heron yet for a' that!
  The independent patriot,
    The honest man, and a' that.

Tho' wit and worth, in either sex,
  Saint Mary's Isle can shaw that,
Wi' Dukes and Lords let Selkirk mix.
  And weel does Selkirk fa' that.
    For a' that, and a' that,
    Here's Heron yet for a' that!

III   M

The independent commoner
  Shall be the man for a' that.

But why should we to Nobles jouk,*
  And is't against the law, that ?
For why, a Lord may be a gowk, †
  Wi' ribband, star and a' that,
    For a' that, and a' that,
    Here's Heron yet for a' that !
A Lord may be a lousy loun,
  Wi' ribband, star and a' that.

A beardless boy comes o'er the hills,
  Wi' uncle's purse and a' that ;
But we'll hae ane frae mang oursels,
  A man we ken, and a' that.
    For a' that, and a' that,
    Here's Heron yet for a' that !
For we're not to be bought and sold,
  Like naigs, ‡ and nowte, § and a' that.

Then let us drink—The Stewartry,
  Kerroughtree's laird, and a' that,
Our representative to be,
  For weel he's worthy a' that.
    For a' that, and a' that,
    Here's Heron yet for a' that !
A House of Commons such as he,
  They wad be blest that saw that.

[The death of General Stewart, M.P. for the Stewartry of Kirkcudbright, in January 1795, created a vacancy in the representation, and in the course of February and March a contest for the election caused much local excitement, in which Burns mixed with his customary zeal.]

---

* crouch.   † fool.   ‡ horses.   § cattle.

BALLAD SECOND—ELECTION DAY.

Tune—" Fy, let us a' to the Bridal."

Fy, let us a' to Kirkcudbright,
  For there will be bickerin' there ;
For Murray's *light horse* are to muster,
  And O how the heroes will swear !
And there will be *Murray*, Commander,[1]
  And Gordon,[2] the battle to win ;
Like brothers they'll stand by each other,
  Sae knit in alliance and kin.

And there will be black-nebbit *Johnie*,[3]
  The tongue o' the trump to them a' ;
An he get na Hell for his haddin,
  The Deil gets na justice ava ·
And there will be *Kempleton's* birkie,[4]
  A boy no sae black at the bane ;
But as to his fine *Nabob* fortune,
  We'll e'en let the subject alane.

And there will be Wigton's new Sheriff ;[5]
  Dame Justice fu' brawly has sped,
She's gotten the heart of a *Bushby*,
  But, Lord ! what's become o' the head ?
And there will be *Cardoness*, Esquire,[6]
  Sae mighty in *Cardoness'* eyes ;

---

[1] Mr Murray of Broughton. This gentleman had left his wife and eloped with a lady of rank.

[2] Thos. Gordon of Balmaghie, the Tory candidate, a nephew of Murray.

[3] John Bushby, " honest man."

[4] William Bushby of Kempleton, a brother of John, who lost a fortune by Douglas Heron & Co.'s Bank, and retrieved it by going to the East Indies, and trading there.

[5] Mr Bushby Maitland, son of John, and newly appointed sheriff of Wigtonshire. He figures in the epistle of Esopus to Maria.

[6] David Maxwell of Cardoness.

A wight that will weather damnation,
   The Devil the prey will despise.

And there will be *Douglasses* doughty,[1]
   New christening towns far and near ;
Abjuring their democrat doings,
   By kissin' the —— o' a Peer :
And there will be folk frae *Saint Mary's*[2]
   A *house* o' great merit and note ;
The deil ane but honors them highly—
   The deil ane will gie them his vote !

And there will be *Kenmure* sae gen'rous,[3]
   Whose honor is proof to the storm,
To save them from stark reprobation,
   He lent them his name in the Firm,
And there will be lads o' the gospel,
   Muirhead wha's as *gude* as he's *true ;*[4]
And there will be Buittle's *Apostle,*[5]
   Wha's mair o' the black than the blue.

And there will be *Logan M'Dowall,*[6]
   Sculdudd'ry an' he will be there,
And also the *Wild Scot o' Galloway,*
   Sogering, gunpowder *Blair.*[7]
But we winna mention Redcastle,[8]
   The *body,* e'en let him escape !
He'd venture the gallows for siller,
   An 'twere na the cost o' the rape.

---

[1] The Messrs Douglas, brothers, of Carlinwark and Orchardton. They had just obtained a royal warrant to alter the name of Carlinwark to "Castle Douglas."

[2] The Earl of Selkirk's family, with whom the poet was in good terms; but in this instance they sided with the Tory interest.

[3] Mr Gordon of Kenmure, with whom Burns was also in good terms.

[4] Rev. Mr Muirhead, of Urr, a proud man, and a high Tory.

[5] Rev. George Maxwell of Buittle, another high Tory.

[6] Colonel M'Dowall of Logan : for *Sculduddery*, see Glossary.

[7] Mr Blair of Dunskey.   [8] Walter Sloan Lawrie, of Redcastle.

But where is the Doggerbank hero,[1]
  That made "Hogan Mogan" to skulk?
Poor *Keith's* gane to h–ll to be fuel,
  The auld rotten wreck of a Hulk.
And where is our King's Lord Lieutenant,
  Sae fam'd for his *gratefu'* return?
The birkie is gettin' his Questions
  To say in Saint Stephen's the morn.

But mark ye! there's trusty *Kerroughtree,*[2]
  Whose honor was ever his law;
If the Virtues were pack'd in a parcel,
  His worth might be sample for a';
And strang an' respectfu's his backing,
  The maist o' the lairds wi' him stand;
Nae gipsy-like nominal barons,[3]
  Wha's property's paper—not land.

And there, frae the Niddisdale borders,
  The *Maxwells* will gather in droves,
Teugh *Jockie,*[4] staunch *Geordie,*[5] an' *Wellwood,*[6]
  That griens for the fishes and loaves;
And there will be *Heron,* the Major,[7]
  Wha'll ne'er be forgot in the *Greys;*
Our flatt'ry we'll keep for some other,
  HIM, only it's justice to praise.

---

[1] These four lines, published now for the first time, are from a fragment of the poet's MS. of this ballad, in the possession of the publisher of these volumes. A battle between the English and the Dutch was fought at the Doggerbank on August 5th, 1781.

[2] Patrick Heron, of Kerroughtree, the Whig candidate.

[3] This refers to the fictitious electors, so common before the Reform Act of 1832, popularly called "paper," or "faggot voters."

[4] John Maxwell, Esq. of Terraughty.

[5] George Maxwell of Carruchan.

[6] Mr Wellwood Maxwell.

[7] Major Heron, brother of the Whig candidate.

And there will be maiden *Kilkerran*,[1]
  And also *Barskimming's* gude Knight,[2]
And there will be roarin *Birtwhistle*,[3]
  Yet luckily roars i' the right.
And there'll be Stamp Office *Johnie*,[4]
  (Tak tent how ye purchase a dram!)
And there will be gay *Cassencarry*,
  And there'll be gleg Colonel *Tam*.[5]

And there'll be wealthy young *Richard*,[6]
  Dame Fortune should hing by the neck,
For prodigal, thriftless bestowing—
  His merit had won him respect.
And there will be rich brother *Nabobs*,[7]
  (Tho' *Nabobs*, yet men not the worst,)
And there will be *Collieston's* whiskers,[8]
  And *Quintin*[9]—a lad o' the first.

Then hey! the *chaste* Interest o' Broughton,
  And hey! for the blessin's 'twill bring;
It may send *Balmaghie* to the Commons,
  In Sodom 'twould make him a king;
And hey! for the sanctified Murray,
  Our land wha wi' chapels has stor'd;
He founder'd his horse among harlots,
  But gied the auld naig to the Lord.

[The various copies of this ballad differ widely in arrangement of the verses.

After printing this ballad in his last edition, Chambers adds: -"Though Burns, we may well believe, had no view to his own interest in writing

[1] Sir Adam Fergusson of Kilkerran.
[2] Sir William Miller of Barskimming, afterwards Lord Glenlee.
[3] Mr Alex. Birtwhistle of Kirkcudbright.
[4] John Syme, Esq., Distributor of Stamps for Dumfries.
[5] Colonel Goldie, of Goldielea.
[6] Richard Oswald, Esq. of Auchincruive.   [9] Messrs Hannay.
  Mr Copeland of Collieston.
[?] Mr Quintin M'Adam, of Craigingillan.

these diatribes, it appears there did result from them some little glimpse of a hope of promotion. Mr Heron, hearing of them, and having perused one, wrote to Mr Syme, with some references to the poet, as if it were not impossible that he might be able to advance his interests."]

BALLAD THIRD.

JOHN BUSHBY'S LAMENTATION.

Tune—" Babes in the Wood."

'TWAS in the seventeen hunder year
    O' grace, and ninety-five,
That year I was the wae'est man
    Of ony man alive.

In March the three-an'-twentieth morn,
    The sun raise clear an' bright ;
But oh ! I was a waefu' man,
    Ere to-fa' o' the night.

Yerl Galloway lang did rule this land,
    Wi' *equal* right and fame,
And thereto was his kinsmen join'd,
    The Murray's noble name.

Yerl Galloway's man o' men was I,
    And chief o' Broughton's host ;
So twa blind beggars, on a string,
    The faithfu' tyke will trust.

But now Yerl Galloway's sceptre's broke,
    And Broughton's wi' the slain,
And I my ancient craft may try,
    Sin' honesty is gane.

'Twas by the banks o' bonie Dee,
    Beside Kirkcudbright's towers,

The Stewart and the Murray there,
 Did muster a' their powers.

Then Murray on the auld grey yaud,
 Wi' *winged spurs* did ride,
That auld grey yaud a' Nidsdale rade,
 He staw upon Nidside.[1]

An there had na been the Yerl himsel,
 O there had been nae play ;
But Garlies was to London gane,
 And say the kye might stray.

And there was Balmaghie, I ween,
 In front rank he wad shine ;
But Balmaghie had better been
 Drinkin' Madeira wine.

And frae Glenkens cam to our aid
 A chief o' doughty deed ;
In case that worth should wanted be,
 O' Kenmure we had need.

And by our banners march'd Muirhead,
 And Buittle was na slack ;
Whase haly priesthood nane could stain,
 For wha could dye the black ?

And there was grave squire Cardoness,
 Look'd on till a' was done ;
Sae in the tower o' Cardoness
 A howlet sits at noon.

---

[1] An allusion to the lady with whom Murray eloped—a member of the house of Johnston, whose well-known crest is a winged spur.

And there led I the Bushby clan,
  My gamesome billie, Will,
And my son Maitland, wise as brave,
  My footsteps follow'd still.

The Douglas and the Heron's name,
  We set nought to their score ;
The Douglas and the Heron's name,
  Had felt our weight before.

But Douglasses o' weight had we,
  The pair o' lusty lairds,
For building cot-houses sae fam'd,
  And christenin' kail-yards.

And then Redcastle drew his sword,
  That ne'er was stain'd wi' gore,
Save on a wand'rer lame and blind,
  To drive him frae his door.

And last cam creepin Collieston,
  Was mair in fear than wrath ;
Ae knave was constant in his mind--
  To keep that knave frae scaith.

    *   *   *   *

[Our readers are likely to agree with us in thinking that Burns appears
to no great advantage in his electioneering verses; at same time, in an
edition professing to give all his poetical works, it might be considered un-
warrantable to omit these, however obscure their allusions, and purely local
their interest. Mr Lockhart remarks that "after the *Excise inquiry*, Burns
took care, no doubt, to avoid similar scrapes ; but he had no reluctance to
meddle largely and zealously in the squabbles of county politics and con-
tested elections ; and thus by merely espousing the cause of the Whig
candidates, he kept up very effectually the spleen which the Tories had
originally conceived against him on tolerably legitimate grounds."]

INSCRIPTION FOR AN ALTAR OF INDEPENDENCE,

AT KERROUGHTREE, THE SEAT OF MR HERON.

THOU of an independent mind,
  With soul resolv'd, with soul resign'd ;
Prepar'd Power's proudest frown to brave,
  Who wilt not be, nor have a slave ;
Virtue alone who dost revere,
  Thy own reproach alone dost fear—
Approach this shrine, and worship here.

[On 21st June of 1794 the poet thus wrote to Mr David M'Culloch of Ardwell :—" My dear sir, my long-projected journey through your country is at last fixed ; and on Wednesday next, if you have nothing of importance to do, take a saunter down to Gateshouse about two or three o'clock, and I shall be happy to take a draught of M'Kune's best with you. Collector Syme will be at Glen's about that time, and will meet us at dish-of-tea hour. Syme goes also to Kerroughtree, and let me remind you of your kind promise to accompany me there. I will need all my friends I can muster, for I am indeed ill at ease whenever I approach your honourables and right honourables."

Chambers notices that the above letter is " valuable as showing that at least a Whig country gentleman deemed Burns presentable at this time before good society." We conceive that as the poet never visited Kerroughtree after the summer of 1794, the inscription in the text is very likely to have been a composition of that year.]

THE CARDIN O'T, THE SPINNIN O'T.

I COFT a stane o' haslock woo,*
  To mak a wab † to Johnie, o't ;
For Johnie is my only jo,
  I loe him best of onie yet.

---

* soft wool from the throat of the sheep.   † wab.

Chorus—The cardin o't, the spinnin o't,
　　　　The warpin o't, the winnin o't ;
　　　　When ilka ell cost me a groat,
　　　　The tailor staw the lynin o't.

For tho' his locks be lyart * grey,
　　And tho' his brow be beld † aboon ;
Yet I hae seen him on a day,
　　The pride of a' the parishen. ‡
　　　　　The cardin o't, &c.

[The original of this tender little snatch of song is in the British Museum
The word "wab" in the second line has been hitherto misprinted "wat."]

THE COOPER O' CUDDY.

Tune—"Bab at the bowster."

Chorus—WE'LL hide the Cooper behint the door,
　　　　Behint the door, behint the door,
　　　　We'll hide the Cooper behint the door,
　　　　And cover him under a mawn, § O.

The Cooper o' Cuddy came here awa,
He ca'd the girrs‖ out o'er us a' ;
An' our gudewife has gotten a ca',
　　That's anger'd the silly gudeman O.
　　　　We'll hide the Cooper, &c.

He sought them out, he sought them in,
Wi' deil hae her ! an' deil hae him !
But the body he was sae doited ¶ and blin,
　　He wist na where he was gaun O.
　　　　We'll hide the Cooper, &c.

They cooper'd at e'en, they cooper'd at morn,
Till our gudeman has gotten the scorn ;

---

* mixed black and grey.　　　　† bald.　　　　‡ plural of parish.
§ basket without lid or handle.　　‖ hoops.　　　¶ stupid.

On ilka brow she's planted a horn,
　　And swears that there they sall stan' O
　　We'll hide the Cooper, &c.

[Nothing more need be said regarding this song, than that it is undoubtedly by Burns, and his MS. of it is in the British Museum.]

THE LASS THAT MADE THE BED TO ME.

WHEN Januar' wind was blawin cauld,
　　As to the north I took my way,
The mirksome night did me enfauld,
　　I knew na whare to lodge till day :
By my gude luck a maid I met,
　　Just in the middle o' my care,
And kindly she did me invite
　　To walk into a chamber fair.

I bow'd fu' low unto this maid,
　　And thank'd her for her courtesie ;
I bow'd fu' low unto this maid,
　　An' bade her make a bed to me ;
She made the bed baith large and wide,
　　Wi' twa white hands she spread it doun ;
She put the cup to her rosy lips,
　　And drank —' Young man, now sleep ye soun'.'

Chorus—The bonie lass made the bed to me,
　　　　　The braw lass made the bed to me,
　　　　　I'll ne'er forget till the day I die,
　　　　　The lass that made the bed to me.

She snatch'd the candle in her hand,
　　And frae my chamber went wi' speed ;
But I call'd her quickly back again,
　　To lay some mair below my head :

A cod she laid below my head,
 And servèd me with due respect,
And, to salute her wi' a kiss,
 I put my arms about her neck.
   The bonie lass, &c.

" Haud aff your hands, young man!" she said,
 " And dinna sae uncivil be ;
Gif ye hae ony luve for me,
 O wrang na my virginitie."
Her hair was like the links o' gowd,
 Her teeth were like the ivorie,
Her cheeks like lilies dipt in wine,
 The lass that made the bed to me :
   The bonie lass, &c.

Her bosom was the driven snaw,
 Twa drifted heaps sae fair to see ;
Her limbs the polish'd marble stane,
 The lass that made the bed to me.
I kiss'd her o'er and o'er again,
 And ay she wist na what to say :
I laid her 'tween me and the wa' ;
 The lassie thocht na lang till day.
   The bonie lass, &c.

Upon the morrow when we raise,
 I thank'd her for her courtesie ;
But ay she blush'd and ay she sigh'd,
 And said, ' Alas, ye've ruin'd me.'
I clasp'd her waist, and kiss'd her syne,
 While the tear stood twinkling in her e'e ;
I said, my lassie, dinna cry,
 For ye ay shall make the bed to me.
   The bonie lass, &c.

She took her mither's holland sheets,
 An made them a' in sarks to me ;

Blythe and merry may she be,
　The lass that made the bed to me.
Chorus—The bonie lass made the bed to me,
　　　　The braw lass made the bed to me;
　　　　I'll ne'er forget till the day I die,
　　　　The lass that made the bed to me.

[The chorus and concluding four lines of the above ballad are pointed out
by Burns in his note thereon, as forming part of the ancient song. He
seems to refer to a common-place production, preserved by Tom D'Urfey,
called "The Cumberland Lass," in which we thus read :—

　　　" She took her mother's winding sheet,
　　　　And cut it into sarks for me;
　　　　Blythe and merry may she be,
　　　　The lass that made the bed to me."

Burns tells us that the original ballad "was composed on an amour of
Charles II., when skulking in the North about Aberdeen, in the time of the
Usurpation. He formed *une petite affaire* with a daughter of the House of
Port-Letham, who was" "the lass that made the bed" to him.]

HAD I THE WYTE? SHE BADE ME.

HAD I the wyte,* had I the wyte,
　Had I the wyte? she bade me,
She watch'd me by the hie-gate side,
　And up the loan she shaw'd me.
And when I wadna venture in,
　A coward loon she ca'd me :
Had Kirk an' State been in the gate,
　I'd lighted when she bade me.

Sae craftilie she took me ben,
　And bade me mak nae clatter;
'For our ramgunshoch,† glum ‡ gudeman
　Is o'er ayont the water.'

---

　* blame.　　　　　　† ram-stam.　　　　　‡ sulky.

Whae'er shall say I wanted grace,
    When I did kiss and dawte * her,
Let him be planted in my place,
    Syne say, I was the fautor. †

Could I for shame, could I for shame,
    Could I for shame refus'd her ;
And wadna manhood been to blame,
    Had I unkindly used her !
He claw'd ‡ her wi' the ripplin-kame, §
    And blae and bluidy bruis'd her ;
When sic a husband was frae hame,
    What wife but wad excus'd her !

I dighted ‖ aye her e'en sae blue,
    An' bann'd ¶ the cruel randy, **
And weel I wat, her willin mou
    Was sweet as sugar-candie.
At gloamin-shot, †† it was I wot,
    I lighted—on the Monday ;
But I cam thro' the Tyseday's ‡‡ dew,
    To wanton Willie's brandy.

[Bordering on indelicacy as this performance does, it is purity itself beside the old model that suggested it.]

DOES HAUGHTY GAUL INVASION THREAT?

Tune—" Push about the Jorum."

DOES haughty Gaul invasion threat?
    Then let the louns beware, Sir ;
There's WOODEN WALLS upon our seas,
    And VOLUNTEERS on shore, Sir :

---

* pet.	† defaulter.	‡ assaulted.
§ wool-dresser's comb.	‖ wiped.	¶ cursed.
** blusterer.	†† dusk.	‡‡ Tuesdays.

The *Nith* shall run to *Corsincon*,[1]
   And *Criffel*[2] sink in *Solway*,
Ere we permit a Foreign Foe
   On British ground to rally !
We'll ne'er permit a Foreign Foe
   On British ground to rally !

O let us not, like snarling curs,
   In wrangling be divided,
Till, slap ! come in an *unco loun*,
   And wi' a rung decide it !
Be Britain still to Britain true,
   Amang ourselves united ;
For never but by *British hands*
   Maun *British wrangs* be righted !
No ! never but by *British hands*
   Shall *British wrangs* be righted !

The *Kettle* o' the Kirk and State,
   Perhaps a *clout*[3] may fail in't ;
But deil a *foreign* tinkler loun
   Shall ever ca' a nail in't.
Our FATHER'S BLUDE the *Kettle* bought,
   And wha wad dare to spoil it ;
By Heav'ns ! the sacrilegious dog
   Shall fuel be to boil it !
By Heav'ns ! the sacrilegious dog
   Shall fuel be to boil it !

The wretch that would a *tyrant* own,
   And the wretch, his true-born brother,
Who would set the *Mob* aboon the *Throne*,
   May they be damn'd together !

---

[1] Corsincon, a high hill at the source of the river Nith.
[2] Criffel, a mountain at the mouth of the same river.
[3] *i.e.*, It may require repair, as a tinkler "clouts a broken cauldron."

Who will not sing 'God save the King,'
 Shall hang as high's the steeple ;
But while we sing 'God save the King,'
 We'll ne'er forget THE PEOPLE !
But while we sing 'God save the King,'
 We'll ne'er forget THE PEOPLE !

[In the early part of 1795, two companies of volunteers were raised by Dumfries, as its quota for defending the fatherland, while the bulk of the regular army was engaged abroad. Many of the liberal residents who had incurred the suspicion of the government were fain to enrol themselves in these corps, in order to shew they were well affected towards their country. Syme, Maxwell, and others of the poet's friends, became volunteers. The ballad appeared in the *Dumfries Journal* of 5th May, as well as in the May number of the *Scots Magazine;* and printed copies of it, in form of a sheet-song, set to music by Mr Stephen Clarke, were soon distributed to members of the corps to which the poet belonged.]

ADDRESS TO THE WOODLARK.

Tune —"Loch Erroch Side."

O STAY, sweet warbling woodlark, stay,
Nor quit for me the trembling spray,
A hapless lover courts thy lay,
 Thy soothing, fond complaining.
Again, again that tender part,
That I may catch thy melting art ;
For surely that wad touch her heart
 Wha kills me wi' disdaining.

Say, was thy little mate unkind,
And heard thee as the careless wind?
Oh, nocht but love and sorrow join'd,
 Sic notes o' woe could wauken !
Thou tells o' never-ending care ;
O' speechless grief, and dark despair :
For pity's sake, sweet bird, nae mair !
 Or my poor heart is broken.

III.   N

[This fine lyric appears to have been forwarded to Thomson in May, 1795, a month during which he seems to have been more than usually prolific in song. There is in possession of the publisher of these volumes a pencil manuscript in the poet's hand, containing what are evidently his first thoughts while conceiving and executing this pathetic effusion. It reads as follows :—

SONG.—COMPOSED ON HEARING A BIRD SING WHILE MUSING ON CHLORIS.

Sing on, sweet songster o' the brier,
Nae stealthy traitor-foot is near;
O soothe a hapless Lover's ear,
    And dear as life I'll prize thee.

Again, again that tender part,
That I may learn thy melting art,
For surely that would touch the heart,
    O' her that still denies me.

Oh was thy mistress, too, unkind,
And heard thee as the careless wind?
For nocht but Love and Sorrow join'd
    Sic notes of woe could wauken.

The closing four lines correspond with the text.]

SONG.—ON CHLORIS BEING ILL.

Tune—"Ay wauken O."

Chorus—LONG, long the night,
        Heavy comes the morrow
    While my soul's delight
        Is on her bed of sorrow.

Can I cease to care?
    Can I cease to languish,
While my darling Fair
    Is on the couch of anguish?
        Long, long, &c.

Ev'ry hope is fled,
    Ev'ry fear is terror;

Slumber ev'n I dread,
Ev'ry dream is horror.
Long, long, &c.

Hear me, Powers Divine !
Oh, in pity, hear me !
Take aught else of mine,
But my Chloris spare me !
Long, long, &c.

[This effusion was sent to Thomson in May 1795. Onward to the close of August of that year (but no farther), Jean Lorimer (or "Chloris") continued to be goddess of the poet's lyrical adoration. In the early part of August, Mr Robert Cleghorn, Farmer, Saughton Mills, near Edinburgh, accompanied by two other Midlothian farmers, named respectively, John Allan, and Robert Wight, paid Burns a visit at Dumfries, and were introduced to Chloris, as the following extract from a hitherto inedited letter of Burns, addressed to the father of that young woman, will show :—"*Dumfries, Tuesday morning.*—My dear Sir, I called for you yesternight both at your own house, and at your favourite lady's—Mrs Hislop of the Globe, but could not find you. I want you to dine with me to-day. I have two honest Midlothian Farmers with me, who have travelled three-score miles to renew old friendship with the poet, and I promise you a pleasant party, a plateful of Hotch-Potch, and a bottle of good, sound port. Mrs Burns desired me yesternight to beg the favour of Jeany to come and partake with her, and she was so obliging as to promise that she would. If you can come, I shall take it very kind.—Yours, ROBERT BURNS. (Dinner at three.) To Mr William Lorimer, senior, Farmer."

The above proves the intimacy that existed between the poet's family and that of the Lorimers, and indicates, moreover, that the tenderness evinced by Burns for Chloris was of no clandestine kind.]

HOW CRUEL ARE THE PARENTS.

Altered from an old English song.

Tune—"John Anderson, my jo."

How cruel are the parents
Who riches only prize,
And to the wealthy booby
Poor Woman sacrifice !

Meanwhile, the hapless Daughter
 Has but a choice of strife ;
To shun a tyrant Father's hate—
 Become a wretched Wife.

The ravening hawk pursuing,
 The trembling dove thus flies,
To shun impelling ruin,
 Awhile her pinions tries ;
Till, of escape despairing,
 No shelter or retreat,
She trusts the ruthless Falconer,
 And drops beneath his feet.

[After a pretty extensive search for the original of this and a few other old English songs which the poet thus paraphrased or adapted for Thomson's publication, we have been unable to find them. The post-mark shews that this and the song following were forwarded to Thomson on 9th May 1795.]

YONDER POMP OF COSTLY FASHION.

Air—" Deil tak the wars."

MARK yonder pomp of costly fashion
 Round the wealthy, titled bride :
But when compar'd with real passion,
 Poor is all that princely pride.
          Mark yonder, &c. (*four lines repeated*).

What are the showy treasures,
 What are the noisy pleasures ?
The gay, gaudy glare of vanity and art :
 The polish'd jewel's blaze
 May draw the wond'ring gaze ;
 And courtly grandeur bright
 The fancy may delight,
But never, never can come near the heart.

But did you see my dearest Chloris,
　　In simplicity's array ;
Lovely as yonder sweet opening flower is,
　　Shrinking from the gaze of day,
　　　　　But did you see, &c.

O then, the heart alarming,
And all resistless charming,
In Love's delightful fetters she chains the willing soul!
　Ambition would disown
　The world's imperial crown,
　Ev'n Avarice would deny,
　His worshipp'd deity,
And feel thro' every vein Love's raptures roll.

["Well! this is not amiss," said the poet in sending the foregoing. "You see how I answer your orders. Your tailor could not be more punctual. I am just now in a high fit of poetising, provided that the strait-jacket of criticism don't cure me. If you can, in a post or two, administer a little of the intoxicating potion of your applause, it will raise your humble servant's frenzy to any height you want. I am at this moment 'holding high converse' with the Muses, and have not a word to throw away on such a Prosaic dog as you are.—*R. B.*"]

'TWAS NA HER BONIE BLUE E'E.

Tune—"Laddie, lie near me."

'Twas na her bonie blue e'e was my ruin,
Fair tho' she be, that was ne'er my undoin' ;
'Twas the dear smile when nae body did mind us,
'Twas the bewitching, sweet, stoun glance o' kindness.
'Twas the bewitching, sweet, stoun glance o' kindness.

Sair do I fear that to hope is denied me,
Sair do I fear that despair maun abide me,
But tho' fell fortune should fate us to sever,
Queen shall she be in my bosom for ever :
Queen shall she be in my bosom for ever.

Chloris, I'm thine wi' a passion sincerest,
And thou hast plighted me love o' the dearest !
And thou'rt the angel that never can alter,
Sooner the sun in his motion would falter :
Sooner the sun in his motion would falter.

THEIR GROVES O' SWEET MYRTLE.

Tune—"Humours of Glen."

THEIR groves o' sweet myrtle let Foreign Lands reckon,
  Where bright-beaming summers exalt the perfume ;
Far dearer to me yon lone glen o' green breckan,
  Wi' the burn stealing under the lang, yellow broom.
Far dearer to me are yon humble broom bowers,
  Where the blue-bell and gowan lurk, lowly, unseen :
For there, lightly tripping, among the wild flowers,
  A-list'ning the linnet, aft wanders my Jean.

Tho' rich is the breeze in their gay, sunny vallies,
  And cauld Caledonia's blast on the wave ;
Their sweet-scented woodlands that skirt the proud palace,
  What are they?—the haunt of the Tyrant and Slave.
The Slave's spicy forests, and gold-bubbling fountains,
  The brave Caledonian views wi' disdain ;
He wanders as free as the winds of his mountains,
  Save Love's willing fetters—the chains o' his Jean.

FORLORN, MY LOVE, NO COMFORT NEAR.

Air—"Let me in this ae night."

FORLORN, my Love, no comfort near,
Far, far from thee, I wander here ;
Far, far from thee, the fate severe,
  At which I most repine, Love.

Chorus—O wert thou, Love, but near me !
 But near, near, near me,
 How kindly thou would'st cheer me,
  And mingle sighs with mine, Love.

 Around me scowls a wintry sky,
 Blasting each bud of hope and joy ;
 And shelter, shade, nor home have I ;
  Save in these arms of thine, Love.
   O wert thou, &c.

 Cold, alter'd friendship's cruel part,
 To poison Fortune's ruthless dart—
 Let me not break thy faithful heart,
  And say that fate is mine, Love.
   O wert thou, &c.

 But, dreary tho' the moments fleet,
 O let me think we yet shall meet ;
 That only ray of solace sweet,
  Can on thy Chloris shine, Love !
   O wert thou, &c.

[This pathetic song, put into the lips of Chloris, was, like the six preceding ones, sent to Thomson in May 1795. In transmitting it the poet
asked, "How do you like the foregoing ? I have written it within this
hour, so much for the *speed* of my Pegasus ; but what say you to his
bottom?" It would appear that Thomson urged objections of some kind to
verse third ; for in his letter of August 3rd, 1795, Burns wrote, "Your
objections are just as to that verse of my song. I hope the following
alteration will please you :—

   Cold, alter'd friends, with cruel art,
   Poisoning fell Misfortune's dart ;
   Let me not break thy faithful heart,
    And say that fate is mine, Love."]

FRAGMENT.—WHY, WHY TELL THE LOVER.

Tune—" Caledonian Hunt's delight."

WHY, why tell the lover
　　Bliss he never must enjoy?
Why, why undeceive him,
　　And give all his hopes the lie?
O why, while fancy, raptur'd, slumbers,
　　" Chloris, Chloris," all the theme,
Why, why would'st thou, cruel —
　　Wake thy lover from his dream.

THE BRAW WOOER.

Tune—" The Lothian Lassie."

LAST May, a braw wooer cam doun the lang glen,
　　And sair wi' his love he did deave me;
I said, there was naething I hated like men—
　　The deuce gae wi'm, to believe me, believe me;
　　The deuce gae wi'm to believe me.

He spake o' the darts in my bonie black e'en,
　　And vow'd for my love he was diein,
I said, he might die when he liket for Jean—
　　The Lord forgie me for liein, for liein;
　　The Lord forgie me for liein!

A weel-stocket mailen, himsel for the laird,
　　And marriage aff-hand, were his proffers;
I never loot on that I kenn'd it, or car'd;
　　But thought I might hae waur offers, waur offers;
　　But thought I might hae waur offers.

Marshall Brown
N. Y.

But what wad ye think ?—in a fortnight or less ··
  The deil tak his taste to gae near her!
He up the *Gate-slack* to my black cousin, Bess—
  Guess ye how, the jad ! I could bear her, could bear
    her ;
  Guess ye how, the jad ! I could bear her.

But a' the niest week, as I petted wi' care,
  I gaed to the tryst o' Dalgarnock ;
And wha but my fine fickle wooer was there,
  I glowr'd as I'd seen a warlock, a warlock,
  I glowr'd as I'd seen a warlock.

But owre my left shouther I gae him a blink,
  Lest neibours might say I was saucy ;
My wooer he caper'd as he'd been in drink,
  And vow'd I was his dear lassie, dear lassie,
  And vow'd I was his dear lassie.

I spier'd for my cousin fu' couthy and sweet,
  Gin she had recover'd her hearin,
And how her new shoon fit her auld schachl't feet,
  But heavens ! how he fell a swearin, a swearin,
  But heavens ! how he fell a swearin.

He beggèd, for gudesake, I wad be his wife,
  Or else I wad kill him wi' sorrow ;
So e'en to preserve the poor body in life,
  I think I maun wed him to-morrow, to-morrow ;
  I think I maun wed him to-morrow.

[This is a "pearl of great price" among the songs of Burns, and has been
a popular favourite ever since it made its appearance. The melody selected
for it is in every way calculated to give effect to the humour and *naïveté* of
the words. Thomson objected to the localities "Gate-slack" and "Dalgarnock," and the poet explained that *Gate-slack* is a romantic pass among the

Lowther Hills on the confines of Dumfriesshire, and that *Dalgarnock* is an equally romantic spot near the Nith, where still are to be seen a ruined church and burial-ground. He at length yielded to an alteration of the former, thus :—

" He up the lang loan to my black cousin, Bess.'

Dr Currie very properly observed on this point that " It is always a pity to throw out anything that gives locality to our poet's verses."]

THIS IS NO MY AIN LASSIE.

Tune—'' This is no my house."

Chorus—THIS is no my ain lassie,
Fair tho' the lassie be ;
Weel ken I my ain lassie,
Kind love is in her e'e.

I see a form, I see a face,
Ye weel may wi' the fairest place ;
It wants, to me, the witching grace,
The kind love that's in her e'e.
This is no my ain, &c.

She's bonie, blooming, straight, and tall,
And lang has had my heart in thrall ;
And ay it charms my very saul,
The kind love that's in her e'e.
This is no my ain, &c.

A thief sae pawkie is my Jean,
To steal a blink, by a' unseen ;
But gleg as light are lover's een,
When kind love is in the e'e.
This is no my ain, &c.

It may escape the courtly sparks,
It may escape the learned clerks ;
But well the watching lover marks
The kind love that's in her eye.
　　　　This is no my ain, &c.

[This fine song was transmitted to Thomson, along with the two that immediately follow, on 3rd August, 1795; after which date, there was silence in the heaven of song for half a year. With exception of a note addressed to the father of "Chloris" early in August, and a short letter to Cleghorn, on the 21st of that month, there does not exist a scrap of the poet's writing in prose or verse that we can pronounce to have been penned by him, between 3rd August, and the close of December, 1795.]

O BONIE WAS YON ROSY BRIER.

O BONIE was yon rosy brier,
　　That blooms sae far frae haunt o' man ;
And bonie she, and ah, how dear !
　　It shaded frae the e'enin sun.

Yon rosebuds in the morning dew,
　　How pure, amang the leaves sae green ;
But purer was the lover's vow
　　They witness'd in their shade yestreen.

All in its rude and prickly bower,
　　That crimson rose, how sweet and fair ;
But love is far a sweeter flower,
　　Amid life's thorny path o' care.

The pathless wild, and wimpling burn,
　　Wi' Chloris in my arms, be mine ;
And I the warld nor wish nor scorn,
　　Its joys and griefs alike resign.

[This is apparently the last song of Burns which was inspired by the charms of Jean Lorimer, and he never excelled it in purity of sentiment and lyric beauty. The bard seems to have intended these as Scottish verses to the air, " I wish my love was in a mire."]

SCOTTISH SONG INSCRIBED TO
ALEXANDER CUNNINGHAM.

Now spring has clad the grove in green,
　　And strew'd the lea wi' flowers ;
The furrow'd, waving corn is seen
　　Rejoice in fostering showers.
While ilka thing in nature join
　　Their sorrows to forego,
O why thus all alone are mine
　　The weary steps o' woe !

The trout in yonder wimplin burn
　　That glides, a silver dart,
And, safe beneath the shady thorn,
　　Defies the angler's art—
My life was ance that careless stream,
　　That wanton trout was I ;
But Love, wi' unrelenting beam,
　　Has scorch'd my fountains dry.

That little floweret's peaceful lot,
　　In yonder cliff that grows,
Which, save the linnet's flight, I wot,
　　Nae ruder visit knows,
Was mine, till Love has o'er me past,
　　And blighted a' my bloom ;
And now, beneath the withering blast,
　　My youth and joy consume.

The waken'd lav'rock warbling springs,
　　And climbs the early sky,
Winnowing blythe his dewy wings
　　In morning's rosy eye ;

As little reck'd I sorrow's power,
    Until the flowery snare
O' witching Love, in luckless hour,
    Made me the thrall o' care.

O had my fate been Greenland snows,
    Or Afric's burning zone,
Wi' man and nature leagu'd my foes,
    So Peggy ne'er I'd known !
The wretch whose doom is ' hope nae mair '
    What tongue his woes can tell ;
Within whase bosom, save Despair,
    Nae kinder spirits dwell.

[These five double stanzas, together with the preceding song and some verses inscribed to Chloris, form the contents of one sheet transcribed by the poet for his "very much valued friend Mr Cunningham" on 3rd August 1795, and signed "COILA." It is addressed at the end thus :—
"To Mr Cunningham—*Une bagatelle de l'amitie.*"
On 20th January thereafter, the poet, as if just wakened out of a trance, thus addressed Mrs Riddell—"The Muses have not quite forsaken me. The following detached stanzas I intend to interweave in some disastrous tale of a Shepherd, 'Despairing beside a clear stream.' *L'amour, toujours l'amour.*" He then transcribes the three central verses of the above song, with variation.]

O THAT'S THE LASSIE O' MY HEART.

Tune—"Morag."

O WAT ye wha that lo'es me,
    And has my heart a keeping?
O sweet is she that lo'es me,
    As dews o' summer weeping,
    In tears the rosebuds steeping !

Chorus—O that's the lassie o' my heart,
    My lassie ever dearer ;
    O she's the queen o' womankind,
    And ne'er a ane to peer her.

If thou shalt meet a lassie,
  In grace and beauty charming,
That e'en thy chosen lassie,
  Erewhile thy breast sae warming,
  Had ne'er sic power alarming;
    O that's the lassie, &c.

If thou hadst heard her talking,
  (And thy attention's plighted),
That ilka body talking,
  But her, by thee is slighted,
And thou art all-delighted;
    O that's the lassie, &c.

If thou hast met this Fair One,
  When frae her thou hast parted,
If every other Fair One
  But her, thou hast deserted,
  And thou art broken-hearted;
    O that's the lassie o' my heart,
    My lassie ever dearer;
    O that's the queen o' womankind,
    And ne'er a ane to peer her.

[Thomson, in October 1794, had asked Burns about the authorship of several songs in the second volume of *The Museum,* and on the 19th of that month, he thus replied:—" The *Young Highland Rover* (Morag) is also mine; but it is not worthy of the fine air." The poet appears to have kept in his view the desirability of making an effort to compose a superior song to this melody; and accordingly there is evidence that about the beginning of August 1795, he had given birth to the above admirable effusion. About that time Mr Robert Cleghorn, accompanied by two Midlothian farmers, paid a visit to the poet in Dumfries, when this song, with other recent productions, was submitted to them. Burns entertained these visitors to a set dinner in his house, on which occasion, besides Dr Maxwell, Dr Mundell, and other gentlemen, Jean Lorimer, and her father, were present.

Mr Cleghorn, on his return to Edinburgh, sent Burns a handsome copy of the Poems of Gawin Douglas, and at same time requested to be favoured with a copy of the song in the text. A sudden and severe illness, of which the poet became the victim immediately after the loss of his only daughter in autumn, prevented him from answering Cleghorn till January 1796, when he transcribed the song and wrote to his friend explaining his hapless condition.]

INSCRIPTION,

WRITTEN ON THE BLANK LEAF OF A COPY OF THE LAST
EDITION OF MY POEMS, PRESENTED TO THE LADY
WHOM, IN SO MANY FICTITIOUS REVERIES OF
PASSION, BUT WITH THE MOST ARDENT SENTI-
MENTS OF REAL FRIENDSHIP, I HAVE SO OFTEN
SUNG UNDER THE NAME OF—"CHLORIS."

'TIS Friendship's pledge, my young, fair Friend,
    Nor thou the gift refuse,
Nor with unwilling ear attend
    The moralising Muse.

Since thou, in all thy youth and charms,
    Must bid the world adieu,
(A world 'gainst Peace in constant arms)
    To join the Friendly Few.

Since, thy gay morn of life o'ercast,
    Chill came the tempest's lour ;
(And ne'er Misfortune's eastern blast
    Did nip a fairer flower.)

Since life's gay scenes must charm no more,
    Still much is left behind,
Still nobler wealth hast thou in store—
    The comforts of the mind!

Thine is the self-approving glow,
    Of conscious Honor's part ;
And (dearest gift of Heaven below)
    Thine Friendship's truest heart.

The joys refin'd of Sense and Taste,
  With every Muse to rove :
And doubly were the Poet blest,
  These joys could he improve.

R. B.

[These verses to Chloris form the concluding portion of the sheet before referred to, which the poet addressed to his friend Mr Cunningham on 3rd August 1795.

Poor "Chloris" henceforth disappears from the scene. Within twelve short months after this period, the heart of her minstrel ceased to beat and his lyre was for ever unstrung. Her father sank into poverty, and she became a cheerless wanderer. The last seven years of her life were passed in Edinburgh. A few friends turned up for her in that city ; and there still exists an affecting note in her handwriting, returning thanks for some little kindnesses bestowed. The words are these :—"Burns's *Chloris* is infinitely oblidged to Mrs ———— for her kind attention in sending the newspapers, and feels pleased and flattered by having so much said and done in her behalf. Ruth was kind and generously treated by Boaz ; perhaps Burns's *Chloris* may enjoy a similar fate in the fields of men of talent and worth.—*March 2nd,* 1825."

She died in September 1831, at the age of fifty-six, in a humble lodging in Middleton's Entry, Potterrow (a locality which does not now exist), and her remains were interred in Newington burying-ground.]

FRAGMENT.—LEEZIE LINDSAY.

WILL ye go to the Hielands, Leezie Lindsay,
  Will ye go to the Hielands wi' me ?
Will ye go to the Hielands, Leezie Lindsay,
  My pride and my darling to be.

[Leaving the Bard for several months in the oblivious position in which his first Biographer and Editor placed him, we shall now endeavour to fill up the intervening blank with gleanings from the fifth and sixth volumes of Johnson's *Musical Museum,* for which work Burns continued to send little snatches of song till near the close of his life. Unfortunately the correspondence between the poet and Mr Johnson has not been preserved in the connected form in which we have the Thomson correspondence, and therefore the dates of our author's contributions to the *Museum* cannot be fixed with positive certainty. Such of these as have not already found a place in this and preceding volumes, we now present in their robable order of composition.

Of the fragment in the text with its corresponding music, Stenhouse says :—"This beautiful old air was communicated by Burns. The stanza to which it is adapted was written by him, and he intended to have added some more verses, as appears from Johnson's memorandum written on the original MS., ' Mr Burns is to send words.' "

The singing of the late John Wilson, Scottish Vocalist, made this song very popular. The following are the additional words he adopted for extending it : we cannot say who manufactured them :—

> " To gang to the Hielands wi' you, Sir,
>   I dinna see how that may be ;
> For I ken na the gate ye are gangin,
>   Nor ken I the lad I'm gaun wi'
>
> O Leezie, lass, ye maun ken little,
>   If sae that ye dinna ken me ;
> My name is Lord Ronald Macdonald,
>   A chieftain o' high degree.
>
> She has kilted her coats o' green satin,
>   She has kilted them up to the knee,
> And she's aff wi' Lord Ronald Macdonald
>   His pride and his darling to be."]

FRAGMENT.—THE WREN'S NEST.

> THE Robin to the Wren's nest
>   Cam keekin in, cam keekin in ;
> O weel's me on your auld pow,
>   Wad ye be in, wad ye be in?
> Thou's ne'er get leave to lie without,
>   And I within, and I within,
> Sae lang's I hae an auld clout
>   To rowe ye in, to rowe ye in.

[This is a little ditty with which Mrs Burns used to divert her children by singing it over to them. The poet got the melody noted down for the *Museum*, where it is given (No. 406), with these words, which appear to be the introductory portion of a similar fragment published by David Herd, and re-produced in the *Museum* (No. 483) as follows :—

Air—" The Wren, or Lennox's love to Blantyre."

The Wren she lies in Care's bed, in Care's bed, in Care's bed,
The Wren she lies in Care's bed, in meikle dule and pyne, jo

When in cam' Robin Redbreast, when in cam' Robin Redbreast,
When in cam' Robin Redbreast, wi' sugar-saps and wine, jo.

Now maiden, will ye taste o' this, taste o' this, taste o' this?
Now maiden, will ye taste o' this, it's sugar-saps and wine, jo.
Na, ne'er a drap, Robin, Robin, Robin,
Na, ne'er a drap, Robin, tho' it were ne'er sae fine, jo.

Then whare's the ring that I gied ye, that I gied ye, that I gied ye,
Say whare's the ring that I gied ye, ye little cutty queen, jo!
I gied it till a soger, a soger, a soger,
I gied it till a soger, was ance a love o' mine, jo.

He promis'd to be back in Spring, to wed his little Jenny Wren,
But Spring and Simmer baith are gane, and here am I my lane, jo.
The Winter winds 'ill chill me thro', they'll chill me thro', chill me thro',
Ye'll think upon your broken vow, when I am dead and gane, jo.

Our main inducement for inserting this nursery ballad here, arises out of
a little incident recorded by Chambers on the authority of Mrs Thomson
(the Jessie Lewars who attended Burns so kindly during his fatal illness).
"One morning the poet offered, if she would play him any tune of which
she was fond, and for which she desired new verses, to gratify her in that
wish to the best of his ability. She accordingly played the air called 'The
Wren's Nest,' and as soon as his ear got familiar with the tune, he sat down,
and in a few minutes produced the admired song, 'O wert thou in the cauld
blast.' "
The air played by Jessie Lewars was not "The Wren's Nest" (No. 406)
but "The Wren," No. 483 of Johnson. The fifth volume of the *Museum*,
where they both appear, was not then published, but the proof sheets may
have been in the poet's possession. On the score of the melody, No. 406,
Clarke has made the following note:—"This tune is only a bad set of
Johny's Gray Breeks."]

NEWS, LASSES, NEWS.

THERE'S news, lasses, news.
    Gude news I've to tell !
There's a boatfu' o' lads
    Come to our town to sell.

Chorus—The wean wants a cradle,
            And the cradle wants a cod :
        I'll no gang to my bed,
            Until I get a nod.

Father, quo' she, Mither, quo' she,
  Do what you can,
I'll no gang to my bed,
  Until I get a man.
                    The wean, &c.

I hae as gude a craft rig
  As made o' yird and stane ;
And waly fa' the ley-crap,
  For I maun till'd again.
                    The wean, &c.

[This curious ditty is barely intelligible, even to a Scotsman, unless he
has been bred at the plough-tail. We suspect that the words were written
merely to preserve a pretty little melody which our bard recovered.]

CROWDIE EVER MAIR.

O THAT I had ne'er been married,
  I wad never had nae care,
Now I've gotten wife an' weans,
  An' they cry " Crowdie " * evermair.

  Chorus—Ance crowdie, twice crowdie,
        Three times crowdie in a day ;
      Gin ye " crowdie " ony mair,
        Ye'll crowdie a' my meal away.

Waefu' Want and Hunger fley † me,
  Glowrin by the hallan en' ‡ ;
Sair I fecht them at the door,
  But ay I'm eerie § they come ben.
          Ance crowdie, &c.

[In a letter to Mrs Dunlop, dated 15th December 1793, the poet, anticipating what might be his condition when laid on a death-bed, quotes the

---

* oatmeal brose, but used as a general term for food.
† frighten.   ‡ cottage doorway.   § apprehensive.

opening stanza and the chorus of this song, as part of an "old Scots ballad."
"I see," he said, "a train of helpless little folks—me and my exertions all
their stay ; (and on what a brittle thread does the life of man hang !) If I
am nipt off at the command of fate, even in all the vigour of manhood, as I
am (such things happen every day), Gracious God ! what would become of
my little flock? . . . But I shall run distracted if I think any longer on the
subject !"   On his death-bed, these fears were all realized—"Alas, Clarke,
I begin to fear the worst ! As to my individual self, I am tranquil (I would
despise myself if I were not); but Burns's poor widow, and half a dozen of
dear little ones—helpless orphans—there I am weak as a woman's tear !
Enough of this ! 'Tis half my disease !"]

MALLY'S MEEK, MALLY'S SWEET.

Chorus—MALLY'S meek, Mally's sweet,
　　　　Mally's modest and discreet ;
　　　Mally's rare, Mally's fair,
　　　Mally's every way complete.

As I was walking up the street,
　A barefit maid I chanc'd to meet ;
But O the road was very hard
　For that fair maiden's tender feet.
　　　Mally's meek, &c.

It were mair meet that those fine feet
　Were weel laced up in silken shoon ;
An' 'twere more fit that she should sit
　Within yon chariot gilt aboon,
　　　Mally's meek, &c.

Her yellow hair, beyond compare,
　Comes trinklin down her swan-like neck,
And her two eyes, like stars in skies,
　Would keep a sinking ship frae wreck,
　　　Mally's meek, &c.

JOCKEY'S TAEN THE PARTING KISS.

Air—"Bonie lass tak a man."

JOCKEY'S taen the parting kiss,
  O'er the mountains he is gane,
And with him is a' my bliss,
  Nought but griefs with me remain,
Spare my Love, ye winds that blaw,
  Plashy sleets and beating rain !
Spare my Love, thou feath'ry snaw,
  Drifting o'er the frozen plain !

When the shades of evening creep
  O'er the day's fair, gladsome e'e,
Sound and safely may he sleep,
  Sweetly blythe his waukening be.
He will think on her he loves,
  Fondly he'll repeat her name ;
For where'er he distant roves,
  Jockey's heart is still the same.

[The poet is now languishing on a bed of sore sickness and distress. Hopelessly barred from participating in the delights of which he so lately sung :—

> "The pathless wild and wimpling burn,
> Wi' Chloris in my arms be mine,"

he is compelled to regard himself as having taken the parting kiss, and "gone over the mountains" away from the sight and the society of her whose smile gave alacrity and vigour to his musings. However, he has not parted with his "singing robes," and here he indites and puts into the lips of the absent fair one a song—not a glad one—but breathing of nature in every line :—

> "Sound and safely may he sleep,
> Sweetly blythe his waukening be."

He has told us that this beautiful "blessing" was his own mother's favourite "Good Night" at parting—"A sound sleep an' a blythe waukening ;" so it was the very last expression her son was likely to forget.

VERSES TO COLLECTOR MITCHELL.

FRIEND of the Poet, tried and leal,
Wha, wanting thee, might beg or steal;
Alake, alake, the meikle deil
    Wi' a' his witches
Are at it, skelpin jig and reel,
      In my poor pouches?*

I modestly fu' fain wad hint it,
That *One-pound-one*, I sairly want it;
If wi' the hizzie † down ye sent it,
    It would be kind;
And while my heart wi' life-blood dunted, ‡
    I'd bear't in mind.

So may the Auld year gang out moanin
To see the New come laden, groanin,
Wi' double plenty o'er the loanin,
    To thee and thine:
Domestic peace and comforts crownin
    The hale design.

POSTSCRIPT.

Ye've heard this while how I've been licket,
And by fell Death was nearly nicket;
Grim loon! he got me by the fecket, §
    And sair me sheuk;
But by gude luck I lap a wicket,
    And turn'd a neuk.

But by that health, I've got a share o't,
And by that life, I'm promis'd mair o't,

---

* pockets.   † servant girl.   ‡ throbbed.   § vest, under woollen shirt

My hale and weel, I'll tak a care o't,
        A tentier * way ;
Then farewell folly, hide and hair o't,
        For ance and ay !

[Collector Mitchell, from whom the poet in the foregoing lines modestly
borrows a guinea, was an intelligent person, and Burns was wont to submit
his compositions to the test of his critical acumen. Chambers informs us
that he was well-educated, with a design to follow the profession of a
minister. These verses, from allusions contained in them, must have been
penned at the close of 1795. How long the poet's illness had continued or
what were the characteristics of his trouble can only now be guessed at; for
no particulars regarding these have been handed down for the information
of posterity. His health was evidently now getting into a convalescent
state ; and from the close of January till the month of April 1796 he seems
to have moved about with some hope of permanent physical improvement.]

THE DEAN OF FACULTY.

A NEW BALLAD.

Tune—"The Dragon of Wantley."

DIRE was the hate at old Harlaw,
        That Scot to Scot did carry ;
And dire the discord Langside saw
        For beauteous, hapless Mary :
But Scot to Scot ne'er met so hot,
        Or were more in fury seen, Sir,
Then 'twixt Hal and Bob for the famous job,
        Who should be the Faculty's Dean, Sir.

This Hal for genius, wit and lore,
        Among the first was number'd ;
But pious Bob, 'mid learning's store,
        Commandment the tenth remember'd :

---

* more guarded.

Yet simple Bob the victory got,
　　And wan his heart's desire,
Which shews that heaven can boil the pot,
　　Tho' the devil piss in the fire.

Squire Hal, besides, had in this case
　　Pretensions rather brassy ;
For talents, to deserve a place,
　　Are qualifications saucy.
So their worships of the Faculty,
　　Quite sick of merit's rudeness,
Chose one who should owe it all, d'ye see,
　　To their gratis grace and goodness.

As once on Pisgah, purg'd was the sight
　　Of a son of Circumcision,
So may be, on this Pisgah height,
　　Bob's purblind mental vision—
Nay, Bobby's *mouth* may be open'd yet,
　　Till for eloquence you hail him,
And swear that he has the angel met
　　That met the ass of Balaam.

In your heretic sins may you live and die,
　　Ye heretic Eight-and-Thirty !
But accept, ye sublime Majority,
　　My congratulations hearty.
With your honors, as with a certain king,
　　In your servants this is striking,
The more incapacity they bring,
　　The more they're to your liking.

[The history of this production seems to be that, towards the close of
1795, in consequence of bad harvests and other causes, there was manifested
much popular discontent, which gave uneasiness to the ministry. In the
Adelphi Theatre of Edinburgh, a public meeting was convened to discuss
politics and adopt means to alleviate the general distress, at which the Hon.
Henry Erskine, Dean of the Faculty of Advocates, presided. Great offence

was thereby given to the Conservative majority in the Parliament House, who resolved to set up an opposition candidate for the office of " Dean" at the ensuing election. The contest was decided on 12th January 1796, when Robert Dundas of Arniston, by a large majority, supplanted the Whig favourite.

Burns, besides having a real respect for Erskine, remembered an old grudge against Dundas, and vented his feelings in the above verses, which display the wit and vigour of his best days.]

EPISTLE TO COLONEL DE PEYSTER.

My honor'd Colonel, deep I feel
Your interest in the Poet's weal;
Ah ! now sma' heart hae I to speel *
              The steep Parnassus,
Surrounded thus by bolus pill,
              And potion glasses.

O what a canty warld were it,
Would pain and care and sickness spare it;
And Fortune favor worth and merit
              As they deserve ;
And ay rowth † o' roast-beef and claret,
              Syne, wha wad starve?

Dame Life, tho' fiction out may trick her,
And in paste gems and frippery deck her;
Oh ! flickering, feeble, and unsicker ‡
              I've found her still,
Ay wavering like the willow-wicker,
              'Tween good and ill.

Then that curst carmagnole, auld Satan,
Watches like baudrons § by a ratton
Our sinfu' saul to get a claut‖ on,
              Wi' felon ire ;

---

* climb.   † abundance.   ‡ insecure.   § the cat.   ‖ clutch.

Syne, whip ! his tail ye'll ne'er cast saut on,
     He's aff like fire.

Ah Nick ! ah Nick ! it is na fair,
First shewing us the tempting ware,
Bright wines, and bonie lasses rare,
     To put us daft ;
Syne weave, unseen, thy spider snare
     O hell's damned waft.

Poor Man, the flie, aft bizzes by,
And aft, as chance he comes thee nigh,
Thy damn'd auld elbow yeuks * wi' joy
     And hellish pleasure ;
Already In thy fancy's eye,
     Thy sicker † treasure.

Soon, heels o'er gowdie, ‡ in he gangs,
And, like a sheep-head on a tangs,
Thy girning laugh enjoys his pangs,
     And murdering wrestle,
As, dangling in the wind, he hangs
     A gibbet's tassle.

But lest you think I am uncivil
To plague you with this draunting drivel,
Abjuring a' intentions evil,
     I quat my pen,
The Lord preserve us frae the devil !
     Amen ! Amen !

[Colonel Arentz Schulyer de Peyster, Major Commandant of the Dumfriesshire corps of Volunteers, although seventy years of age at this date,
survived Burns upwards of a quarter century. He died and was buried in
Dumfries in November 1822, his age being ninety-six. He was of French
extraction, if not a native of France, but served as a British Officer in Upper
Canada during the American war. On retiring from service, he settled down
in Dumfries, the native place of his wife, who was a daughter of Provost
Blair ; the wife of Burns's friend, John M'Murdo of Drumlanrig, was
another of Provost Blair's daughters.]

---

* itches.   † secured.   ‡ heels o'er head.

A LASS WI' A TOCHER.

Tune—" Ballinamona Ora."

AWA wi' your witchcraft o' Beauty's alarms,
The slender bit Beauty you grasp in your arms,
O, gie me the lass that has acres o' charms,
O, gie me the lass wi' the weel-stockit farms.

> *Chorus*—Then hey, for a lass wi' a tocher,
> Then hey, for a lass wi' a tocher ;
> Then hey, for a lass wi' a tocher ;
> Then nice yellow guineas for me.

Your Beauty's a flower, in the morning that blows,
And withers the faster, the faster it grows :
But the rapturous charm o' the bonie green knowes,
Ilk spring they're new deckit wi' bonie white yowes.
> Then hey, for a lass, &c.

And e'en when this Beauty your bosom hath blest
The brightest o' Beauty may cloy when possess'd ;
But the sweet, yellow darlings wi' Geordie impress'd,
The langer ye hae them, the mair they're carest.
> Then hey, for a lass, &c.

[After a pause of six months, the Thomson correspondence was resumed for a brief period in February 1796. Mr Thomson wrote on the 5th of that month intimating his intention to publish an octavo edition of his collection, and requesting Burns to furnish words for a few Irish airs mentioned. The song in the text was the first result.]

HERON ELECTION BALLAD, NO. IV.

THE TROGGER.

Tune—" Buy Broom Besoms."

WHA will buy my troggin, fine election ware,
Broken trade o' Broughton, a' in high repair?
> *Chorus*—Buy braw troggin frae the banks o' Dee :
> Wha wants troggin let him come to me.

There's a noble Earl's fame and high renown,[1]
For an auld sang—it's thought the gudes were stown—
    Buy braw troggin, &c.

Here's the worth o' Broughton[2] in a needle's e'e ;
Here's a reputation tint by Balmaghie.[3]
    Buy braw troggin, &c.

Here's its stuff and lining, Cardoness's head,[4]
Fine for a soger, a' the wale o' lead.
    Buy braw troggin, &c.

Here a little wadset, Buittle's[5] scrap o' truth,
Pawn'd in a gin-shop, quenching holy drouth.
    Buy braw troggin, &c.

Here's an honest conscience might a prince adorn ;
Frae the downs o' Tinwald,[6] so was never worn.
    Buy braw troggin, &c.

Here's armorial bearings frae the manse o' Urr ;
The crest, a sour crab-apple, rotten at the core.[7]
    Buy braw troggin, &c.

Here is Satan's picture, like a bizzard gled,
Pouncing poor Redcastle,[8] sprawlin like a taed.
    Buy braw troggin, &c.

Here's the font where Douglas[9] stane and mortar names ;
Lately used at Caily christening Murray's crimes.
    Buy braw troggin, &c.

---

[1] The Earl of Galloway.   [2] Mr Murray of Broughton.
[3] Gordon of Balmaghie.   [4] Maxwell of Cardoness.
[5] Rev. Geo. Maxwell of Buittle.   [6] John Bushby of Tinwald.
[7] Rev. Jas. Muirhead of Urr, who talked of himself as "The Muirhead,' and displayed family heraldry.
[8] Walter Sloan Lawrie of Redcastle.
[9] Douglas of Carlinwark, who changed the name of that town to *Castle Douglas.*

Here's the worth and wisdom Coilieston[1] can boast ;
By a thievish midge they had been nearly lost.
　　　Buy braw troggin, &c.

Here is Murray's fragments o' the ten commands ;
Gifted by black Jock[2] to get them aff his hands.
　　　Buy braw troggin, &c.

Saw ye e'er sic troggin ? if to buy ye're slack,
Hornie's[3] turnin chapman—he'll buy a' the pack.
　　　Buy braw troggin, &c.

[This is the fourth of the series of Heron Election Ballads. Mr Heron
gained the Election, but he had scarcely entered on parliamentary duties
when a dissolution occurred. "Troggers" are a set of vagrant traffickers
who travel with a donkey and cart laden with all kinds of wares which they
may gather in their journeys, and which they hawk for money or barter.]

COMPLIMENTARY VERSICLES TO JESSIE LEWARS.

THE TOAST.

Fill me with the rosy wine,
Call a toast, a toast divine ;
Give the Poet's darling flame,
Lovely Jessie be her name ;
Then thou mayest freely boast,
Thou hast given a peerless toast.

[From about the middle of April, Burns was rarely able to leave his
room ; and during a considerable portion of each day he had to keep his
bed. One day he took up a crystal goblet, and inscribed " The Toast"
upon it with his diamond, and presented it to his kind attendant, Miss
Lewars.]

---

[1] Copland of Collieston.　　　[2] John Bushby.　　　[3] the Devil.

THE MENAGERIE.

Talk not to me of savages,
　From Afric's burning sun ;
No savage e'er could rend my heart,
　As, Jessie, thou hast done :
But Jessie's lovely hand in mine,
　A mutual faith to plight,
Not even to view the heavenly choir,
　Would be so blest a sight.

[Mr Brown, the surgeon, on one of his visits to the poet, brought an
advertising sheet describing the contents of a menagerie of wild beasts then
being exhibited in Dumfries. Burns seeing Miss Lewars occupied in
perusing the bill, asked for a sight of it, and he immediately wrote the
above lines on the back of it, with a red pencil.]

JESSIE'S ILLNESS.

Say, sages, what's the charm on earth
　Can turn Death's dart aside !
It is not purity and worth,
　Else Jessie had not died.

ON HER RECOVERY.

But rarely seen since Nature's birth,
　The natives of the sky ;
Yet still one seraph's left on earth,
　For Jessie did not die.

[Jessie Lewars, a sister of John Lewars, the poet's fellow-exciseman, was
an amiable young woman, who acted the part of a ministering angel in the
household of Burns during this period of distress. Chambers observes that
" it is curious to find him, even in his present melancholy circumstances,
imagining himself as the lover of his wife's kind-hearted young friend ; as if
the position of the mistress were the most exalted in which his fancy could
place any woman he admired, or towards whom he desired to express
gratitude."]

O LAY THY LOOF IN MINE, LASS.

Chorus—O LAY thy loof * in mine, lass,
  In mine, lass, in mine, lass ;
  And swear on thy white hand, lass,
   That thou wilt be my ain.

A slave to Love's unbounded sway,
He aft has wrought me meikle wae ;
But now he is my deadly fae, †
 Unless thou be my ain.
   O lay thy loof, &c.

There's mony a lass has broke my rest,
That for a blink ‡ I hae lo'ed best ;
But thou art Queen within my breast,
 For ever to remain.
   O lay thy loof, &c.

[The above little song is so very similar in character to the two popular lyrics addressed to Jessie Lewars which immediately follow, that we are disposed to regard it as another of those effusions elicited by the poet's regard for her at this period.]

A HEALTH TO ANE I LOE DEAR.

Chorus—HERE'S a health to ane I loe dear,
  Here's a health to ane I loe dear ;
  Thou art sweet as the smile when fond lovers
   meet,
  And soft as their parting tear—Jessy.

Altho' thou maun never be mine,
 Altho' even hope is denied ;

---

* palm of the hand. † foe. ‡ short period.

'Tis sweeter for thee despairing,
   Than ought in the world beside—Jessy.
     Here's a health, &c.

I mourn thro' the gay, gaudy day,
   As hopeless I muse on thy charms ;
But welcome the dream o' sweet slumber,
   For then I am lockt in thine arms—Jessy.
     Here's a health, &c.

I guess by the dear angel smile,
   I guess by the love-rolling e'e ;
But why urge the tender confession,
   'Gainst Fortune's fell, cruel decree ? Jessy.
     Here's a health, &c.

[This beautiful lyric Currie believed to be "the last finished offspring" of Burns's Muse. Seldom has Burns excelled this love-song in elegance of expression, poetic sentiment, and perfect lyrical execution. Jessie Lewars, the subject of the verses, was married about three years after this period, to Mr James Thomson, writer in Dumfries—3rd June 1799 being the date of the marriage. A family of five sons and two daughters was the result of the union. She survived her husband, and spent the years of her widowhood at Maxwelltown near Dumfries. It will be remembered that, at the great Burns-Festival held near the Ayr Monument on 6th August 1844, Jessie Lewars and her husband sat next to the relatives of the Poet, on the right hand of the chairman. In her death she was not far separated from them, for her tombstone is fixed in the wall, close to the Mausoleum of the Bard. We there read that her husband died on 5th May 1849, aged 75, and that she died on 26th May 1855, aged 77.]

O WERT THOU IN THE CAULD BLAST.

O WERT thou in the cauld blast,
   On yonder lea, on yonder lea,
My plaidie to the angry airt,
   I'd shelter thee, I'd shelter thee ;
Or did Misfortune's bitter storms
   Around thee blaw, around thee blaw,

Thy bield should be my bosom,
  To share it a', to share it a'.

Or were I in the wildest waste,
  Sae black and bare, sae black and bare,
The desert were a Paradise,
  If thou wert there, if thou wert there;
Or were I Monarch o' the globe,
  Wi' thee to reign, wi' thee to reign,
The brightest jewel in my crown
  Wad be my Queen, wad be my Queen.

[Mendelssohn composed a melody for the words in the text, which he arranged as a Duet. It is described by Chambers as "an air of great pathos, 'such as the meeting soul may pierce,' in which the great German composer seems to have divined the peculiar feeling, beyond all common love, which Burns breathed into the song."]

INSCRIPTION TO MISS JESSY LEWARS

ON A COPY OF THE SCOTS MUSICAL MUSEUM, IN FOUR VOLUMES, PRESENTED TO HER BY BURNS.

THINE be the volumes, Jessy fair,
And with them take the Poet's prayer,
That Fate may, in her fairest page,
With ev'ry kindliest, best presage
Of future bliss, enrol thy name:
With native worth and spotless fame,
And wakeful caution, still aware
Of ill—but chief, Man's felon snare;
All blameless joys on earth we find,
And all the treasures of the mind—
These be thy guardian and reward;
So prays thy faithful friend, the Bard.

DUMFRIES, *June 26th*, 1796.

[The first volume of this presentation copy of the *Museum* (so far as published in the life-time of Burns) was exhibited, bearing the above inscription on its fly-leaf, at Dumfries, on the occasion of the Burns Centenary in 1859. In the bard's published correspondence is a letter from him to Johnson, the original of which bears to have been delivered by post on 17th June 1796. It concludes thus :—"My wife has a very particular friend, a young lady who sings well, to whom she wishes to present the *Scots Musical Museum.* If you have a spare copy, will you be so obliging as to send it by the very first *Fly*, as I am anxious to have it soon."

Cromek, who first published the letter in 1808, says in a foot-note : "In this humble and delicate manner did poor Burns ask for the copy of a Work to which he had gratuitously contributed not less than 184 original, altered, and collected songs!" Allan Cunningham, who personally knew nothing of the transaction, thus rashly ventured to remark in his latest edition :— "Will it be believed that this humble request was not complied with!" This calumny was repeated in that biographer's note to a later letter of the bard, thus :—"Few of the last requests of the poet were effectual : Clarke, it is believed, did not send the second pound-note he wrote for : Johnson did not send the copy of the *Museum* which he requested, and the Com-missioners of Excise refused the continuance of his full salary."

We gladly aid in wiping away the injustice thus done to Johnson, who, although poor, was known to be a generous man, and greatly esteemed by Burns. In the Edinburgh Subscription list, which was opened after the poet's death for the benefit of his family, we find the name of "James Johnson, engraver," set down for Four pounds; while George Thomson subscribes no more than Two guineas.]

FAIREST MAID ON DEVON BANKS.

Tune—"Rothiemurchie."

*Chorus—*FAIREST maid on Devon banks,
    Crystal Devon, winding Devon,
    Wilt thou lay that frown aside,
    And smile as thou wert wont to do?

Full well thou know'st I love thee dear,
Couldst thou to malice lend an ear !
O did not Love exclaim : ' Forbear,
    Nor use a faithful lover so.'
        Fairest maid, &c.

Then come, thou fairest of the fair,
Those wonted smiles, O let me share ;

And by thy beauteous self I swear,
No love but thine my heart shall know.
Fairest maid, &c.

[This last strain of the great master of lyric eloquence is dated from
" Brow, on the Solway Frith, 12th July 1796," and he died on 21st of same
month.   There were two fair maids on Devon banks, whose charms he had
celebrated in 1787, namely Charlotte Hamilton, and Peggy Chalmers.   We
cannot bring ourselves to conceive that he ever had much love for Charlotte,
although he praised her beauty highly; whereas, it is manifest from some
observations which dropped from Clarinda, that he did dream of a common-
sense, practical passion for Peggy Chalmers, afterwards Mrs Lewis Hay.
That lady herself, when living in widowhood, at Edinburgh, in the early
part of this century, informed Thomas Campbell, the poet, that Burns had
made her a serious proposal of marriage.[1]   He must at one period have
been impressed with the notion that he had declined in her favour through
the slander of tale-bearers, and this ruling thought is strongly expressed in
the above song :—

" Could'st thou to malice lend an ear!
O did not love exclaim : ' Forbear,
Nor use a faithful lover so.'"

Burns left Dumfries for Brow on 4th July, and returned home on the 18th.
On the 21st, early in the day, all was over.]

---

[1] We state this on the information of Dr Carruthers of Inverness, who
had it personally from Campbell.

GLOSSARY.

A', all.
Aback, backwards.
Abeigh, or *abiegh*, at a distance.
Aboon, above, up.
Abread, abroad, in sight.
Abreed, in breadth.
Ae, one; usually *prou.* yac.
Aff, off.
Aff-loof, off-hand.
Afore, before.
Aft, oft.
Aften, often.
Agee, or *ajee*, on one side.
Agley, off the right line.
Aiblins, perhaps.
Ain, own.
Airles, hiring money.
Airl-penny, a silver penny given as airles.
Airn, iron, a mason's chisel.
Airt, region of the earth or sky.
Aith, an oath.
Aits, oats.
Aiver, an old horse.
Aizle, a hot cinder.
Alake, alas.
Alane, alone.
Amaist, almost.
Amang, among.
An', and.
An, if. See *gif, gin.*
Ance, once.
Ane, one.
Anent, concerning, about.
Anither, another.
Ase, ashes of wood.

Asteer, stirring.
Attour, moreover, besides.
Atween, between.
Atweel no, by no means.
Aught, eight; possession.
Auld, old.
Auld-farran', or *auld-farrant*, sagacious, prudent, cunning.
Auld-shoon, old shoes.
Aumous, alms.
Ava, at all.
Awa, away, begone.
Awfu', awful.
Awn, the beard of corn.
Awnie, bearded.
Ayont, beyond.

Ba', ball.
Babie-clouts, child's first clothes.
Backets, buckets.
Backlins-comin, coming back.
Back-yett, private gate.
Bad, did bid.
Baggie, the belly.
Baide, endured, did stay.
Bainie, with large bones.
Bairin, laying bare.
Bairn, a child.
Baith, both.
Baiveridge, hansel drink.
Ballets, ballants, ballads.
Ban, to swear, or curse.
Bane, bone; *banie*, see *bainie.*
Bang, to drive, to excel.
Bannock, flat soft cake.

Bardie, diminutive of bard.
Barefit, barefooted.
Barket, barked.
Barkin, barking.
Barley-bree, barley-broo, juice of barley, malt liquor.
Barmie, like barm.
Batch, a crew, a gang.
Batts, botts, a disease in horses.
Bauckie-bird, the bat.
Baudrons, a cat.
Bauk, a cross beam.
Bauks, rafters.
Bauld, bold.
Baws'nt, having a white stripe down the face—of horses, dogs, and cattle.
Be, or *bee*, give over, cease.
Bear, barley.
Bearded-bear, barley with its bristly head.
Beastie, diminutive of beast.
Beet, beek, to add fuel to a fire.
Befa', to befall or happen.
Beld, bald.
Bellys, bellows.
Belyve, by and by.
Ben, into the parlour.
Benmost-bore, the inmost corner.
Bent, coarse grass.
Bethanket, grace after meat.
Beuk, a book.
Bicker, a wooden dish, a short rapid race.
Bickering, hurrying, quarrelling.
Biel', or *bield*, shelter.
Bien, wealthy, snug.
Big, to build.
Biggin, building, a house.
Biggit, built.
Bill, a bull.
Billie, a brother, a companion.
Bing, a heap of grain, potatoes, &c.
Birdie-cocks, young cocks.

Birk, birch.
Birkie, a conceited fellow.
Birnie, wiry.
Birring, the noise of partridges, &c., when they rise.
Birses, bristles.
Bit, nick of time, place.
Bizz, a bustle, to buzz.
Black's the grun, as black as the ground.
Blastet, worthless.
Blastie, a shrivelled dwarf, a term of contempt, full of mischief.
Blate, bashful, sheepish.
Blather, bladder ; nonsense.
Blathrie, idle talk, flattery.
Blaud, to slap.
Blaudin-shower, a heavy rain.
Blaw, to blow, to boast.
Bleer't, eyes dim with weeping.
Bleer my een, dim my eyes.
Bleeze, flame ; *bleezin*, flaming.
Blellum, nonsense.
Blether, to talk idly.
Bleth'rin, talking idly.
Blink, a little while, a smiling look.
Blinkin, smirking.
Blinker, a term of contempt.
Blirt and blearie, outburst of grief.
Blue-gown, beggars who got annually, on the king's birthday, a blue cloak or gown with a badge.
Bluid, or *blude*, blood.
Blype, a shred, a large piece.
Bobbit, danced.
Bock, to vomit.
Bocket, gushed, vomited.
Bodle, two pennies Scots.
Bogie, a morass.
Bonie, bonnie, bonny, handsome.

Bonnock, or *bannock,* a thick cake of bread.

Boord, a board.

Boortree, the shrub elder.

Boost, behoved, must needs.

Bore, a hole in a wall.

Botch, an angry tumour.

Bother, to make a fuss.

Bousing, or *bowsing,* drinking.

Bouk, body, bulk.

Bow-hough'd, out-kneed.

Bow-kail, cabbage.

Bowd, bended, crooked.

Brachens, or *breckens,* ferns.

Brae, a declivity.

Braid, broad.

Braik, a harrow to break clods.

Braindge, to run rashly forward.

Braindg't, "*the horse braindg't,*" plunged in the harness.

Brak, broke, became insolent.

Brankie, gaudy, spruce.

Branks, a wooden curb for horses.

Brash, a sudden illness.

Brats, coarse clothes, children.

Brattle, a short race, hurry.

Braw, gallant, handsome, fine, expensively dressed.

Brawlys, or *brawlyns,* very well.

Braxies, diseased sheep.

Breastet, or *breastit,* sprung up or forward.

Breastie, diminutive of breast.

Brechame, a horse-collar.

Bree, juice, liquid.

Breef, an irresistible spell.

Breeks, breeches.

Brent, smooth and polished.

Brent-new, brand-new, in fashion.

Brewin, brewing, gathering.

Brig, a bridge.

Brisket, the breast, the bosom.

Brither, a brother.

Brock, a badger.

Brogue, a hum, a trick.

Broo, broth, liquid, water.

Broose, a race at country weddings.

Brose, a dish made of oatmeal seasoned.

Browst, ale, as much as is brewed at a time.

Brugh, a burgh ; a lunar halo.

Bruilyie, a broil, combustion.

Brunstane, brimstone.

Brunt, did burn, burnt.

Brust, to burst, burst.

Buchan-bullers, the waves off the coast of Buchan.

Buckskin, an inhabitant of Virginia.

Buff our Beef, thrash us soundly.

Buff and blue, the Whig livery.

Buirdly, stout made.

Bum-clock, the humming beetle.

Bummin, humming as bees.

Bummle, to blunder, to drone.

Bummle, or *bummler,* a blunderer.

Bunker, a window - seat, or chest.

Bure, did bear.

Burn, burnie, small stream.

Burn-e-win', the blacksmith.

Burr-thistle, the thistle of Scotland.

Buskit, dressed.

But, without, void of.

But and ben, the country kitchen and parlour.

By, beyond.

Byke, a bee-hive.

Byre, a cow-house.

Ca', to call, to drive.

Ca't, or *ca'd,* called, driven, calved.

Cadger, a carrier.

Cadie, or *caddie*, a message-goer.
Caff, chaff.
Caird, a tinker.
Cairn, loose heap of stones.
Calf-ward, an enclosure for calves.
Calimanco, thick cotton cloth worn by ladies.
Callan, or *callant*, a boy.
Caller, or *cauler*, fresh and cool.
Callet, a follower of a camp.
Cam, came.
Canna, cannot.
Cannie, gentle, mild.
Cannilie, dexterously, gently.
Cantie, or *canty*, cheerful.
Cantraip, a charm, a spell.
Cap-stane, a cape-stone, key-stone.
Cark, *carking*, anxious.
Carl, or *carle*, an old man.
Carl-hemp, male stalk of hemp.
Caries, cards.
Castock, the stalk of a cabbage.
Caudron, a cauldron.
Cauk and keel, chalk and red clay.
Cauld, cold.
Caup, a cup, a quaich.
Cavie, a hen-coop.
Chantin, chanting.
Chanter, drone of a bagpipe.
Chap, a person, a fellow.
Chaup, a stroke, a blow.
Cheeket, cheeked.
Cheek for chow, side by side.
Cheep, a chirp, to chirp.
Chiel, *chield*, or *cheel*, a young fellow.
Chimla, or *chimlie*, fire-place.
Chimla-lug, the fire-side.
Chirps, cries of a young bird.
Chittering, shivering.

Chockin, choking.
Chow, to chew.
Chuckie, a brood-hen.
Chuffie, fat faced.
Clachan, hamlet.
Claise, or *claes*, clothes.
Claith, cloth.
Claithing, clothing.
Clap, *clapper*, the clapper of a mill.
Clarkit, wrote.
Clartie, dirty, filthy.
Clash, an idle tale.
Clatter, an idle story.
Claught, snatched at.
Claut, to scrape.
Clauted, scraped clean.
Claver, clover.
Clavers and havers, nonsense.
Claw, to scratch.
Cleckin, a brood of chickens.
Cleed, to clothe.
Cleek, hook, snatch.
Clegs, the gad flies.
Clinkin, jerking, clinking.
Clinkin down, sitting down hastily.
Clinkum bell, the church bell-ringer.
Clips, wool-shears.
Clishmaclaver, idle conversation.
Clock, to hatch, a beetle.
Clockin, clucking of a hen.
Cloot, the hoof of a cow, &c.
Clootie, the devil.
Clour, a contusion.
Clout, to repair.
Cluds, clouds.
Clunk, the sound of drinking from a bottle.
Coaxin, wheedling.
Coble, a fishing boat.
Cod, a pillow.
Coft, bought.
Cog, a wooden dish.

Coila, from Kyle, a district in Ayrshire, so called, saith tradition, from Coil, or Coilus, a Pictish monarch.

Collie, a sheep dog.

Collie-shangie, an Irish row.

Comin, coming.

Commaun, command.

Convoyed, accompanied.

Cood, the cud.

Coof, a blockhead, a ninny.

Cookit, appeared and disappeared by fits.

Cooser, a stallion,

Coost, did cast.

Coot, the ancle.

Coolie, a wooden dish.

Corbies, carrion crows.

Core, corps, party.

Corn't, fed with oats.

Couthie, kind, loving.

Cove, a cave.

Cowe, to keep under.

Cowp, to barter, to tumble over.

Cowpet, tumbled over.

Cowrin, cowering.

Cowte, a colt.

Cozie, coziely, snug, snugly.

Crabbit, crabbed, fretful.

Crack, conversation, to converse.

Crackin, conversing.

Craig, craigie, a high rock, the neck.

Craiks, cries, the corn rail.

Crambo-clink, or *crambo-jingle*, doggrel verses.

Crank, the noise of an ungreased wheel.

Crankous, fretful, captious,

Cranreuch, the hoar-frost.

Crap, a crop, to crop.

Craw, a crow of a cock.

Creel, a basket.

Creeshie, greasy.

Cronie, a friend, a gossip.

Crood, or *croud*, to coo as a dove.

Croon, a hollow moan.

Crooning, humming.

Crouchie, crooked-backed.

Crouse, cheerful, courageous.

Crousely, cheerfully, courageously.

Crowdie, a *brose* made of oatmeal, hot water, and butter.

Crowdie-time, meal-time.

Crowlin, crawling hatefully.

Crummie's nicks, marks on cows' horns.

Crummie, or *crombie*, a cow with crooked horns.

Crummock, a staff with a crooked head. See *Cummock*.

Crump-crumpin, hard and brittle.

Crunt, a blow on the head with a cudgel.

Crushin, crushing.

Cuddle, to clasp fondly.

Cuif, see *coof*.

Cummock, or *crummock*, a staff with a crooked head.

Curch, or *curchie*, kerchief.

Curchie, a curtsey.

Curler, a player at curling.

Curling, a game on the ice.

Curmurring, murmuring.

Curpan, the crupper, the rump.

Curple, the rear of a person or animal.

Cushat, the dove, or woodpigeon.

Cutty, short.

Cutty-stool, or *creepie-chair*, stool of repentance.

Dadie, or *daddie*, a father.

Daffin, merriment, foolishness.

Daft, merry, giddy, foolish.

Daft-buckie, mad fish.
Daimen, rare, now and then.
Daimen-icker, an ear of corn occasionally.
Dainty, good-humoured.
Dancin, dancing.
Dandered, wandered.
Dappl't, dappled.
Darklins, darkling, without light.
Daud, or *dawd,* a large piece of bread, &c., to thrash to abuse.
Daudin-showers, rain urged by wind.
Daur, to dare ; *daur't,* dared ; *daurna,* dare not.
Daurg, or *daurk,* a day's labour.
Daut, or *dawt,* to fondle, to caress.
Dautet, dawtit, fondled, caressed.
Davoc, diminutive of Davie.
Dawin, dawning of the day.
Dead-sweer, very loath, averse.
Dearies, sweethearts.
Dearthfu', dear, expensive.
Deave, to deafen.
Deil-ma-care, no matter for all that.
Deleerit, delirious.
Descrive, to describe, to perceive.
Deuks, ducks.
Devle, or *devel,* a stunning blow.
Dight, to wipe, to clean corn from chaff.
Dimpl't, dimpled.
Ding, to excel.
Dink, neat, lady-like.
Dinna, do not.
Dirl, a sudden tremulous stroke.
Disrespecket, disrespected.
Distain, stain.

Dizzen or *dizz'n,* a dozen.
Dochter, daughter.
Doided, silly from age.
Dolt, stupified, crazed, also a fool.
Donsie, affectedly neat and trim.
Doo, dove, pigeon.
Doodle, to dandle.
Dool, sorrow ; to " *sing dool,*" to lament, to mourn.
Dorty, saucy, nice.
Douse, or *douce,* sober, wise, prudent.
Doucely, soberly, prudently.
Dought, was or were able.
Doup, backside, end of a candle.
Doup-skelper, striker on the breech.
Dour and din, sullen and sallow.
Douser, more prudent.
Dow, am or are able, can.
Dowff, pithless, frivolous.
Dowie, worn with grief.
Downa, not able, cannot.
Doylt, or *doylte,* wearied.
Dozen, stupified, benumbed.
Drab, a young female beggar.
Drap, a drop, to drop.
Drappin, dropping.
Drauntin, drawling,
Dreep, to ooze, to drop.
Dreigh, tedious.
Dribble, drizzling slaver.
Driddle, the motion of a bad violinist, or dancer.
Drinkin, drinking.
Droddum, the breech.
Drone, part of a bagpipe.
Droop rumpl't, that droops at the crupper.
Drouket, or *droukit,* wet.
Drouth, thirst, drought.
Drucken, druken, drunken.

Drumly, muddy.

Drummock, or *drammock*, oat meal and cold water mixed.

Drunt, pet, sour humour.

Dryin, drying.

Dub, a small pond.

Duds, rags, clothes.

Duddie, ragged.

Dung, worsted, pushed.

Dunsh, a heavy push.

Dunted, throbbed, beaten.

Dusht, overcome with fear.

Dyvor, bankrupt.

E'e, or *ee*, the eye.

Een, the eyes.

E'e-bree, the eyebrow.

E'en, *e'enin*, the evening.

E'en, as ; *e'en's* even as.

Eerie, frighted, haunted.

Eild, old age.

Elbuck, the elbow.

Eldrich, ghastly, elvish.

En', end.

Enbrugh, or *Embrugh*, Edinburgh.

Eneugh, and *eneuch*, enough.

Ensuin, ensuing.

Especial, especially.

Ether-stone, stone formed by adders.

Ettle, to try, attempt, aim.

Eydent, diligent, busy.

Fa', fall, lot, to fall, fate.

Fa' that, deserve that.

Faddom't, fathomed.

Faes, foes.

Faem, foam of the sea.

Faiket, forgiven or excused.

Fain, desirous of.

Fairin, present from a fair.

Fallow, fellow.

Fand, did find.

Fareweel, fareweel, adieu.

Farl, a cake of bread.

Fash, trouble, care.

Fasheous, troublesome.

Fasht, troubled.

Fasten e'en, Fasten's even.

Fathrals, or *fatt'rels*, ribbon ends.

Faught, fight.

Fauld, and *fald*, a fold for sheep.

Faut, or *faute*, fault.

Fawsont, decent, seemly.

Fearfu', fearful, frightful.

Fear't, affrighted.

Feat, neat, spruce, clever.

Fecht, to fight.

Fecht'n, fighting.

Feck, number, quantity.

Fecket, an under-waistcoat.

Feckfu', large, brawny, stout.

Feckless, puny, weak, silly.

Feckly, mostly.

Feg, a fig.

Fegs, faith, an exclamation.

Feide, feud, enmity.

Fell, keen, biting.

Felly, relentless.

Fend, *fen'*, to make a shift.

Ferlie, or *ferley*, to wonder.

Fetch, to pull by fits.

Fetch't, pulled intermittently.

Fey, strange.

Fidge, to fidget ; *fidgin*, fidgeting.

Fidgin-fain, tickled with pleasure.

Fien-ma-care, the devil may care.

Fient, fiend, a petty oath.

Fier, sound, healthy.

Fierrie, fiery, bustling active.

Fissle, a bustle.

Fit, foot or footstep.

Fittie-lan, the near horse of the hindmost pair in the plough.

Fizz, to make a hissing noise, fuss.

Flaffin, the motion of rags in the wind ; of wings.

Flaite, did flyte or scold.

Flannen, flannel.

Flang, threw with violence.

Fleech, supplicate ; *fleechin*, supplicating.

Fleesh, a fleece.

Fleg, a fright, a random blow.

Flether, to flatter.

Flethrin, flattering.

Fley, to scare, to frighten.

Fley'd, scared, frightened.

Flichter, *flichtering*, to flutter.

Flinders, shreds, broken pieces.

Flingin-tree, a flail.

Flisk, to fret at the yoke.

Flisket, fretted ; *flisky*, skittish.

Flittering, fluttering, vibrating.

Flunkie, a servant in livery.

Flyte, *flyting*, scold, scolding.

Foor, hastened, progressed.

Foord, a ford.

Foorsday, Thursday.

Forbears, forefathers.

Forby, or *forbye*, besides.

Forfain, jaded, forlorn.

Forgie, to give.

Forjesket, jaded.

Forniawed, worn out.

Fou, or *fu'*, full, drunk.

Foughten, *forfoughten*, troubled, fatigued.

Foul-thief, the devil.

Fouth, plenty, enough.

Fow, a bushel, also a pitchfork.

Frae, from.

Freath, froth.

Frien', friend.

Fud, tail of a hare.

Fuff, to blow intermittently.

Fulyie, foul matter.

Funnie, full of merriment.

Fur-ahin, the hindmost horse on the right hand when ploughing.

Furder, further, succeed.

Furm, a form, a bench.

Fusionless, spiritless.

Fyfteen, fifteen.

Fyke, trifling cares.

Fyle, to soil, to dirty.

Fyl't, soiled, dirtied.

Gab, the mouth ; to speak pertly.

Gaberlunyie, a beggar.

Gae, to go ; *gaed*, went ; *gane* or *gaen*, gone ; *gaun*, going.

Gaet or *gate*, way, manner, road.

Gairs, coloured insertions on wearing apparel.

Gang, to go, to walk.

Gangrel, a wandering person.

Gar, to make, to force to ; *gar't*, forced to.

Garten, a garter.

Gash, wise, sagacious, talkative.

Gatty, failing in body, swelled.

Gaucy, or *gawcie*, large, plump.

Gaud, and *gad*, a rod or goad.

Gaudsman, one who drives the horses at the plough.

Gaunted, yawned, longed.

Gawkie, a thoughtless person.

Gaylies, and *gaylins*, pretty well.

Gear, riches, goods of any kind.

Geck, to toss the head in scorn.

Ged, a pike.

Ged's hole, the grave.

Gentles, great folks.

Genty, elegant, well-bred.

Geordie, a guinea.

Get, a child, a young one

Ghaist, a ghost.

Gie, to give ; *gied*, gave ; *gien*, given.

Gif, if ; see *gin*, also *an*.

Giftie, diminutive of gift.

Giglets, laughing youths.

Gillie, diminutive of gill; Gaelic for boy.

Gilpey, a half-grown boy or girl.

Gimmer, a ewe two years old.

Gin, if ; see *gif*, also *an*.

Gipsey, a young girl.

Girdle, a round iron plate on which cakes are fired.

Girn, to grin, to twist the features in rage, agony, &c. ; a snare for birds.

Girnin, grinning.

Girran, a little vigorous animal.

Gizz, a periwig, the face.

Glaikit, inattentive, foolish.

Glaive, a sword.

Glaizie, smooth, like glass.

Glaum'd, grasped.

Gled, a species of hawk.

Gleg, sharp, ready.

Gley, a squint, to squint.

Gleyde, an old horse.

Glib - gabbit, that speaks smoothly and readily.

Glieb, a portion of ground.

Glint, to peep as light, quickly.

Glintin, peeping.

Glinted by, went brightly past.

Gloamin, the twilight.

Gloamin-shot, twilight musing.

Glow'r, to stare.

Glowrin, gazing.

Glum, displeased.

Glunch, a frown ; to frown.

Goavan, moving vacantly.

Gor-cocks, moor-cocks.

Gowan, the flower of the daisy.

Gowany, covered with daisies.

Gowd, gold.

Gowff, the game of golf.

Gowk, the cuckoo.

Gowl, to howl ; *gowling*, howling.

Grain, or *grane*, to groan.

Graip, a pronged instrument.

Graith, accoutrements, furniture.

Graizle, to move like unoiled machinery.

Grannie, grandmother.

Grape, to grope ; *grapet*, groped.

Grat, did greet, or shed tears.

Great, *grit*, intimate, familiar.

Gree, to agree.

Green-graff, green grave.

Greet, to shed tears, to weep.

Greetin, weeping.

Grey-nick-quill, a bad quill.

Griens, longs, desires.

Grieve, steward.

Grippet, seized, catched.

Grissle, gristle, or stump.

Groaning-maut, drink at a lying-in.

Groset, or *grosel*, a gooseberry.

Grousome, loathsome, grim.

Grumph, a grunt; to grunt.

Grumphie, a sow.

Grumphin, grunting.

Grun', ground.

Grunstane, a grindstone.

Gruntle, the snout, a grunting noise.

Grunzie, a pig-shaped mouth.

Grushie, thick, of thriving growth.

Gude, the Supreme Being.

Gude auld-has-been, once excellent.

Gude, or *guid*, good.

Gudes, or *guids*, commodities.

Gude or *guid e'en*, good evening.

Gude or *guidfather*, and *gude-mother*, father-in-law, and mother-in-law.

Gudeman and *gudewife*, the master and mistress of the house.

Gude - willie, hearty, with a will.

Gully, or *gullie*, a large knife.

Gulravage, running wild with joy.

Gumlie, muddy, drumly.

Gumption, discernment.

Gusty, *gustfu'*, tasteful.

Gut-scraper, a fiddler.

Gutcher, grandsire.

Ha', hall.

Haddin, house, home.

Hae, to have, to accept.

Haen, had.

Haet, *fient haet*, a petty oath.

Haffet, the side of the head.

Hafflins, not fully grown.

Hag, a scar, moss ground.

Haggis, an oatmeal pudding.

Hain, to spare, to save; *hain'd*, spared.

Hain'd gear, hoarded money.

Hairst, harvest.

Haith, a petty oath.

Haivers, nonsense.

Hal', or *hald*, an abiding place.

Hale, whole, tight, healthy.

Hallan, a rustic porch.

Haly, holy.

Hame, home ; *hamely*, familiar.

Han'-afore, see *Lan'-afore*.

Han's breed, hand's breadth.

Hansel-throne, throne when first occupied.

Hap, an outer garment.

Hap-shackled, bound fore and hindfoot.

Hap-step-an'-loup, hop, skip, and leap.

Happer, a hopper, the hopper of a mill.

Happin, hopping.

Harigals, heart, liver, and lungs.

Harkit, hearkened.

Harn, a very coarse linen.

Hash, a term of contempt.

Hastit, hastened.

Haud, to hold.

Haughs, low-lying, rich land.

Haurl, to pull violently.

Haurlin, pulling roughly.

Haver-meal, coarsely ground meal

Haveril, *havcrel*, a quarter-wit.

Havins, good manners.

Hawkie, a cow.

Healsome, healthful, wholesome.

Heapit, heaped.

Hear't, hear it.

Hearse, hoarse.

Heather, or *hether*, heath.

Hech, a sigh of weariness.

Hecht, promised.

Heels-owre-gowdie, topsy-turvy.

Heeze, to elevate, to raise, to lift.

Hellim, the rudder or helm.

Herrin, herring.

Herry, to plunder.

Herryment, devastation.

Hersel, herself.

Het, hot, heated.

Heugh, hollow under a crag; *coal - heugh*, a coal-pit; *lowan heugh*, a blazing pit.

Hilch, to halt; *hilchin*, halting.

Hiney, honey.

Hing, to hang ; *hang*, hung.

Hirple, to walk with difficulty.

Hirplin, limping.

Hirsel, as many cattle or sheep as one person can attend.

Histie, dry, chapt, barren.

Hitch, a loop, a stop, a knot.

Hizzie, a wild young girl.

Hoddin, hobbling.

Hoddin-grey, woollen cloth of a coarse quality.

Hoggie, a one-year-old sheep.

Hog-score, the distance-line in curling.

Hog-shouther, to justle.

Hoodie-craw, a carrion crow.

Hool, outer skin or husk.

Hoolie, or *hooly*, slowly, leisurely.

Hoord, a hoard, to hoard.

Hoordet, hoarded.

Horn, a drinking tumbler made of horn.

Hornie, the devil.

Host, or *hoast*, to cough roughly.

Hostin, coughing.

Hotch'd, moved excitedly.

Houghmagandie, fornication.

Howlet, an owl.

Housie, diminutive of house.

Hove, *hoved*, to heave, swollen.

Howdie, a midwife.

Howe, a hollow or dell.

Howebackit, sunk in the back.

Howff, a house of resort.

Howk, to dig.

Howkin, digging deep.

Howket, digged.

Hoy, *hoy't*, to urge, urged.

Hoyse, to pull upwards.

Hoyte, motion between a trot and gallop.

Huchall'd, moving with a hilch.

Hughoc, diminutive of Hugh.

Hums and hankers, mumbles and hesitates.

Hunkers, the hams.

Hurcheon, a hedgehog.

Hurdies, the crupper, the hips.

Hushion, a stocking wanting the foot, worn on the arm.

I', in.

Icker, an ear of corn.

Ier-oe, a great-grandchild.

Ilk, or *ilka*, each, every.

Ill-deedie, mischievous.

Ill o't, awkward at it.

Ill-willie, malicious; opposite of *Gude-willie*.

Indentin, indenting.

Ingine, genius, ingenuity.

Ingle, fire, fireplace.

Ingle-lowe, light from the fire.

I rede ye, I advise ye, I warn ye.

I'se, I shall or will.

Ither, other, one another.

Jad, giddy young woman.

Jauk, to dally at work, to trifle.

Jaukin, trifling, dallying.

Jauner, idle talk, slack-jaw.

Jaup, a jerk of any liquid.

Jaw, coarse raillery; *jaw-hole*, a sink for foul water.

Jillet, a jilt, a giddy girl.

Jimp, slender waisted, handsome.

Jinglin, jingling.

Jink, to dodge.

Jinkin, dodging.

Jink an' diddle, tremulous movement.

Jinker, a gay sprightly girl.

Jirt, a jerk, to squirt.

Jocteleg, a kind of knife.

Jokin, joking.

Jouk, to stoop.

Jow, pealing sound of a bell.

Jumpin, jumping.

Jundie, a push with the elbow.

Kae, a daw.

Kail, colewort, a kind of broth.
Kailrunt, the stem of colewort.
Kain, fowls, &c., paid as rent.
Kebars, rafters. See "*Bauks.*"
Kebbuck, a cheese.
Keckle, joyous cry.
Keek, a sly look, to peep.
Kennin, knowledge, a small matter.
Ket, a matted fleece of wool.
Key, a pier or harbour.
Kiaugh, carking anxiety.
Kilt, to truss up the clothes.
Kimmer, a young girl, a gossip.
Kin, or *kith*, kindred.
Kin', kind.
Kintra, *kintry*, country.
Kirn, the harvest supper, a churn.
Kirsen, to christen, to baptize.
Kist, chest, a shop counter.
Kitchen, anything that is eaten as a relish with bread.
Kith, or *kin*, kindred.
Kittle, to tickle, ticklish.
Kittlen, a young cat.
Kiutlin, cuddling, fondling.
Kiutle, to cuddle.
Knaggie, like knags, or points of rocks.
Knap, to strike or break.
Knappin-hammer, a hammer for breaking stones.
Knurlin, knotty.
Knowe, a small round hillock.
Kye, cows, kine.
Kyte, the belly.
Kythe, to discover.

Labor, or *labaur*, toil; to thrash or plough.
Laddie, diminutive of lad.
Laggen, the angle between the side and the bottom of a wooden dish.
Laigh, low.

Lairin, *lairie*, wading in mud, &c., miry.
Laith, loath.
Laithfu', bashful.
Lallans, the Lowlands.
Lambie, diminutive of lamb.
Lammas moon, harvest moon.
Lampit, a limpet.
Lan', land, estate.
Lan'-afore, or *han'-afore*, foremost horse in the plough.
Lan'-ahin, or *han'-ahin*, the hindmost horse in the plough.
Lane, lone ; *my lane*, *thy lane*, myself alone, thyself alone.
Lanely, lonely.
Lang, long ; to long, to weary.
Langsyne, long ago, time long past.
Lap, did leap.
Late and air, late and early.
Laughin, laughing.
Lave, the rest.
Lav'rock, the lark.
Lawlan', lowland.
Lay my dead, attribute my death.
Lea, unploughed land.
Lea'e, or *lea'*, to leave.
Leal, loyal, true, faithful.
Lear, learning, lore.
Lee-lang, live-long.
Leesome luve, lawful love.
Leeze me on, a phrase of endearment.
Leister, a three-pronged and barbed dart for striking fish.
Leugh, did laugh.
Leuk, a look, to look.
Libbet, castrated.
Lick, to beat ; *licket*, beaten.
Lift, sky, firmament.
Lightly, sneeringly.
Lilt, a ballad, a tune ; to sing.

Limmer, a kept mistress.
Limp't, limped, hobbled.
Link, to trip along ; *linkin*, tripping along.
Linn, a waterfall, a cascade.
Lint, flax ; *lint i' the bell*, flax in flower.
Lintwhite, a linnet ; *lint-white*, flaxen.
Livin, living.
Loan, loaning, a narrow way between hedges, or low dykes.
Loof, the palm of the hand.
Loot, did let.
Loove, or *luve*, love ; to *lo'e*, to love.
Losh, man! rustic exclamation.
Loun, or *loon*, a low fellow.
Louper-like, *lan'-louper*, a stranger of a suspected character.
Lout, or *loot*, to stoop down.
Lowin, flaming.
Lowin-drouth, burning desire for drink.
Lowe, a flame, to flame.
Lowrie, or *tod lowrie*, the fox.
Lowse, to loose ; *lowsed*, unbound, loosed.
Lug, the ear.
Lug of the law, at the ear of the judge.
Lugget, having a handle.
Luggie, a small wooden dish with a handle.
Lum, chimney ; *lum-head*, chimney-top.
Lunt, a column of smoke.
Lyart, grey.

Mae, and *mair*, more.
Maggot's-meat, food for the worms.
Mahoun, Satan, false Prophet.
Mailen, a farm.

Maist, most, almost.
Maistly, for the greater part.
Mak, to make ; *makin*, making.
Mally, Molly, Mary.
Mang, among.
Manse, the minister's house.
Manteele, a mantle.
Mark, *merk*, a Scottish coin.
Marled, party-coloured.
Mar's year, the year 1715.
Martial chuck, soldier's follower.
Mashlum, mixed corn, messlin.
Mask, to infuse.
Maskin-pat, teapot.
Maukin, a hare.
Maun, must ; *maunna*, must not.
Maut, malt.
Mavis, the thrush.
Maw, to mow ; *mawin*, mowing.
Mawn, a basket without a handle, used for holding seed, &c.
Meere, or *meare*, a mare.
Melder, a load of corn for the mill.
Mell, to meddle ; also a mallet.
Melvie, to soil with meal.
Men', to mend.
Mense, good manners, decorum.
Menseless, ill-bred, rude, impudent.
Merle, the blackbird.
Messan, a small dog, a mongrel.
Middin, a dunghill.
Middin-creels, manure panniers.
Milkin-shiel, a place where cows or ewes are brought to be milked.
Mim, affectedly meek.

III.   Q

Mim-mou'd, gentle-mouthed.
Min', to remember.
Minawae, minuet.
Minnie, mother, dam.
Mirk, dark; darkness.
Misca', to abuse, to call names.
Misca'd, abused, slandered.
Mishanter, misadventure.
Mislear'd unmannerly.
Misteuk, mistook.
Mither, mother.
Mixtie - maxtie, confusedly mixed.
Moudiwort, a mole.
Moistify, to moisten, to soak.
Mools, earth, mould.
Mony, or *monie*, many.
Moop, to nibble.
Moorlan', belonging to moors.
Morn, to-morrow.
Mottie, full of motes.
Mou', the mouth.
Mousie, diminutive of mouse.
Muckle, or *meikle*, great, much.
Muses'-stank, muses'-rill.
Musie, diminutive of Muse.
Muslin-kail, thin broth.
Mutchkin, an English pint.
Mysel, myself.

Na, no, not, nor.
Nae, or *na*, no, not any.
Naething, nothing.
Naig, a horse, a nag.
Nane, none.
Nappy, strong ale.
Neglecket, or *negleckit*, neglected.
Neebor, or *neibor*, a neighbour.
Neuk, nook.
Niest, nighest, next.
Nieve, *nief*, the fist.
Nievefu', handful.
Niffer, an exchange, to barter.
Niger, a negro.

Nit, a nut.
Norland, belonging to the north.
Notic't, noticed.
Nowte, nolt, oxen, black cattle.

O', of.
O boot, into the bargain.
O't, of it.
Ony, or *onie*, any.
Or, is often used for ere, before.
Orra-duddies, superfluous rags.
Ourie, shivering, outlying.
Oursel, *oursels*, ourselves.
Outlers, cattle unhoused.
O'ergang, to tread on.
O'erlay, an upper cravat.
Ower, *owre*, or *ow'r*, over.
Owsen, oxen.
Oxter'd, supported under the arm.

Pack, intimate, familiar; twelve stone of wool.
Paidle, *paidlin*, to walk in water.
Painch, paunch.
Paitrick, a partridge.
Pang, to cram.
Parle, courtship.
Parishen, parish.
Parritch, or *porritch*, oatmeal pudding.
Pat, did put; a pot.
Pattle, or *pettle*, a small spade to clean the plough.
Paughty, proud, haughty.
Paukie, cunning, sly.
Pay't, paid, beat.
Peat-reek, smoke of peats; a sort of whisky.
Pech, to breathe short as in asthma; *pechin*, breathing short.
Peghan, the crop, the stomach.

Pennie, riches; *penny-fee*, small money wages; *penny-wheep*, small beer.
Pet, a favourite.
Pettle, to cherish.
Philabeg, the Highland kilt.
Phraise, fair speeches.
Phraisin, flattering.
Pibroch, a martial air on the bagpipe.
Pickle, a grain of corn.
Pigmy-scraper, little fiddler.
Pine, or *pyne*, pain, uneasiness.
Pingle, trouble, difficulty.
Pint-stowp, a two-quart measure.
Plack, an old Scotch coin.
Plackless, pennyless.
Plaidie, diminutive of plaid.
Platie, diminutive of plate.
Plew, or *pleugh*, a plough.
Pliskie, a trick.
Pock, a meal-bag.
Poind, to seize cattle, &c., for debt.
Poortith, poverty.
Posie, a nosegay, a garland.
Pou, to pull; *pou'd*, pulled.
Pouk, to pluck.
Poussie, a hare or cat.
Pout, a polt, a chick.
Pou't, did pull.
Poutherie, *pouthery*, like powder.
Pow, the head, the skull.
Pownie, a little horse, a pony.
Powther, or *pouther*, gunpowder.
Preclair, supereminent.
Preen, a pin.
Prent, printing, print.
Prie, to taste.
Prief, proof.
Prig, to cheapen, to dispute.
Priggin, cheapening.
Primsie, demure, precise.

Propone, to lay down, to propose.
Pund, pound.
Pyet, a magpie.
Pyle, peel, skin.
'Pystle, epistle.

Quaick, cry of a duck.
Quat, quit; to quit.
Quauk, to quake; *quaukin*, quaking.
Quech, or *quaich*, a drinking-cup.
Quey, a young cow.
Quines, queans, young women.

Ragweed, herb, ragwort.
Raible, to rattle nonsense.
Rair, to roar; *rairin*, or *roarin*, roaring.
Raize, to madden, to inflame.
Ramfeezled, fatigued, overpowered.
Rampin, or *rampaugin*, raging.
Ram-stam, thoughtless, forward.
Randie, a shrew.
Rantin, joyous.
Raploch, coarse cloth.
Rarely, excellently, very well.
Rash, a rush; *rash-buss*, a bush of rushes.
Ratton, a rat.
Raucle, rash, reckless.
Raught, or *rax'd*, reached.
Raw, a row.
Rax, to stretch, to reach out.
Ream, cream, froth.
Reamin, brimful, frothing.
Reave, or *rieve*, take by force.
Rebute, repulse, rebuke, rebuff.
Reck, to heed.
Rede, counsel; to counsel, to discourse.
Red-peats, burning turfs.
Red-wat-shod, walking in blood.

Red-wud, stark mad.
Ree, half drunk, fuddled, wild.
Reek, smoke.
Reekin, smoking; *reckit*, smoked.
Reestit, arrested.
Remead, remedy.
Requite, requited.
Restricket, restricted.
Rew, to smile, to take pity on.
Rickles, shocks of corn, stooks.
Riddle, sieve.
Rief-randies, sturdy thieves.
Rig, a ridge.
Rin, to run, to melt; *rinnin*, running.
Rink, a curling term.
Rip, a handful of unthreshed corn.
Ripplin-kame, instrument for dressing flax.
Risket, a noise like the tearing of roots.
Rock, or *roke*, the distaff.
Rockin, evening gathering.
Rood, or *rude*, the cross.
Roon, a shred.
Roose, to praise.
Roun', round.
Roupet, hoarse with a cold.
Row, to roll, to wrap.
Row't, rolled, wrapped.
Rowtin, lowing.
Rowte, to low, to bellow.
Rowth, plenty.
Rozet, rosin.
Rumble-gumption, common-sense.
Run-deils, downright devils.
Rung, a cudgel.
Runkled, wrinkled.
Runt, the stem of colewort.
Ruth, compassion.
Ryke, reach; *raught*, reached.

Sae, so.

Saft, soft.
Sair, to serve, a sore; *sairie*, sorrowful.
Sairly, sorely; much.
Sair't, served.
Sang, a song.
Sark, a shirt; *sarket*, provided in shirts.
Saugh, willow.
Saugh-woodies, willow-wands.
Saul, soul.
Saumont, salmon.
Saunt, saint; *sauntet*, dead and glorified.
Saut, salt; *sautet*, salted.
Saw, to sow; *sawin*, sowing.
Sax, six; *saxty*, sixty.
Scar, to scare; *scaur*, apt to be scared; a precipitous bank of rock or earth.
Scaud, to scald.
Scauld, to scold; *scawl*, a scold.
Scone, a kind of bread.
Sconnor, or *scunner*, a loathing.
Scraich, to scream.
Screed, to tear, a rent.
Scrieve, to glide swiftly.
Scrievin, gleesomely.
Scrimp, scant.
Scrimpet, scanty.
Scroggie, covered with underwood.
Sculduddrie, loose talk; fornication.
Seizin, seizing.
Sel, self; *a body's sel*, one's self.
Sell't, did sell.
Sen', to send.
Servan', servant.
Sets, *sets off*, goes away; fits, becomes.
Settlin', settling; *to get a settlin'*, to be frightened into quietness.
Shaird, a shred, a shard.

Shangin', a stick attached to a dog's tail.

Shank it, walk it; *shanks*, legs.

Shauchl t-feet, loose, ill-shaped feet.

Shaul, shallow.

Shaver, a barber, a wag.

Shavie, an ill turn.

Shaw, to show; a small wood.

Sheen, bright, shining.

Sheep-shank, to think one's self nae sheep-shank, to be conceited.

Sherra-muir, Sherriff-Muir.

Sheugh, a ditch, a trench, a sluice.

Shiel, shealing, a shepherd's cottage.

Shill, shrill; clear sharp sound.

Shog, a push off at one side.

Shool, a shovel.

Shoon, shoes.

Shore, to offer, to threaten.

Shor'd, half offered and threatened.

Shot, one traverse of the shuttle from side to side of the web.

Shouther, the shoulder.

Sic, such; *sic-like*, such as.

Sicker, sure, steady.

Sidelins, sidelong, slanting.

Silken-snood, a fillet of silk.

Siller, silver, money, white.

Simmer, summer.

Sin, a son.

Sin', since; *sinsyne*, since then.

Skaith, injury.

Skellum, a worthless fellow.

Skelp, to slap.

Skelpin, striking, walking rapidly.

Skelpie-limmer, a female scold.

Skiegh, proud, saucy, mettled.

Skinkin, thin, like soup-meagre.

Skirl, to cry, to shriek shrilly.

Skirlin, shrieking, crying.

Skirl't, shrieked.

Sklent, slant.

Sklented, ran, or hit obliquely.

Skouth, vent, free action.

Skreigh, skriegh, a scream.

Skyrin, party-coloured.

Skyte, worthless fellow; to slide rapidly off.

Slade, did slide.

Slae, sloe.

Slap, a gate, a breach in a fence.

Slaw, slow.

Slee, sly; *slee'st*, slyest.

Sleeket, sleek, sly.

Sliddery, slippery.

Slip-shod, loose shod.

Sloken, to quench, to slake.

Slype, a wet furrow from the plough.

Slypet-o'er, fell over, as above.

Sma', small.

Smeddum, dust, mettle, sense.

Smiddy, smithy.

Smirking, good-natured, smiling.

Smoor, to smother; *smoor'd*, smothered.

Smoutie, obscene: *smoutie phiz*, sooty aspect.

Smytrie, a small collection.

Snapper, mistake in walking, &c.

Snash, impertinence.

Snaw, snow, to snow.

Snaw-broo, melted snow.

Snawie, snowy.

Sneck, the latch of a door.

Sned, to lop, to cut off.

Sned besoms, to cut brooms.

Sneeshin, snuff; *sneeshin-mill* snuff-box.

Snell, and *snelly,* bitter, biting.
Snick-drawin, trick-contriving.
Snirt, snirtle, concealed laughter.
Snool, sneak.
Snoove, to go creepingly.
Snorin, snoring.
Snowk, to scent or snuff as a dog.
Snowket, scented, snuffed.
Sobbin, or *sabbin,* sobbing.
Sodger, or *soger,* a soldier.
Sonsie, lucky, jolly.
Soom, to swim.
Souk, to suck.
Souple, flexible, swift.
Souter, a shoemaker.
Sowens, or *so'ns,* a Scots dish.
Sowp, a spoonful.
Sowth, to whistle over a tune.
Sowther, to solder.
Spae, to prophesy, to divine.
Spails, chips, splinters.
Spairin, sparing.
Spairge, to dash with mire.
Spak, did speak.
Spaul, a limb.
Spates, speats, sudden floods.
Spaviet, having the spavin.
Speel, to climb.
Spence, the country parlour.
Spier, to ask, to inquire.
Spinnin-graith, wheel and roke and lint.
Splatter, to splutter; a splutter.
Spleuchan, a tobacco pouch.
Splore, a frolic, noise, riot.
Sprachl'd, scrambled.
Sprattle, to scramble.
Spreckl'd, spotted, speckled.
Spring, quick air in music.
Spret, a tough-rooted plant.
Sprettie, full of sprets.
Spunk, fire, mettle, wit, spark.
Spunkie, mettlesome, fiery.
Spurtle, a stick used in making porridge.

Squad, a squadron.
Squatter, to flutter in water.
Squattle, to sprawl.
Squeel, a scream, a screech.
Stacher, to stagger.
Stack, a rick of corn, &c.
Staggie, diminutive of stag.
Staig, a two-year-old horse.
Stalwart, stately, strong.
Stampin, stamping.
Stane, a stone.
Stang, sting, stung.
Stank, a pool of standing water.
Stan't, to stand, did stand.
Stap, stop, stave.
Stapple, a plug, or stopper.
Stark, stout, potent.
Staukin, walking with dignity.
Staumrel, a blockhead, half-witted.
Staw, did steal, to surfeit.
Steek, to shut; a stitch.
Steer, to molest, to stir.
Steeve, firm, compacted.
Stegh, to cram the belly; *steghin,* cramming.
Stell, a still—commonly a smuggler's.
Sten, to rear as a horse.
Stents, dues of any kind.
Stey, steep; *steyest,* steepest.
Stibble, stubble; *stibble-rig,* the reaper in harvest who takes the lead.
Stick-an'-stow, totally, altogether.
Stilt, a crutch; to limp, to halt.
Stilts, poles for crossing a river.
Stimpart, eighth part of a bushel.
Stinkin, foul smelling.
Stirk, a cow or bullock a year old.

Stock, a plant of colewort, cabbages.

Stockin, stocking.

Stook, twelve sheaves.

Stoor, hollow sounding, hoarse.

Stot, an ox.

Stound, sudden pang of the heart.

Stoup, or *stowp*, narrow jug with a handle, for holding liquids.

Stoure, or *stowr*, dust in motion.

Stown, stolen; *stowlins*, by stealth.

Stoyte, the walking of one drunk.

Strack, did strike.

Strae, straw; *to die a fair strae death*, to die in bed.

Straik, to stroke: *straiket*, stroked.

Strappin, tall, handsome, vigorous.

Strath, low alluvial land, a holm.

Straught, straight.

Stravagin, wandering without aim.

Streek, to stretch; *strœkit*, stretched.

Striddle, to straddle.

Stroan't, spouted, pissed.

Stroup, the spout.

Strunt, spirituous liquor of any kind; to walk sturdily, to be affronted.

Studdie, the anvil.

Stuff, corn or pulse of any kind.

Stumpie, diminutive of stump.

Sturt, trouble; *sturtin*, affrighted.

Styme, a glimmer of light.

Sucker, sugar.

Sud, *shou'd*, should.

Sugh, the continued sighing.

Sumph, a pluckless fellow.

Suthron, an Englishman.

Swaird, sward; the smooth grass.

Swall'd, swelled.

Swank, stately, jolly.

Swankie, or *swanker*, a strapping youth.

Swap, an exchange; to barter, to coup.

Swarf'd, swooned.

Swat, did sweat.

Swatch, a sample.

Swats, drink, new ale or wort.

Sweer, lazy, averse; *dead-swcer*, extremely averse.

Swinge, to beat, to whip.

Swirl, a curve, an eddying blast or pool, a knot in wood.

Swith, or *swith awa*, get away.

Swither, to hesitate.

Swoor, or *swure*, swore, did swear.

Swurd, a sword.

Sybow, a thick-necked onion.

Syne, since, ago, then.

Tackets, broad-headed nails.

Tae, a toe.

Taet, a small quantity.

Tak, to take; *takin*, taking.

Tangle, a sea-weed used as salad.

Tap, the top; *tap-pickle*, ear of corn.

Tapetless, heedless, foolish.

Targe, a shield; *targe them tightly*, cross-question them severely.

Tarrow, to murmur.

Tarry-breeks, a sailor.

Tassie, a drinking-cup.

Tauld, or *tald*, told.

Taupie, a foolish person.

Tawie, that allows itself peaceably to be handled (spoken of a cow, horse, &c.).

Tawted, or *tawtie*, matted together.

Teethless bawtie, toothless cur.

Ten-hours'-bite, a slight feed to the horse while in the yoke in the forenoon.

Tent, a field pulpit; heed, caution; *to tak tent*, to take heed.

Tentie, heedful, cautious.

Tentless, heedless, careless.

Teugh, tough.

Thack, thatch; *thack an raep*, all kinds of necessaries, particularly clothing.

Thae, those; distinct from *they*.

Thairms, small guts, fiddle-strings.

Thanket, or *thankit*, thanked.

Theeket, thatched.

Thegither, together.

Themsel, themselves.

Thick, intimate, familiar.

Thigger, a seeker of alms, a *sorner*.

Thinkin, thinking.

Thir, these; opposed to *thae*, those.

Thirl, to thrill; to bind to a bargain.

Thirl'd, thrilled, vibrated; bound.

Thole, to suffer, to endure.

Thowe, a thaw, to thaw.

Thowless, slack, lazy.

Thrang, throng, busy; a crowd.

Thrapple, throat, windpipe.

Thraw, a twist, a contradiction.

Thraw, to sprain, to twist, to contradict.

Thrawin, twisting; *thrawn*, twisted.

Threap, or *threep*, to assert.

Threshin, thrashing; *threshin-tree*, a flail.

Thretteen, thirteen; *thretty*, thirty.

Thrissle, thistle.

Through, to go on with, to make out.

Throuther, or *through-ither*, pell-mell, confusedly.

Thrum, sound of a spinning-wheel in motion; thread at end of a web.

Thud, to make a thumping noise.

Thummart, foumart, polecat.

Thumpit, thumped; did beat.

Thysel, thyself.

Till't, to it; *fa' till't*, begin.

Timmer, timber; a tree.

Timmer-prop't, supported by timber.

Tine, or *tyne*, to loose; *tint*, lost.

Tinkler, a tinker.

Tip, or *toop*, a ram.

Tippence, twopence, money.

Tirl, to make a slight noise.

Tirlin, uncovering; *tirlet*, uncovered.

Tither, the other.

Tittlin, whispering and laughing.

Tittle, to whisper, to prate idly.

Tocher, marriage portion; *tocher bands*, marriage bonds.

Tod, a fox; *Tod i' the fauld*, fox in the fold.

Toddle, to totter, like the walk of a child; *todlen-dow*, toddling dove.

To-fa', a building added, a lean-to, a place of refuge; *to fa' o' the nicht*, when twilight darkens into night; pron. *tu-fa* (French *u*).

Too, also.

Toom, empty; *toomed*, emptied.

Toop, a ram; *pron.* as with French *u*.

Toss, a toast.

Tosie, ruddy with strong liquor.

Tout, the blast of a horn.

Touzle, to ruffle in romping.

Tow, a rope.

Towmond, a twelvemonth.

Towsie, rough, shaggy.

Toy, an old fashion of female head-dress.

Toyte, to totter like old age.

Trams, shafts; *barrow trams*, the handles of a barrow.

Transmugrifi'd, metamorphosed.

Trashtrie, trash, rubbish.

Trickie, or *tricksie*, full of tricks.

Trig, spruce, neat.

Trimly, cleverly, excellently.

Trinle, the wheel of a barrow.

Trintle, to roll, to trundle.

Trinklin, trickling.

Troggers, wandering merchants.

Troggin, goods to truck or dispose of.

Trow, to believe.

Trowth, truth; a petty oath.

Trysts or *trystes*, appointments.

Tumbler-wheels, the wheels of a low cart.

Tug, raw hide or rope.

Tulyie, a quarrel.

Twa, two.

Twa-three, a few, two or three.

'Twad, it would.

Twal, twelve.

Twine, to twist.

Twin, to part with; to give up.

Twistle, twisting.

Tyke, a dog.

Tysday, Tuesday.

Unback'd filly, a mare hitherto unsaddled.

Unco, strange, uncouth, very great, prodigious.

Unco, as an adverb, very; "*unco pack an' thick thegither*," very intimate and friendly.

Uncos, news; strange things or persons.

Undoin, undoing, ruin.

Unfauld, unfold.

Unkenn'd, unknown.

Unsicker, uncertain, insecure.

Unskaith'd, undamaged, unhurt.

Upo', upon.

Vap'rin, vapouring, boasting idly.

Vauntie, joyous.

Vera, very.

Virl, a ring round a column. &c.

Vogie, vain.

Wa', wall; *wa's*, walls.

Wabster, a weaver.

Wad, would; to bet; a bet, a pledge.

Wadna, would not.

Wadset, a mortgage.

Wae, woe; *waefu'*, sorrowful.

Waefu'-woodie, hangman's rope.

Waesucks! wae's me! alas! O the pity!

Wa'flower, wallflower.

Waft, woof.

Wair, or *ware*, to expend.
Wair'd on, spent upon.
Wale, choice, to choose.
Wal'd, chose, chosen.
Walie, ample, large, jolly; also an exclamation of distress.
Wame, the belly.
Wanchansie, unlucky.
Wanrest, *wanrestfu'*, restless, unrestful.
Wark, work.
Wark-lume, a tool to work with.
Warl', or *warld*, the world.
Warld's-worm, a miser.
Warlock, a wizard.
Warly, worldly.
Warran', a warrant; to warrant.
Warsle, or *warstle*, to wrestle.
Warsl'd, or *warstl'd*, wrestled.
Warst, worst.
Wastrie, prodigality.
Wat, or *weet*, wet.
Wat, *I wat*, I know, I wot.
Wattle, a twig, a wand.
Wauble, to swing, to reel.
Waught, a copious drink.
Wauket, thickened.
Waukin, waking, watching.
Waukrife, not apt to sleep.
Waur, worse, to worst; *waur't*, worsted.
Wean, or *weanie*, a child.
Wearie, exhausted.
Weary-widdle, toilsome contest.
Weason, weasand, windpipe.
Weavin the stockin, to knit stockings.
Wecht, weight, solidity.
Wee, little; *wee bit*, a small matter.
Weeder-clips, instrument for removing weeds.

Weel, well; *weelfare*, welfare.
Weet, rain, wetness; to wet.
We'se, we shall.
Wha, who.
Whaizle, to wheeze.
Whalpet, whelped.
Whang, a leathern thong, a thick slice of cheese, bread, &c.
Whar, *whare*, where; *whar-e'er*, wherever.
Whase, whose; *wha's*, who is.
What-reck, nevertheless.
Wheep, to fly nimbly.
Whid, a lie.
Whiddin, running as a hare.
Whigmaleeries, fancies.
Whilk, which.
Whingin, complaining.
Whirligigums, useless ornaments.
Whisht, silence; *to hold one's whist*, to be silent.
Whisk, to sweep, to lash.
Whisket or *whiskit*, switched.
Whiskin beard, a beard like the whiskers of a cat.
Whissle, a whistle, to whistle.
Whitter, a hearty draught of liquor.
Whittle, a knife.
Whunstane, a whinstone.
Whyles, or *whiles*, sometimes.
Wi', with.
Wick, a term in curling.
Widdie, a rope.
Widdifu', one who merits hanging.
Wiel, a small whirlpool.
Wifie, *wifikie*, diminutive for wife.
Wight, a man, a person.
Wight, stout, enduring.
Wight an' wilfu', strong and obstinate.

Willyart-glower, a bewildered stare.

Wimple, to meander, *wimpl't*, meandered.

Wimplin, meandering.

Win', the wind.

Win', to wind, to winnow.

Win't, winded as a bottom of yarn.

Winna, will not.

Winnock, a window.

Winsome, gay, hearty, attractive.

Wintle, a staggering motion.

Winze, a curse or imprecation.

Wiss, to wish.

Withouten, without.

Wizen'd, dried, shrunk.

Woer-babs, the garter knitted below the knee with a couple of loops.

Wonner, a wonder.

Won, to dwell.

Woo, to court, to make love to.

Woo', wool.

Wordy, worthy.

Worset, worsted.

Wrack, to teaze, to vex, to destroy.

Wraith, a spirit, a ghost.

Wrang, wrong, to wrong.

Wud, wild, mad; *red wud*, stark, mad.

Wumble, a wimble, or gimlet.

Wyliecoat, a flannel vest.

Wyte, blame, to blame.

Yaud, an old horse.

Ye, this pronoun is frequently used for *thou.*

Yealings, coevals.

Yearns, eagles; otherwise, *cairns*

Yell, barren, that gives no milk.

Yerk, to lash, to jerk, to excite.

Yerket, or yerkit, jerked.

Yestreen, yesternight.

Yett, a gate.

Yeuks, itches.

Yill, ale.

Yirl, earl.

Yince, once; *yin*, one.

Yird, earth; *yirded*, earthed, buried.

Yitt-meal, oat meal.

Yokin, yoking.

Yont, ayont, beyond.

Yirr, a quick, startling sound.

Young guidman, a new married man.

Yowe, a ewe; *yowie*, diminutive of *yowe.*

Yule, Christmas.

INDEX OF FIRST LINES

IN VOLS. I. II. III.

TURNBULL AND SPEARS, PRINTERS, EDINBURGH.

EDINBURGH ILLUSTRATED EDITION OF THE
POEMS AND SONGS OF ROBERT BURNS
COMPLETE · CHRONOLOGICALLY ARRANGED
NOTES, GLOSSARIES, AND INDEX BY W. SCOTT
DOUGLAS · AND LIFE BY PROFESSOR NICHOL ·
WITH TWELVE PHOTOGRAVURES AFTER
DRAWINGS BY MARSHALL BROWN · IN
FOUR VOLUMES

"They say best men are moulded out of faults,
 And, for the most, become much more the better
 For being a little bad."
                    —*Measure for Measure*, Act v. Scene I.

"Salve vetustæ vitæ imago
 Et specimen venientis Ævi."—G. BUCHANAN.

ROBERT BURNS

A SUMMARY OF HIS CAREER AND GENIUS

BY THE LATE

JOHN NICHOL, M.A., LL.D.

Professor of English Literature
In the University of Glasgow

PUBLISHED BY
JAMES THIN
EDINBURGH 1896

LIST OF ILLUSTRATIONS

NOTE

Mr Nichol's Essay on *Burns* was first printed in 1882, for the subscribers to Mr Scott Douglas's edition of the *Works*. It is now published without any material alteration : some corrections have been introduced from marginal notes in the author's copy.

It was Mr Nichol's intention to revise the essay for a projected volume of literary studies ; but the original plan was never carried out. The essay on *Carlyle*, which was to have come second in order, was enlarged into an independent book for the series of *English Men of Letters*, and the revision of the present work was not completed. Although the essay as it stands cannot be taken as representing the author's final judgment, it is published with the authority of Mr Nichol's representatives, and (it is believed) in accordance with his wishes.

W. P. KER.

9th June 1896.

A

I

INTRODUCTORY

In a bibliography, scarcely inferior in variety to that which has gathered around Shakespeare, there is a tract with the heading, "Men who have failed." Its purpose is apparent ; we can construct the sermon from the text, as Cuvier reconstructed a monster from the inspection of a bone : but the title, as applied, is false. Whatever Burns' merits or demerits as a man, the vital part of his career was a swift success, and, what is of more moment, a lasting one. Every decade in which his presence recedes, his power grows : his passionate strength has overleapt the barriers of his dialect. Almost every British critic, during the last half century, has pelted or hailed him : everything that should be said of him, and everything that should not, has been said, often clumsily, often disconnectedly, yet on the whole exhaustively ;

so that little remains but to correct conflicting
exaggerations.   Burns has suffered from two
sets of assailants.   The "unco guid," who
" compound for " social meanness and religious
malice, by damning other things " they have
no mind to," had a score against him, which,
during his life and after, they did their best to
pay : and they believed him to be worse than
he was because they wished it.   The "unco"
bad were keen to exaggerate his weakness, that
they might throw over their own vulgar vices
the shield of a great name.   On the other
hand, the idolatry of a nation, prone to canonise
its illustrious dead, has oppositely erred.   "No
poet, from the blind singer of Troy downwards,
is his peer ;"   "What would become of the
civilised world were his writings obliterated ? "—
such are the common-places of festival speeches,
of journalists patriotically inspired.   He has
been worshipped, shouted about, preached at,
pointed to as a warning, held forth as an
example.   "The roar of his drunkards" has
proclaimed him a saint ; the grim moralist, to
the zealot's joy, has denounced him as the
chief of sinners.   It is as natural as harmless
that a recent accomplished biographer, selected

on the Heraclitean principle of contrasts, should sigh over his " Socinian tendencies," and daintily regret the publication of his quenchless satires : it is inevitable that a literary censor, whose writings are sometimes models of style, always mirrors of complacency, should label his wood-notes as hardly superfine. He has had plenty of praise, plenty of blame, enough of " allow-ances," far more than enough of patronage : he has rarely had—what few men have often—simple justice.

" The work of Burns," says his first editor, " may be considered as a monument not to his own name only but to the expiring genius of an ancient and independent nation." The antithesis of our chief latinist better represents the attitude of our chief poet, who was at once the last of the old and the first of the new. He came in the autumn or evening of our northern literature, but around him was the freshness of the morning and the May. Like Chaucer, he stood on the edge of two eras, and was a prophet as well as a recorder, em-balming and exalting legend and song, affront-ing and rending inveterate superstitions ; the chief satirist as well as the lyrist of his race.

A Jacobite and a Jacobin, holding out hands to "Charlie" over the straits and to Washington across the Atlantic, the monument of his verse, "vetustæ vitæ imago," bears a beacon "venientis ævi." Pupil of Ramsay, master of Tannahill, it is natural that Chloris and Damon should linger in his pages beside Jean and Gavin and Davie, and the beggars at Nanse's splore. Everyone of judgment sees that his most underived and passionate work was his best, that his fame rests more firmly on the records of his freest moods ; more on the Songs and the Satires, and "Tam O'Shanter," and the "Jolly Beggars," than on the "Cotter's Saturday Night." But to realise his relation to the thought and music of his country requires a study of his antecedents.

Burns was an educated, but not a learned man, and he drew next to nothing from our early literature. Of the old Ballads, despite his residence in the border land, he made comparatively little use. The seventeenth century had little to give him ; when the strife of Covenanter and Cavalier held the hearts and threatened the lives of men, the northern Muses were dumb. Poetry was shrivelled under the

frown of Presbyteries. The stream of native
song had been flowing, under black weeds, till
it came to light again in the Jacobite minstrelsy,—where the spirit of the hills first makes
itself felt in the voices of the plain,—in the
pastorals of Ramsay, the fresh canvass of
Thomson and Beattie, and the sketches of
native life by Fergusson. From these, his
generously acknowledged masters, Burns inherited much ; most from the ill-starred genius
of the last. The loves, animosities, and temptations of the two poets were akin ; they were
both, almost to boasting, devotees of independence ; both keen patriots, they were alike
inspired with hatred of their country's besetting
sin, hypocrisy ; but there is, on a smaller scale,
the same difference between them that there
is between Chaucer and Shakespeare. " The
Farmer's Ingle " is a quaint picture of a rustic
fireside north of the Tweed, but " The Cotter's
Saturday Night " is a store of household words
for every Scottish home in the nineteenth, as
it was in the eighteenth century ; " Plainstaines
and Causey " prattle, with playful humour, of
the freaks and follies of the society that moves
over them ; but about the bridges that span

the Ayr there is thrown the moonlight of the
fairies of the "Midsummer Night." In greater
measure, Burns was the heir of the nameless
minstrels, on whose ungraven tombs he throws
a wreath of laurels wet with grateful tears.
But he likewise exalts them, idealising their
plain-spoken pathos or laughter, making their
local interests universal and abiding.

He was enabled to do so by the fact of his
being inspired by the spirit of the Future as
well as of the Past. He lived when the
so-called "Romantic" literary movement had
been initiated by the publication of Percy's
Reliques, Macpherson's Ossian, and the immortal forgeries of the most precocious genius
in our tongue. Burns never names Chatterton,
—probably because he could not read his
masterpieces,—but they have many points of
contact. Both were emphatically Bards, as
opposed to the poets of culture by whom they
were, in the eighteenth century, almost ex-
clusively preceded ; both were "sleepless souls,"
but their themes lay far apart. The mysteri-
ously stranded child to whose dingy garret
there came visions of armies in the air, the
flapping of ravens' wings, the sound of seas

in a tumult like that of Kubla Khan, is the ancestor of Coleridge on his magic side: Burns, of Wordsworth, to whom he bequeathed his pathetic interpretation of nature; and of Byron, the inheritor of his " passions wild and strong." They are together petrels of the storm that, shaking " thrones, princedoms, powers, dominions," converted Versailles into a moral Pompeii, and drove the classic canons of art into a museum of antiquities. The " Freedom dreste in blodde steyned veste" of the one is like the " stalwart ghaist" with the " sacred-poesie-Libertie" of the other. But if the Rowley poems had any influence on Burns, it came indirectly through Cowper, who may have borrowed the Olney Hymn, " God moves in a mysterious way," from Chatterton's, beginning, " O God, whose thunder shakes the sky," and handed on the same devotional mood to the author of the prayer—

> " O thou Great Being what Thou art
> Surpasses me to know."

The same breath blows through diverse instruments that have, as regards religion, the same note of scorn for insincerity, and beneath

it one major key of perplexity, awe, and resig-
nation.   The defiance that rises in Queen Mab
and the Revolt of Islam almost to the shrill-
ness of a shriek, the lurid light of the red star
of Cain, belong to a later age.

William Cowper—a reed shaken with the
wind, and yet a prophet — a terror-stricken
" castaway," and yet the most conspicuous
leader of a revolt, found in Scotland a vice-
gerent greater than himself,—a mighty mass of
manhood, who, free from the intellectual fetters
that bound, the ghastly clouds that obscured,
his elder contemporary, struck more ringing
blows, and soared into a higher heaven.

Finally—*pace* Mr Carlyle to the contrary—
the condition of our literature at the time was,
on the whole, favourable to the appearance of
our greatest interpreter.   It has been the fashion
to talk contemptuously of the men who, though
with different ideas of finish, reared many of
the foundations upon which we build ; but, if
we except Poetry and Physical Science, the
eighteenth century produced most of what the
nineteenth is content to criticise.   " In its latter
half," says Mr Charles Scott in a paper display-
ing rare insight and sympathy, " Scotland was

at the culmination of its intellectual glory. It never stood higher relatively to the rest of Europe." After supporting his assertion by the names of Hume, Robertson, Reid, Stewart, and Adam Smith, he proceeds, " The Bench, the Bar, and the Pulpit were adorned by men who, sometimes rough and quaint, were always vigorous and original. We had in those days the greatest statesmen Britain has seen . . . the approach of the French Revolution had stirred the blood of the people . . . their great poet alone was wanting. The hour struck and the man appeared."

II

SURVEY OF BURNS' LIFE

I.—*First Period, Alloway*, 1759—1766.
(*Æt.* 1-7.)

BURNS was qualified to be a national poet by
his start from the meeting of all the waters of
his country's literature, no less so by the circumstances of his birth and the grasp of his genius.
Scion of a family on the North-East, members
of which, by his own account, had shared the
fortunes of the Earl Marischal, he was born
and lived in the South-West among the descendants of the Covenanters. He was a peasant
more in virtue of his prevailing themes than by
his actual rank. Addressing every grade from
the Prince of Wales to roadside tramps, the
"annals of the poor" are dearest to the heart
of one who was often by painful experience
familiar with their sorrows. But Burns himself,
save latterly as a government official, never did

13

a day's work for others than himself and his family. His father's status as a tenant farmer in the Lowlands was equivalent to that of an English yeoman. His own position in society, in the lower section of the middle class, went with his education and his free spirit to make him as much at ease in the reception rooms of the aristocracy as in the lanes of Mauchline. Everything conspired to make him what he was, a national rather than a peasant poet. In one of the passages in which he almost petulantly resents the claims of rank, he speaks of his " ancient but ignoble blood." In the same spirit Béranger, answering those who " criticise the paltry de " before his name, rejoices in being " a very scamp of common stamp." But both were only half in earnest, and neither without some pride in their ancestors. Those of Burns can be traced at least to the latter years of the seventeenth century, when they are found well settled in the Mearns. It is worthy of note that the poet's grandfather, inspired by a zeal which characterised his descendants, built the first school-house in the district of his farm. His third son, William, born in 1721, continued to reside in Kincardineshire till 1748, when he migrated southwards as a gardener; in 1749 laying out the Edinburgh meadows, and from 1750 onwards similarly engaged in Ayrshire, till, having taken a lease of seven acres in Alloway, he built on them, largely with his own hands, the "auld clay biggin" of two rooms, to which, in 1757, at the age of thirty-six, he brought home his bride, Agnes Brown of Maybole. In this house—now almost a Mecca to northern patriots—Robert, the first offspring of the marriage, was born on the 25th January 1759.

For the little record left of the cottage life at Alloway, we are indebted to three sometimes conflicting authorities:—Burns' letter to Dr Moore (Aug. 2nd, 1787); that addressed to Mrs Dunlop by his brother Gilbert; and the reminiscences of his tutor, Mr John Murdoch, a young man of rare accomplishments and sagacity, to whom during their childhood, and much to their profit, the education of the family was in large measure committed. The autobiographic sketch is a strange chequer of fancy, philosophy, and recklessness, written in the sunshine of success, crossed by the shade of afflictions, and of follies which the writer was

simultaneously deploring and recommitting. It
is written with great apparent candour, and
with the author's constant force of style ; the
facts, often lighted up by brilliancies of setting,
are sometimes, it may be, magnified in the haze
of imagination. From the blessing or bane of
the excess of this faculty, Gilbert—the only
other junior member of the family who in a
rapid sketch calls for comment—was, in his
maturity at least, singularly free. An intelligent and canny Scot of enlarged mind, he is
studiously proper, respectable, and orthodox,
speaking in one strain of "an atheist, a dema-
gogue, or any vile thing." He is a more or less
sympathetic apologist for his brother's weak-
nesses : but, in the interests of truth or of
popular feeling, he more than once attempts to
disenchant Robert's narrative of an element
of romance. The poet attributes the family
migration southward to political causes, describing his ancestors as "renting lands of the
noble Keiths of Marischal," as having had "the
honour of sharing their fate" and "shaking
hands with ruin for what they esteemed the
cause of their King and their country." Elsewhere the same assertion reappears in verse :—

" My fathers that name have revered on a throne,
    My fathers have fallen to right it ;
Those fathers would spurn their degenerate son,
    That name should he scoffingly slight it."

Gilbert, on the alleged authority of a parish certificate, emphatically asserts that his father had " no concern in the late wicked rebellion." Between the romance of the elder and the caution of the younger brother we have, in this and other instances, no means of deciding. A variation of more interest appears in their diverse estimates of the character of William Burness himself. There is nothing in the poet's prose inconsistent either with the picture of the Cotter, or the noble epitaph ending with Goldsmith's line—" For e'en his failings leaned to Virtue's side." But of these failings Robert was far from being piously unconscious. " I have met with few," he says of his father, " who understood men, their manners and their ways, equal to him ; but stubborn ungainly integrity and headlong ungovernable irascibility are disqualifying circumstances, consequently I was born a very poor man's son." Elsewhere he complains of being the victim of parental prejudice. Gilbert, on the other hand, always

defends his father, saying, "I bless his character
for almost everything in my disposition or
habits I can approve." "He was proud of
Robert's genius, but the latter was not amenable to controul," which indeed appears to have
been the fact. Genius seldom is amenable to
control: nor is dense stupidity. Murdoch,
writing from London in later years, is lavish in
expressions of love and veneration for his old
employer, in whose two-roomed cottage, a
"tabernacle of clay, there dwelt a larger portion
of content than in any palace in Europe."
"He spoke the English language with more
propriety than any man I ever knew with no
greater advantages. This had a very good
effect on the boys, who talked and reasoned
like men long before others. O for a world of
such . . . he was worthy of a place in West-
minster Abbey." Allowing for the exaggerations of filial piety and tutorial gratitude, we
gather that William Burness was, on the whole,
as Mr Carlyle describes him, a man worth going
far to meet, of that force of character which rises
into originality, with a thirst for knowledge and
power of communicating it alike remarkable,
but defective in tact; none farther from Mack-

lin's Scotchman, for instead of "booing" he
was ostentatiously independent, manly to the
core, and religious, with a softened Calvinism,
expressed in his Manual of Belief, fond of
speculation, within limits, and keen in argument. In person he was above common stature,
thin and bent; in essence honesty incarnate.
The secret of Scotland's greatness, says the
Times, is oatmeal; a champion of the Free
Church says it is Sabbatarianism; a zealous
Presbyter, that it is hatred of Prelacy. Does it
not depend as much on the influence of a few
men of such character as we have described?
Murdoch's remaining recollections of the quiet
household, of the father who bequeathed his
proud, quick temper without his strong con-
trolling will, of the mother from whom Robert
inherited his bright eyes and love of song, of
the precocious boys, the gravity of the future
poet, and the gaiety of the douce farmer, of the
early love of books, and the integrity common
to them all, are our only reliable records of the
life at Alloway, unless we refer to this period
the "warlock and spunkie" stories of the old
woman,—germs of the fancies that afterwards
conjured up an eerie "something" on the Tar-

bolton road, and set the ruined kirk "ableeze" with the most wonderful witch dance in litera-ture.

II. — *Second Period, Mount Oliphant,* 1766—1777. *(Æt.* 7-18.)

The happiest days of William Burness went by in the clay cottage. Henceforth, as before, he wrought hard, and practised, as he preached, economy, temperance, and perseverance, but the winds and tides of adversity were ruthless, and he played a losing game. Desirous of cultivating land on his own account, he obtained a lease of Mount Oliphant in 1765, and entered on residence in the following year. The sad story of the bad farm,—"with the poorest soil under cultivation," writes Gilbert in 1800,—of the scanty crops, the inclement seasons, the death of the kind landlord, and the insolent letters of the tyrannic factor, has been often told, best of all by Burns himself, whose character was, during these twelve years, largely formed under influences partly favourable, partly the reverse. At home the children continued to be trained up "in decency and order" by their

father, who, with two exceptions—Robert's fort-
nightly study of French under Murdoch at Ayr,
and some lessons in penmanship at Dalrymple
—took upon himself the whole duty of their
education. This was conducted by candlelight
in the evenings when they had returned from
their labour in the fields, special attention being
paid to arithmetic as a secular, and exposition
of the Scriptures as a religious basis. To these
lessons was added the stimulating effect of the
"good talk" in leisure hours with the few clever
people of the neighbourhood — Mrs Burns,
though much occupied with household matters,
listening appreciatively—and the reading aloud
of some play of Shakespeare or other classic.
Books were William Burness' only luxury; he
never ranked a love of them among the artificial
wants he strove to discourage, and his well-
chosen stock, acquired by the scant savings of
the family or placed at their disposal by the
kindness of friends, was at starting the poet's
greatest advantage. His earliest favourites
were the "Vision of Mirza" and one of
Addison's Hymns. Then followed the life of
Hannibal, lent by Murdoch, and the history of
Sir William Wallace, borrowed from a village

blacksmith. The first sent the boy strutting up and down the room in an excess of martial enthusiasm that was far from being one of the man's prevailing moods, breaking out genuinely in only three of his later songs. The second, doubtless the popular chap-book based on Blind Harry, poured into his veins the " Scotch prejudice " to which he owes so much of his hold over the somewhat self-sufficient race of which he is at once the censor and the trumpeter. Burns was born as Scott was born, before the age of the shrivelling criticism—"the spirit that says ' No ' "—that has robbed us of Coriolanus and Tell, and damped half the fires of national fervour. " The greatest of the Plantagenets " was to him a bogie tyrant ; the firer of the Barns of Ayr, a model of martyred chivalry; and in singleness of heart he chose a fine Sunday to worship in the Leglen Wood, visiting the fabled haunts of his "heroic countryman with as much devout enthusiasm as ever pilgrim did the shrine of Loretto." Among other volumes, borrowed or bought, on the shelves of Loan House were, besides good manuals and grammars of English and French (in which language he displayed remarkable proficiency), Mason's Extracts, a collection of songs, Stackhouse's History of the Bible, from which Burns picked up a fair amount of ancient history, a set of Queen Anne letters, on the study of which he began to write his own carefully and to keep copies of them, the Spectator, Pope's Homer and afterwards his other works, some of the novels of Richardson and Smollett, Allan Ramsay, Hervey's "Meditations," with some plays of Shakespeare and essays of Locke. To these were added at Lochlea, Shenstone, Thomson, Fergusson, Mackenzie's "Man of Feeling," "Tristram Shandy,"—which he devoured at meals, spoon in hand,—with the Mirror, Lounger, &c., and later Macpherson's "Ossian" and Milton. A good library for a farm-house even now, and, if scant for an author, Burns had mastered it. He drew blood from everything he read ; *e.g.,* the style of some of his letters is affected by Sterne to a degree never enough remarked, that of others equally by the English essayists. Above all, he was saturated with the Bible and the Book of Songs, carrying them with him for spare moments in the fields, and lingering over them in his cold little room by night ; "care-

fully noting the true, tender, sublime, or
fustian," and so learning to be a critic, while
stirred by emulation to become himself a lyrist.
His first verses were inspired by a calf-love—
innocent prelude to many of various hues—for
" Handsome Nell," his partner in the labours of
the harvest during his fifteenth autumn, the
tones of whose voice made his " heart-strings
thrill like an Æolian harp."   Save the song, " I
dreamed I lay where flowers were springing," he
wrote nothing more of consequence till six, and
little till ten years later.   His circumstances
were fatal to precocious authorship.   The father
and sons were fighting bravely through their
eleven lean years of struggle, ending in defeat ;
and were, with both physical and moral bad
results, overwrought.   Work on land, in the
open air, is in itself more favourable to mental
activity than the routine drudgery of a teacher
or literary hack ; but the labour to which the
young Burnses were inevitably subjected was
both excessive and premature.   The poet was
always a good and dexterous workman, "at the
plough, scythe, or reap-hook he feared no com-
petitor : " in the later days at Ellisland we have
testimony to his being able at a push to " heave

a heavier stone " than any of his " hands." But
these early efforts were drawing on his capital
and exhausting his fund of strength. At the
age of thirteen he threshed the corn :

> " The thresher's weary flingin'-tree
> The lee-lang day had tired me."
> —*The Vision*, l. 7.

At fifteen he was the principal labourer. The
family kept no servant, and for several years
butcher-meat was unknown in the house. Un-
ceasing toil brought Burns to his sixteenth year.
His robust frame overtasked, his patience was
overtried; despite bursts of buoyancy and the
vague ambition which he pathetically compares
to the groping of the blind Cyclops, his temper
was often exasperated. His shoulders were
bowed, and his nervous system received a fatal
strain ; hence long, dull headaches, palpitations
and sullen fits of hypochondria, with lurid lights
from " the passionate heart," darting at inter-
vals through the cloud. " Μελαγχολικοὶ ἀεὶ ἐν
σφοδρᾷ ὀρέξει." Prosperity has its temptations,
but they are nothing to those of the poetic
temperament goaded by pain within, and chilled
by apathy without. From toils which he associates with those of a galley slave, and the

internal fire craving for sympathy in a freer
atmosphere than even that of his home, there
sprung the spirit of revolt which soon made
headway, and passed not only the bars of
formalism, but the limits of rational self-
restraint.

At this period, despite an awkward shyness
and a morbid dread of ridicule, the poet's social
disposition—"the hypochondriac taint" he calls
it, that made him fly solitude—had led him to
form acquaintance with companions in or near
Ayr, some of whom had superior advantages,
contemplated not without envy. "They did
not know," he bitterly remarks, "enough of
the world to insult the clouterly appearance
of his plough-boy carcase." Two years after
he had committed his first "sin of rhyme,"
Burns, if we accept his own chronology, spent
the summer months at Kirkoswald, studying
mensuration. Here he came in contact with
some of the riotous scenes of that smuggling
coast, took part in them, found himself "no
enemy to social life," and learned "to look
unconcernedly on a large tavern bill." Here
also, when "the sun entered Virgo" (*i.e.*, in
August) he encountered a premonition of his

master spell in " a charming fillette," who, living next door to the school, set him " off at a tangent " from his trigonometry. Nothing came of the affair at the time, but several years later (1783) Burns renewed his acquaintance with the girl (Peggy Thomson), and from a rough former draft rewrote in her honour, " Now westlin' winds," etc. Following the same authority (his own) as to date, we must assign to the early winter of the same year an event by which the serenity of the domestic life—one phase of which is represented in the " Cottar's Saturday Night," the other in the " Twa Dogs "—was interrupted. This event was the poet's persistence, directly against his father's will, in attending a country dancing-school. The motive he assigns, a desire to give his manners a " brush," seems innocent enough ; but the action was typical of his rebellion against the straiter rules of the Scotch moral creed, and is therefore of more importance than at first appears.

It is admitted that, in reaction from the levities of later Romanism, the reformed religion in the north was at first stamped with an excessive austerity, and that, in after days,

the long fight of Presbyterian Calvinism with
the Episcopalian Hierarchy helped to per-
petuate the spirit in which Knox himself,
though by no means so fanatical as many of
his followers, regarded a ball at Holyrood as
"the dance of the seven deadly sins." The
overstrained moral code of the Puritans, laughed
out by the Restoration, discarded as visionary
by the common sense of the Revolution in
England, survived in Scotland in connection
with the penances of the Kirk, so familiar to
the reader of Burns, and still lingers in police
regulations more socially inquisitorial than
those of any other civilized country. The
attempt to "deal with" every form of human
frailty as a legal offence may be laudable in
design; in practice it is apt to generate hypocrisy, deceit, and even crime, as a means of
escape from exposure. But the stricter party
of the Scotch Kirk, during the eighteenth
century, not content with publicly branding
the sins, set its face against the amusements
of the people; it tried to keep them not only
sober and chaste, but constantly sombre; to
close the theatres, to shut the barns, fine the
fiddlers, and set their melodies to psalms.

Under the most depressing circumstances,
Nature will have her way. From the gloom
of a stern creed within, of inclement skies
without, the Scotch peasantry sought relief in
vocal music,—cultivated the more eagerly that
instrumental was banished from the kirks,—in
whisky, and in dancing. The Reformation for
two centuries in our country stifled the other
arts, but not that of Rizzio. Music triumphed
over the spirit of the creed of Calvin, as it is
now encroaching on the precepts of Penn.
The fire in the heart of the Scotch peasantry,
unextinguished by all the dry ashes of the
Catechism, found vent in love songs—many of
those current before the coming of their great
minstrel, of worse than doubtful taste—in which
they are tenfold more prolific than the gayer
French; in rural assignations, where passion
too often set at nought the terrors of the cutty-
stool, and in the village "splore," for which
the dancing-school was a preparation. "This
is," says Dr Currie, in his liveliest passage,
worth quoting as a comment on many of
our author's poems, " usually a barn in winter,
and the arena for the performers a clay
floor. The dome is lighted by candles stuck

in one end of a cloven stick, the other
being thrust into the wall. Young men and
women will walk many miles to these country
schools, and the instant the violin sounds,
fatigue seems to vanish, the toil-worn rustic
becomes erect, his features brighten with sympathy, every nerve seems to thrill with sensa-
tion, and every artery to vibrate with life."
Such was the scene from which William Burness wished to keep back the poet, and from
which the poet would not be kept back. It is
a wise thing to multiply innocent pleasures, the
worst policy to restrict them. Unfortunately
in seeking an innocent pleasure, Burns was
made guilty of a disobedience, and resented
it by a defiance inevitable to his nature. In
taking his first step to be the interpreter of a
nation, he had to cease to be a dutiful son.
He broke the bonds that would not stretch, and
soon revelled in his freedom as a wild colt in a
meadow. From this crisis, he began to find
himself ; his virgin bashfulness was too rapidly
" brushed " away ; his native eloquence gushed
forth like a liberated stream ; in every society
he found himself the light of conversation and
the leader of debate ; and in his hours of leisure

beyond the walls of his home, whether by a dyke-side or in an inn parlour, was surrounded by admiring or astonished groups who confided to him their affairs of the heart, and obtained his assistance in their wooing. At this period, ere reaching "green eighteen," he himself began to manifest a precocious "*penchant à l'adorable moitié du genre humain*"—"My heart was completely tinder, and was eternally lighted up by some goddess or other." According to Gilbert, Robert "idealized his women perpetually:" but he was as fickle as Sterne, and through life found it easier to adore a new mistress than to put on a new coat: a versatility often characteristic of the poetic temperament.

III.—*Third Period, Lochlea*, 1777—1784.
(*Æt.* 18-25.)

William Burness attempted to leave Mount Oliphant at the end of a six years lease, *i.e.*, after a residence of five and a-half years, 1771 ; but, failing, remained five and a-half years longer, at the expiration of which he contrived to reserve means and credit to secure the tenancy of Lochlea, whither the family re-

moved on Whitsunday 1777, and where, for the
first three years of their occupancy, they seem
to have fairly thriven.   Of this space of time
there is little record : to its close belong the
poet's letters to Ellison Begbie—a young
woman, understood to be the Mary Morrison
of his song, to whom he paid his addresses with
a view to marriage, but who, after seriously
entertaining them, to his grave discomfiture
rejected his suit.   In 1780 the brothers established a Bachelors' Club, in which a variety of
social subjects were discussed, though under
some restrictions, with sufficient freedom and
zest to stimulate the ingenuity and sharpen the
wits of the members.   It appears that Robert,
always ambitious of shining, prepared himself
beforehand for the debates.   The next year of
his life was in more than one respect disastrous.
Having been in the habit of raising flax on a
portion of his father's ground, it occurred to
him to go to Irvine to learn to dress it.   For
some time he attacked his new trade with heart
and hope, and, if we may judge by the letter to
his father of Dec. 1781, lived a strictly frugal
and abstinent life : but as they were giving a
welcome carousal to the New-Year (1782), the

shop, in which he had combined with one of his mother's relations, took fire, and Burns was left " like a true poet, without a sixpence." Smarting under this loss, feeling himself jilted at once by Ellison and by fortune, he went through the usual despairs, and resorted to the too common consolations. Meeting with others of the class of seafaring men he had encountered at Kirk-oswald, his eloquence, raised to a feverish heat, shed a lustre over their wild thoughts and ways. By one of those, a Mr Richard Brown, whose romantic adventures captivated his fancy, he was now for the first time—by how many not the last were hard to tell—led to " bound across the strid " of what is technically called virtue. We have here no space, had we inclination, to pry into the details of the story, nor the continual repetitions of it, which marked and marred his career. Home again with a troubled conscience, and a love for company unworthy of him, he found in the Masonic Lodge at Tarbolton an institution unhappily well-suited to his weakness for being first in every circle. In the festivals of that guild he could defy competition : the brethren, justly proud of their new deputy-master, joined with a

right good will in the ballad of John Barleycorn, and shouted till "the kebars sheuk" over the chorus of "The Big-bellied Bottle." Nevertheless these years were not barren. Before going to Irvine, Burns had written "On Cessnock Banks" and "My Nannie O": he brought back from it his early religious pieces, and the volume of Fergusson which first fired him with the definite ambition of being himself a poet.

Between 1781-83 were written the "Lament for Mailie," "Winter: a Dirge," "Remorse," and others in similar strain; also a number of songs, the best known being "The Rigs of Barley" and "Green grow the rashes." These were addressed to various objects; some former flames, as Kirkoswald Peggy, again flit across the horizon, others may have been imaginary. One might as well undertake to trace all the originals of Horace's or Herrick's fancy as those of Burns', for, when he became famous, even married women contended to have sat to him for their portraits. The passion in these songs is more lively than intense; their charm is in the field breeze that blows through them as freshly as in the days of Chaucer. A love for the lower forms of social life was the poet's be-

setting sin,—Nature his healing power. He was fortunate in being placed amid the scenes best suited to nourish a genius which fed on the meadows and glades round the bends of the Ayr, as a bee feeds on flowers, and had no affinity to mountain tops on the one hand, or to cities on the other. Living in full face of the Arran hills, he never names them. He takes refuge from the ridges of Ben Goil and Ben Gnuiss among the woods of Ballochmyle, and in the spirit which inspired his " Mouse " and his " Daisy," turns out of his path, fearing to "disturb the little songsters of the grove." Similarly Chaucer, who travelled in Italy, names neither Alp nor Apennine. Each found his " cheer in the brightness utterly of the glad sun." The gloom of Burns was not by lonely tarn or " steep frowning summit," but in the snow-drift that starves the cattle on the low-land moor, and the winter wind that is like man's ingratitude. A country life saved him as far as he was saved ; two seasons of a city made it stale to him, and he perished in a county town. With the sweetness of the fields came the benign influences of Coila, to which he thus refers : — " My passions, when once

lighted up, raged like so many devils, till they got vent in rhyme, and then the conning over my verses, like a spell, soothed all into quiet." Here the master-lyrist of the last century antici-pates the great mosaic-worker of the present—

> " But for the unquiet heart and brain
> A use in measured language lies,
> The sad mechanic exercise,
> Like dull narcotics numbing pain."

In 1783 the poet, beginning to realise the chances of his fame, commenced his first Common-Place Book, " Observations, hints, songs, scraps of poetry, &c."—it concludes October 1785, with a warning against his own errors (æt. 24-26). The second, begun April 9, 1787, ends August 1790 (æt. 28-31). They are both of consider-able biographical and literary interest.

Meanwhile at the farm affairs were kept going only by strict economy and hard labour, and when a dispute about the terms of the lease resulted in an adverse decision it broke the old man's heart. He died (Feb. 13, 1784, æt. 63) full of sorrows and apprehensions for the gifted son, who wrote for his tomb in Alloway the famous epitaph, and afterwards applied to him the lines of Beattie—

" Is it for this fair virtue oft must strive
With disappointment, penury, and pain ? "

Robert and Gilbert lingered at Lochlea for some time longer, but when the crash came, they were only able, by claiming arrears of wages on their father's estate, to rescue enough to start in joint-tenancy at Mossgiel, about a mile from Mauchline, whither about Whitsunday they migrated with their mother and the rest of the family.

IV.—*Fourth Period, Mossgiel,* 1784—1788.
(*Æt.* 25-29.)

The brothers entered on their new lease with brave hearts ; Robert, in a resolute mood, calculating crops, attending markets, and determined, " in spite of the world, the flesh, and the devil, to be a wise man ; " but the results of bad seed the first year, and a late harvest the second, " overset " his " wisdom." The family seemed to flit from one mound in Ayrshire to another : their new abode also lay high, and the snow during four severe winters was deep on its cold wet clay : consequently the outcome was so scanty that they had to give up part of their bargain, and surrender

some of their stock ; but they had a kind landlord, to whom they were probably indebted for
their ability to struggle on, and abandon the
idea of another migration.   No one has moral-
ised better on "the uses of adversity" than
Burns ; few so finely as when he says that
misfortunes "let us ken oursel'" : yet none
more prone when the pinch came, to blame
his evil star, and to seek shelter from the
world's censure and his own under "overwhelming circumstances."   We have, however,
the direct testimony of Gilbert to his stead-
fastness in one important respect—"His temperance and frugality were everything that
could be desired."   The effect of prevalent
misconception on this point is visible, even in
Mr Carlyle's, in many respects, incomparable
essay.   The poet had at Kirkoswald and Irvine
learned to drink, and he was all his life liable
to social excesses, but it is unfair to say that
"his character for sobriety was destroyed."

Most of his best work was done at Mossgiel,
and inspired by the country around, or in Mauchline itself.   This, the most suggestive of his
haunts, has suffered less than most places from
railway, or pit, or mine, or the importunity of

professional showmen. A new road has been made through the quiet village and a new steeple set in the midst of it, without doing much to mar its homeliness. The Poet, whose renown beyond the Atlantic brought hither Nathaniel Hawthorne, still haunts the streets. Our eyes may yet rest upon the Priory, and on the Corse, where he found the girl, who was his fate, hanging up clothes to dry. We have access to the crib in the Back Causeway to which he brought her home, and to the alehouse of Nanse Tinnock. Whence, through the churchyard, by the graves of the twins and the Armours, of Daddy Auld and his "black bonnet,"—William Fisher,—of the good Gavin and the sister of the ill-fated Peggy Kennedy of Daljarrock, between the site of Moodie's tent and the lunching booths of the Holy Fair, we come to that of Johnny Dow's "Arms," with its "roaring trade," and the windows from which the lovers beckoned across the lane. We pass on the other side to Poosie Nansie's howff, where "the vera girdle rang" with the wildest of vagrant revels, on which we can almost see Burns interloping with his cronies Richmond and Smith, or "setting up" the Cowgate with "Common-

sense " Mackenzie, or loitering along the main
with Lapraik and Kennedy. We picture him
taking the east road and coming over " the
drucken steps " to the racecourse, where (in
April 1784 or '85) he first met " the jewel " of
the " six proper young belles " ; and so back
by the upland fields to watch the gloamin'
growing grey over the Galston moors ; or the
south road to Catrine, where he was entertained and recognised by Dugald Stewart ; or
another to the Whitefoords at Ballochmyle ;
or another to Coilsfield, " the Castle o' Mont-
gomerie," whose banks and braes yet blossom
with his name, to call on his early patron,
afterwards the Earl, Sir Hugh. Lastly, we
loiter down the Faile till it trickles into the
Ayr, by a grove more poetically hallowed than
the fountain of Vaucluse or Julie's bosque.
There is no spot in Scotland so created for a
modern idyl, none leaves us with such an impression of perfect peace as this, where the
river, babbling over a shelf of pebbles to the
left, then hushed through " birch and hawthorn,"
and Narcissus willows, murmuring on, heedless
of the near and noisy world, keeps the memory
green of our minstrel and his Mary.

Burns' life during the years 1784-86 was mainly concerned with three matters—a keen religious controversy, the intimacy that resulted in his marriage, the full blaze and swift recognition of his genius.

The poet, brought up like his countrymen in the Calvinistic theology, was by nature and circumstance soon led to question and "puzzle" the tenets of his ancestors. Proud of his polemic skill, and shining "in conversations between sermons," he at Irvine, if not before, was familiarised with "liberal opinions" in speculation in connection with laxity in life; he continued to hold them in better company.

Ayrshire had been, for some time, the headquarters of a Theological Conservatism, often combined with Radical Politics; but, during this period, several of the pulpits were occupied by men affected by the wider views prevailing in the literary circles of the capital, where Polite Literature, seldom on close terms with Fanaticism, was represented by Robertson, and Blair, and Beattie, and Mackenzie. The clergymen of the "New Licht," or Moderate party, were, compared with their antagonists, men of "light and leading," learning and manners.

They read more, wrote better, and studied their fellows from various points of view. Scholars and gentlemen, personally without reproach, they believed not only in good works, but occasionally in good cheer, made allow-ances for sins of blood, and were inclined to "gently scan their brother man, still gentler sister woman." The representatives of the "Auld Licht" party, on the other hand, were more potent in the pulpit. M'Kinlay and Moodie, Black Jock Russell and Peebles, Father Auld, and Steven "The Calf," never shot over the heads of the people by refer-ences to Aristotle's Ethics or Cicero's Offices: they charmed the mob by the half physical excitement of vehement words and vulgar action: knotty points of faith, which their opponents were apt to slur, they cleared at once " wi' rattlin' and wi' thumpin'," and when patrons, like Glencairn, being men of culture, began in their appointments to be influenced by the regard of like for like, they raised against them the cry of " Patronage "—

> " Come join your counsels and your skills
> To cowe the lairds ;"

a cry, so well chosen in a democratic country

that, despite Bacon's "*exceptis rebus divinis*,"
despite Burns's comment—

> "And get the brutes the power themsels
> To choose their herds,"

it has, after a century's fight, with results yet
to be seen, carried the day. Few criticisms on
the poet have done justice to his friends the
Moderates. Liberal conservatives, with excessive " Economy," as is their wont, have passed
the question by. The orators and pamphleteers
of that offshoot of the Church, whose name is
a masterpiece, almost a miracle, of misnomen-
clature, have been left free to rail at large at a
body of men, on the whole, among the best of
their age. Maligned as " mundane," because
they looked on the round world as a place to
live, not merely to die in ; and held to be
" coarse-minded " because they did not become
hysterical, the historian will give them the
credit of helping to keep the country sane.
That these men appreciated, esteemed, and
invited Burns to their houses has of course
been lamented : even the philosopher and guide
of John Sterling says the poet learned " more
than was good for him " at the tables of the

New Licht, but it is unjust to weight them, on the ground of unauthenticated anecdotes, with the responsibility of his already formed opinions. Accomplished Broad-Church clergymen may have pointed some of the arrows in his quiver, but it was the indecorum of his adversaries and loyalty to his friends that set them flying. By all accounts his landlord, Gavin Hamilton, was of the salt of the earth, upright, genial, " the puir man's friend," himself in word and deed a gentleman ; but he openly espoused the liberal cause, and the Rev. Mr Auld, a person, says Cromek, " of morose and malicious disposition," having had a feud with Hamilton's father, sought every occasion of venting his spite on the son, whose child he refused to christen, for the following reasons :—Hamilton was seen on horseback and ordered his gardener to dig a few potatoes (for which the gardener was afterwards ecclesiastically dealt with) on the Lord's Day, he was heard to whistle on a Fast Day, and said "damn it " before Mr Auld's very face. High social position, stainless life, and benevolence were as nothing against the fact that he played at cards, and on Sundays only went once to church ; the straiter sect already regarded him with venomous looks. Robert Aitken, another staunch friend whose acquaintance Burns made at the Castle, and to whom he dedicated "The Cotter's Saturday Night," on similar grounds, came in for his share of the same narrow virulence. The poet watching his opportunity, found it on one of the frequent occasions when the practice of those severe censors shamed their precept. Hard cash is the touch-stone of religious profession, and two shining Auld Licht divines, being at variance as to their parochial bounds, abused each other, in open court, with more than average theological indecency.

> "Sic twa—O do I live to see't
> Sic famous twa should disagreet,
> An' names like villain, hypocrite,
>   Ilk ither gi'en,
> While new-light herds with laughin' spite
>   Say neither's lee'in."

In this wise, Burns struck from the shoulder, and seizing on Pope's lacerating lines—

> "Blockheads with reason wicked wits abhor,
> But fool with fool is barbarous civil war,"

launched at the Pharisees his "Twa Herds, or Holy Tulzie." By this piece, towards the close of 1784, his reputation as a satirist, next to that of a lyrist his title deed to fame, was made at a stroke. No wonder the liberals, whose weakness lay in lack of demagogic art, clapped their hands and drank their claret, with added relish " upon that day ! " Here was a man of the people, speaking for the people, and making the people hear him, fighting their battle in a manner hitherto unknown among their ranks. The first shot fired, the guns of the battery rattled and rang, volley on volley. " Holy Willie's Prayer," with the Epistles to Goudie, Simpson, and M'Math, " The Holy Fair," besides " The Jolly Beggars " and the " Address to the Deil," inspired in part at least by the same spirit, were written in 1785. To the next year belong " The Ordination," the "Address to the Unco Guid," " The Calf," and the " Dedication to Hamilton,"—a sheaf which some of the admirers of the poet's softer mood would fain pluck out of his volume and cast like tares into the oven. They fail to perceive that, for good or ill, they represent as essential a phase of his genius as the lighter characters of the Canterbury Tales do that of Chaucer. Burns' religious satires are an inalienable part of his work ;

though, for some years after his Edinburgh
success, the fire which prompted them smoul-
dered, it sends out continual sparks in his
letters, and three years later, on the prosecution
of his friend M'Gill, it blazed into the fierce
blast of "The Kirk's Alarm."

"Orthodox, orthodox, wha believe in John Knox,
    Let me sound an alarm to your conscience ;
There's a heretic blast has been blawn in the West,
    That what is no sense, must be nonsense."

A keen adversary and unscrupulous contro-
versialist admits that these lines, once sent
abroad, cannot be suppressed by Bowdlerism.
"Leviathan is not so tamed." No, nor can
Michael's flaming sword be so blunted. It is
hard to say what the writer might not have
done for religious liberty in Scotland, had not
the weight of his judgment been lessened, as
the cogency of Milton's views on Divorce, by
the fact that he was, in part at least, fighting
for his own hand. Speculative opinion has less
to do with some aspects of morality than is
generally supposed ; but it was unfortunate for
the poet that when the Kirk-Session of Mauchline met to look over their artillery they found,

by his own confession, a weak point in his armour.

No biography of Burns can be complete that does not discuss with some detail the delicate matters connected with his relation to the other sex ; but, in the slight survey to which we are confined, it must be enough to glance at the main facts and draw an inference. Philosophical moralists have, with considerable force, asserted that the root of all evil is selfishness; but in practice this takes two directions so distinct that they mark two distinct types of evil, the one exhibited in various forms of dishonesty, hypocrisy, meanness, or fraud ; the other in incontinence of speech, of diet, or in relations of sex. In the worst type, *e.g.*, that of Richardson's Lovelace, that of the deliberate seducer and deserter, they are combined. The chaste commercial rogue, who gives tithes of his plunder, is, as a rule, too tenderly dealt with by the Church ; the man—unfairly not the woman — who yields to every gust, is perhaps too tenderly dealt with by the World. Burns, it must be admitted, was in this respect emphatically "passion's slave," and yet a nation ostentatiously proud of its morality wears him in its " heart

of hearts." He was more reckless in his loves
than Lord Byron ; but he was never treacherous,
like King David, and, in contrast with the arch-
sentimentalist Rousseau, he never sought to
shirk the consequences of his misdeeds. When
accordingly, in November 1784, his " Dear
bought Bess," the result of a *liaison* during the
last days of Lochlea, made her appearance, she
was hailed in " The Welcome " with a sincere
affection, brought up in the family and shared
their fortunes. This event brought Burns within
the range of ecclesiastical censure, which, con-
sidering that it was an established custom, not
to be waived out of respect even for the person
of a poet, he too keenly resented. Shortly before
or after, he was implicated in another affair with
a more serious result. It is dogmatism to pre-
tend certainty as to the date of his first meeting
with his Jean, depending as it does on the original
presence or interpolation of a stanza in the
Epistle to Davie ; but only in the last month
of 1785 must their intimacy have culminated.
Mr Armour, a well-to-do master mason, and
strict " Auld Licht," who hated freedom of
thought and speech when combined with poverty,
from the first set himself against the courtship

D

as a prelude to an undesirable alliance. Burns was accordingly driven to contract a clandestine marriage by acknowledging the girl in writing as his wife; a form still valid. When, however, their relation was discovered, the incensed parents, with a disregard of her honour which forfeits their claim to our respect, persuaded her to destroy her "lines" and repudiate her bargain. By this step, assigned to April 13, 1786, and the transgressor's second appearance, July 9, on the bad eminence of the stool of repentance, with a view to obtain a certificate of bachelorship, both parties—mistakenly as lawyers now maintain—seem to have thought that the irregular alliance was annulled. The poet gave vent to his outraged feelings in "The Lament" and the last stanza of "The Daisy," and finding himself out of friends and favour, holding that "hungry ruin had him in the wind," gave up his share of the farm, resolved to seek refuge in exile, and accepted a situation as bookkeeper to an estate in Jamaica. The Armours' rejecting his overtures of reconciliation and threatening him with legal proceedings put spurs to his intent; he hurried on the publication of his poems, and with the proceeds bought a steerage passage in a ship to sail from Greenock on the 1st September.

Burns expected a wife to go with him or to follow him ; but it was not Jean. Nothing in his career is so startling as the interlineation of his loves ; they played about him like fire-flies ; he seldom remembered to be off with the old before he was on with the new. Allured by two kinds of attraction, those which were mainly sensual seem scarcely to have interfered with others of a higher strain. It is now undoubted that his white rose grew up and bloomed in the midst of his passion-flowers. Of his attachment to Mary Campbell, daughter of a Campbelton sailor, and sometime nurse to the infant son of Gavin Hamilton, he was always chary of speech. There is little record of their intimacy previous to their betrothal on the second Sunday, the 14th of May 1786, when, standing one on either bank of the Faille, they dipped their hands in the brook, and holding between them a Bible, —on the two volumes of which half-obliterated inscriptions still remain,—they swore everlasting fidelity. Shortly after she returned to her native town, where " Will you go to the Indies, my Mary ? " and other songs were sent to her.

Having bespoken a place in Glasgow for Martin-
mas, she went in the autumn to Greenock to
attend a sick brother, and caught from him a
fever which proved fatal at some date before
October 12, when her lair was bought in the
West Kirkyard, now, on her account, the resort
of pilgrims.   Mrs Begg's story of Burns receiving the news of her death has been called
in question; but how deep the buried love lay
in his heart is known to every reader of his
verse.   After flowing on in stillness for three
years, it broke forth as the inspiration of the
most pathetic of his songs—

"Thou lingering star with lessening ray,"—

composed in the course of a windy October
night, when musing and watching the skies
about the corn-ricks at Ellisland.   Three years
later, it may have been about the same harvest
time, even on the same anniversary, the reced-
ing past, with a throng of images, sad and
sweet, again swept over him, and bodied itself
forth in the immortal lyric—

"Ye banks and braes and streams around the Castle
    o' Montgomery,"—

which is the last we hear of Highland Mary.

Meanwhile Burns had arrived at the full consciousness of being a poet, and, though speaking
with almost unbecoming modesty of his rank,
in comparison with Ramsay and Fergusson,
had, by his own statement, as high an opinion
of his work as he ever entertained. His fertility
during the years 1785-86, more especially in the
period between November 1785 and April 1786,
has rarely been equalled. Among the pieces
conceived behind the plough, and transcribed
before he went to sleep in his garret over the
" but and ben " of the farm-house, in addition to
his anti-calvinistic satires and " Dr Hornbook "
(of more local interest), were " The Twa Dogs,"
" The Author's Prayer," " The Vision," and
" The Dream," " Halloween," " The Farmer's
Address to his Mare," " The Cotter's Saturday
Night," the two Epistles to Davie and three to
Lapraik, the lines to a Mouse and to a Daisy,
" Scotch Drink," " Man was made to mourn,"
and " The Jolly Beggars." These, with the
exception of the last, along with some of his
most popular songs, were included in his first
volume. Preparations for publishing it at Kilmarnock began in April ; it appeared on July
31st under the auspices of Hamilton, Aitken,

and other of his friends. The result was an almost instant success, if not a thorough appreciation. Of an edition of 600, at the end of the month only 41 copies remained unsold. This epitome of a genius, so pronounced and so varied, expressing itself so tersely and yet so clearly—for there was not a word in the volume that any Scotch peasant who could read could fail to understand—took its audience by storm, and set all the shores of the West in a murmur of acclaim. It only brought to the author £20 direct return, but it introduced him to the literary world. Mrs Dunlop of Dunlop began with him the correspondence which testifies to a nine years' friendship. Dugald Stewart invited him to his house at Catrine, where he met Lord Daer, and found his first experience of the aristocracy a very pleasant one. Somewhat later Henry Mackenzie gave him a favourable review in the *Lounger*, extracts from which were copied into the London papers. Of Stewart, Burns speaks at all times with affectionate respect ; the philosopher bears as emphatic testimony to the favourable impression made by the first appearance of the poet, and to the high qualities of mind which

he exhibited in their frequent walks together
about the Braid Hills in the subsequent spring
—to the independence of his manners, a consciousness of worth devoid of vanity, and the
fluency, precision, and originality of his speech.
" He had a very strong sense of religion, and
expressed deep regret at the levity with which
he had heard it treated in some convivial
meetings." " All the faculties of his mind
were equally vigorous." " From his conversation I should have pronounced him fitted to
excel in whatever walk of ambition he had
chosen to exert his abilities. He was fond of
remarking on character, shrewd, and often sar-
castic, but extravagant in praise of those he
loved. Dr Robertson thought his prose, con-
sidering his education, more remarkable than
his verse.

From August till the middle of November,
during which time he had written " The Brigs
of Ayr," " The Lass of Ballochmyle," " Tam
Samson's Elegy," and other minor pieces, preparations for the poet's departure were pro-
ceeding. On the 26th of September he writes
to his Montrose cousin that it will not take
place till after harvest ; but, a month later,

he is still bent on the Indies. Coming back over Galston Moor from a visit to that excellent Moderate, his friend, Dr Laurie of Loudon, he wrote " The gloomy night is gath'ring fast," ending " Farewell, the bonie banks of Ayr."

In the interval, incited by Mr Hamilton to venture on a second edition, he was discouraged by the timidity of the Kilmarnock printer ; but an enthusiastic letter, transmitted by Laurie, from the blind poet, Dr Blacklock, and the prospect of the support of the Earl of Glencairn, induced him to stay his steps and try his fortune in the Scotch metropolis. He who had sung " Freedom and whisky gang together," was not to be an overseer of slaves, but an exciseman. He left Mauchline on a pony on the 27th, and reached Edinburgh on the 28th November, with passports that promised him a fair start, in the " pastures new," on which he now, in his twenty-eighth year, broke ground.

V.—*Fifth Period, Edinburgh, Nov.* 1786— *May* 1788. (*Æt.* 27-29.)

In the northern capital of these days there was more of Auld Reekie, less of Modern

Athens; the iron-road had not displaced the
Nor-Loch, the main thoroughfare ran down
from the Castle to Holyrood, and the banks
of the valley were undisfigured by domineering
hotels or the College towers which have roused
Mr Ruskin's wrath. The first sight of a city,
moreover, is as attractive to a countryman, as
the first glimpse of the sea to an inlander. We
can easily imagine that the poet, affected alike
by the picturesque grandeur of the place and its
historical associations, spent the first days after
his arrival in wandering about the quaint old
streets, looking into shop windows, rambling
up Arthur Seat, and gazing over the Frith on
the Lomonds. We can fancy him taking off
his hat at the threshold of Allan Ramsay's
barber shop, or seeking out the " narrow house "
of Fergusson, in Canongate Kirk, and kneeling
to kiss the sod on which he, at his own expense,
erected the memorial to his neglected predecessor. But if he kept apart for a time
from society, it was from choice, not necessity;
armed with introductions to Dr Blacklock and
the Earl of Glencairn, the favour of Mr Stewart,
and that of his amiable critic, Mr Mackenzie,
secured, and the literary world of the place on

tip-toe to see him, he soon became acquainted
with Drs Blair and Gregory, the Tytlers of
Woodhouselee, father and son, Henry Erskine,
Lord Monboddo (who had vaguely guessed
what Mr Darwin is generally held to have
proved), and his daughter, the fair theme of
several of his minor verses. In short, before
a week was over, he found himself, in his
own words, suddenly "translated from the
veriest shades of life" to the centre of the
most distinguished circles. He was by the
scholars of that brilliant time, by the bench
and the bar, by fashion and by beauty, wel-
comed, courted, feasted, and admired. "The
town," wrote Mrs Cockburn towards the close
of the year, "is at present all agog with the
ploughman poet. . . . He has seen Duchess
Gordon and all the gay world. His favourite
for looks and manners is Bess Burnett, no bad
judge indeed." It has been suggested that the
sudden change of life must have been pre-
judicial to his health; but no man was ever
less spoiled by adulation.

When Burns first saw the mental and social
aristocracy of the land, and they saw him,
they met on equal terms. "In the whole
strain of his bearing," we are told, "he mani-

fested his belief that in the society of the most eminent men of his nation he was exactly where he was entitled to be; hardly deigning to flatter them by exhibiting a symptom of being flattered." " I never saw a man," says Scott, " in company with his superiors in station or information more perfectly free from either the reality or the affectation of embarrassment. His address to females was extremely deferential, with a turn either to the pathetic or the humorous, which engaged their attention particularly. . . . He was much caressed in Edinburgh, but the efforts made for his relief were extremely trifling." With all his essential modesty, the poet must have felt a glow of triumph at the impression made by his matchless conversational power; according to Lockhart, who had the reports of auditors, " the most remarkable thing about him." The Duchess of Gordon said he was the only man who ever " carried her off her feet "; Ramsay of Ochtertyre, " I have been in the company of many men of genius, but never witnessed such flashes of intellectual brightness as from him, the impulse of the moment, sparks of celestial fire ; " and the brilliant Maria Riddell, the best friend of his later days, " I hesitate not to affirm —and in vindication of my opinion I appeal to

all who had the advantage of personal acquaintance with him—that poetry was actually not
his *forte* . . . none have ever outshone Burns
in the charm—the sorcery, I would almost call
it—of fascinating conversation. . . . The rapid
lightnings of his eye were always the harbingers
of some flash of genius. . . . His voice alone
could improve upon the magic of his eye." The
poet went home from assemblages of learning,
wit, and grace, where he had been posing pro-
fessors, arguing down lawyers, and turning the
heads of reigning beauties, to share with his
friend Richmond, then a writer's apprentice, a
crib in Baxter's Close, Lawnmarket, for which
they paid together three shillings a week. Not
unfrequently he dropped in by the way upon
gatherings of another sort, knots of boon companions met where the wine went faster and the
humour was more akin to that of the Tarbolton
Lodge. For the chief of these free-thoughted
and loose-worded clubs, nicknamed that of the
Crochallan Fencibles, he afterwards compiled
the collection of unconventional songs *—some

* Burns kept this volume under lock and key, and it was
only printed, with doubtful propriety, for limited circulation,
after his death.

amusing, others only rough — known as the " Merry Muses," to which he contributed a few pieces. Like Chaucer, he owed half his power to the touch of Bohemianism that demands now and then a taste of wild life. The English poet did not meet his Host or Miller among his fellow ambassadors, and the Scotch bard must often have left the company of Drs Blair and Robertson with an irresistible impulse to have his fling among the Rattlin' Willies of the capital, whose example possibly led him to form other connections of a kind to be regretted. But it is hard to see how this could have been prevented by any interposition of his high-class friends, or how, despite Scott's reproach, they could, at this stage, have done anything for the pecuniary relief of a man at once so wayward and so proud. They did him substantial service in facilitating the publication of his poems, and taking measures to ensure their success. Lord Glencairn introduced him to the publisher Creech, and got the members of the Caledonian Hunt to take 100 copies of the second edition. It appeared, 21st April 1787, had nearly 3000 subscribers, and ultimately brought the author about £500; a sum which enabled him, besides handing over a handsome amount, £200, to his brother, to undertake several excursions, and, when the time came, to stock a new farm. This volume, containing most of the pieces in the Kilmarnock impression, with others, as the " Winter Night " (the sole important product of December 1786), was published in the same year, 1787, in London. In 1793 the two-volume edition appeared. It was reprinted in 1794, but not again during the life-time of the poet.

In the spring of 1787, Burns entered into an agreement to aid the engraver Johnson in his " Museum," to the six volumes of which—the last published shortly after his death—he gave about 180 songs. In September 1792 he was invited by Mr George Thomson to supply material for a similar work, the " Melodies of Scotland." On this undertaking also, he entered with alacrity, only stipulating that he should not be required to write in classic English, and contributed in all about 100 songs, wholly original, or so recast from older models as to make them really new.

The leisure of the last nine years of the poet's life, *i.e.*, from 1787 to 1796, was almost wholly

devoted to these two enterprises ; his other
poetic performances being, with one exception,
insignificant. Nothing was said about money,
and his work was, in the one case entirely, in
the other nearly, gratuitous. On the publication of his first half volume, Thomson, with a
note of thanks, sent to Burns a shawl for his
wife, a picture by Allan representing the
" Cotter's Saturday Night," and £5. Such an
acknowledgment of a treasure " above rubies "
has provoked inevitable derision. It has been
pleaded for Thomson that he had then only
received an instalment of a tenth part of the
work, that he was far from affluent, and that he
put the whole of the songs at the disposal of
Dr Currie, when on the poet's death that gentleman was about to edit an edition for the benefit
of his family. At all events, Burns indignantly
stopped any similar advance : he only forbears
returning his correspondent's " pecuniary parcel " because " it might savour of affectation " ;
if he hears a word more of such " debtor and
creditor traffic " he will " spurn the whole transaction " ; his songs are " either below or above
price." Whatever the " *motif* " of this letter—a
point which his inconsistency in money matters

(for he had not hesitated to dun Creech for his due) and his frequent irony, leave doubtful—he abode by his determination never again to write for "cold unfeeling ore." In 1795 when requested by the editor of a high-class London newspaper to furnish weekly an article for the "poetical department" at a remuneration of £52 a year, he refused the offer. It is calculated that, including the profits of the reissue of his poems in 1793, he had up to the date of his death received for the literary labour of fifteen years about £900; less than a third of the sum paid to Moore for "Lalla Rookh," but a hundred times the outcome to Milton of "Paradise Lost." Wisely, in any case, Burns was never seduced by a popularity he feared to be evanescent, to think of literature as a means of livelihood. He adopted, by anticipation, the advice of Sir Walter Scott—never more apposite than now— "let your pen be your pastime, your profession your anchor," and, with the idea of an independence at the plough-tail foremost in his mind, was already negotiating with Mr Patrick Miller of Dalswinton for a tenancy of a farm on the banks of the Nith. With a view to explore the ground, he on May 5th started on the Border tour, with his friend Ainslie of the Crochallans, of most of which we have in his journal a sufficient record. From other sources we learn that, on his return, he arrived at Mossgiel on the 8th of June. "O Robbie," his mother is said to have cried, as she met her son unannounced at the farm-house door. Enough has been said—sometimes rather rhapsodically —of an event so ready for rhetoric. The prodigal had gone into a far country and returned with a laurel crown. In the old homestead all was sunshine; no one suspects maternal tenderness or scrutinises fraternal praise ; but the poet did not receive so graciously the civilities of his "plebeian brethren," who, nine months before, had taken the other side of the street, and were ready to hound him into exile. The adulation of success which follows on insolence to calamity is sure, on another turn of the wheel, to be again reversed ; and Burns was all through the blare and blaze manfully conscious that his triumph was meteoric.

The old Armours were conspicuously deferential, and got the return they deserved in his expression of disgust at their "mean, servile compliance." With the daughter it was different,

E

and he flew, as Professor Wilson naïvely expresses it, "too fervently to the arms of his Jean." After hovering for a few days about Mauchline, he, driven by a wandering impulse or lured by the haunts of his lost Mary, rushed off on an expedition to the West Highlands, that has been called mysterious, because we have no record of it, save a few letters and an epigram composed at Inverary, which shows, as might have been expected, that he did not find the atmosphere of the metropolis of the Argyles congenial. After a month spent, on his return, in Ayrshire, we find him, early in August, back in Edinburgh, where the fame of his volume made him more a lion than ever in the circles of his former friends, and opened to him others. Unmoved by flattery or favour he, in one respect only, betrayed a morbid self-consciousness. He was suspicious of being stared at, intolerant of condescension, and too nervously on his guard against the claims of learning or of rank. This feeling appears in the "Winter Night" and passages of the Common-place Book, in which he takes notes of the "characters and manners" as they rose around him. These pen and ink sketches are, on the whole, conceived in a spirit of friendliness, but they are coloured by a cynical vein, and it is hardly to be wondered at that when extracts—of course the severest—began to be circulated, people did not feel envious of a place among them. There is little to add of the spring and summer of this year save a few records of the poet's impressionableness, generosity, and patriotic enthusiasm. In January he writes to Hamilton that he has almost persuaded a Lothian farmer's daughter to accompany him. In February he applied for and obtained permission to erect the tombstone over Fergusson. In March, answering Mrs Scott of Wauchope, he wrote the famous Epistle, with the well-worn lines beginning, " E'en then a wish, I mind its power," and sent some grateful verses to Glencairn, which, as appears, he did not obtain permission to publish. The memory of that accomplished nobleman rests securely on the stanzas afterwards inspired by the premature close (in 1791) of his generous life, " The bridegroom may forget the bride," than which there has been no finer tribute of genius to worth, since Simonides and Pindar exalted the fame of the kings of Syracuse. In April, in the course of a Prologue for the benefit of the veteran Scotch

Roscius (Mr Wood), Burns, after referring to Hume, Robertson, and Reid, as glories of Caledonia, perpetrated his worst criticism—

" Here Douglas forms wild Shakespeare into plan,"

and in May, writing to Mr Tytler of Woodhouselee on the " Vindication of Mary Stuart," his worst lines—

" Though something like moisture conglobes in my eye,
Let no one misdeem me disloyal."

On the 25th of August he started with the schoolmaster Nicol, another Crochallan, on a three weeks' tour in the Eastern Highlands, in the course of which he visited Queen Mary's birth-room at Linlithgow, the tomb of Sir John the Græme at Falkirk, the Carron Works,— which he compared to the mouth of the Pit,— Bannockburn, scrawling on the window of the inn at Stirling the dangerous stanza spread abroad to his harm—

" The injured Stuart line is gone," &c.,

Strathallan, suggesting the lament, " Thickest night around me dwelling," Dunkeld, Birnam Hill, Aberfeldy, and the ducal residence at Blair, where he met Mr Graham of Fintry

and gave the toast, "Athole's honest men, and
Athole's bonnie lasses." They passed through
Rothiemurchus and Aviemore by Strathspey to
Findhorn and Castle Cawdor, then over Culloden to Forres and Shakespeare's witch muir.
We next find the poet entertained at Castle
Gordon,—an event commemorated in some of
his most graceful English verses,—and hurried
away by the jealous impatience of his companion, then returning by Aberdeen (where he
met some of his relatives and Bishop Skinner,
son of the author of " Tullochgorum," which he
extravagantly pronounced the best of Scotch
songs) : we trace him through Montrose to
Perth and up the Almond Water, looking for
the scene of " Bessie Bell and Mary Gray," and
so by Kinross and Queensferry to Edinburgh.
Ere the month was out he made (Oct. 1787)
with Dr Adair a fourth excursion, the main
point of interest in which is his residence at
Harvieston, and intimacy with Miss Margaret
Chalmers, to whom he in vain offered his hand.
On the same occasion he made the acquaintance
of Mr Ramsay of Ochtertyre on the Teith, knelt
on Bruce's grave in the Cathedral of Dunferm-
line, and then, " from grave to gay," having

persuaded Adair to sit on the stool of repentance, administered to him a parody of his own
rebuke.   At Clackmannan he was knighted by
an ancient lady with the sword of her ancestor,
the good King Robert, and, nothing loath, re-
sponded to her toast, " Hooi uncos ! " *i.e.,* "Awa'
Whigs, awa'."

Burns refers to his Highland trip in particular
as " perfectly inspiring," but its only poetic outcome of much consequence was " Macpherson's
Lament," the death-song of a freebooter (recalling that of Ragnar Lodbrog), on the wild
grandeur of which Mr Carlyle has eloquently
dwelt.   The fact that these expeditions yielded
so little direct harvest may be explained in
part by the business purpose of the first, and
the ill-adjusted companionship of the third ;
more by the prodigious productiveness of the
two previous years, and the social excitement
of the six preceding months.   The soil on which
rich crops grow must sometimes lie fallow.
Add that the spirit of poetry bloweth where
it listeth, that to a mind of emphatically spon-
taneous power the fact of being expected to
write was a bar to inspiration, that Burns,
unlike Scott, only took delight in fine scenery

as a frame to living interests, and we scarcely require to consider the fatigues of travel in the days when a sturdy lexicographer's journey to the Hebrides was a matter of more adventure than is now that of a lady to the Rocky Mountains or the Sandwich Isles.

Back in Edinburgh, the poet shifted to more comfortable quarters in St James' Square, where he lived with Mr Cruikshank, whose daughter is the Rosebud of his Muse. The rest of the year was mainly devoted to negotiations with Johnson, letters about the " Erebean fanatics," who were persecuting Hamilton and M'Gill, and stray verses addressed to Peggy Chalmers. On December 8, thrown from a hackney coach, he sustained an injury serious enough to lay him aside for six weeks, during which he expresses despairing disgust of life, and describes himself as " the sport, the miserable victim of rebellious pride, hypochondriac imagination, agonising sensibility, and Bedlam passion." Poetic natures are rarely stoical, and a man accustomed to walk the fields in the morning, to blaze in society at night, naturally chafes under confinement with a disabled limb. Burns was besides beginning to smart from the fickle-

ness—none the less that he had anticipated it
—of " Fortune beguiling." His day of " grace,
acceptance, and delight " had passed its noon.
The town had had its fill of the prodigy, and
the sough of the Reminiscences made the doors
of the great move more slowly on their hinges.

The proud poet in later days, when the castle
grew cold, sought solace in the " howff"; now
he frequented the Crochallans, or wandered
about the crags. He had been foiled in one
love-suit, and was prosecuting another under
difficulties. Our space will only permit us to
sum the evidence bearing on this strange story.
On December 7th, Burns, at the table of a
common friend, met Mrs M'Lehose, a lady
whose husband had gone to the West Indies
and left her with limited means to bring up two
children in retirement in Potter-row. Handsome, lively, well read, of easy manners and a
ready wit, a writer of verses, sentimental and
yet ardent, she was born in the same year as
Burns, and told him that she shared his dis-
positions, and would have been his twin-brother
had she been a man. Two such beings were
obviously made for one another, and they lost
no time in finding it out. The above-mentioned

accident having prevented their taking tea together, on the following day he received her
condolences with rapture. If he was, as lawyers
maintain, at this time a married man, he did
not know it; but she was aware that she was
only a grass-widow, and she was virtuous.
Their correspondence must therefore be conducted with discretion, and "friendship," not
"love," must be their watchword. How to reconcile the pretence with the reality was the
trouble. Let them take the names of Clarinda
and Sylvander, and exchange their compliments with the pastoral innocence of shepherd
and shepherdess in the Golden Age. So it
went on, letters flying to and fro, like carrier
pigeons, then greetings from windows, visits,
risks, recoilings, fresh assignations, reproaches
and reconciliations, wearisome to us, alternately
tantalising and alluring to the mutually fas-
cinated pair. It is perhaps impossible to get
at the absolute truth in this business, and if
conjecture errs, it ought to be on the side of
charity. One point has been now made plain,
it was no case of mere philandering. Beneath
all Clarinda's verbiage there throbs the pulse of
a real passion, afraid of itself, and yet incapable

of surrendering its object. She knew that she was playing with edge-tools, but she had confidence in the strength of her principles. Sylvander writes more like an artist, never with so much apparent affectation as in many of those letters ; fustian and bombast they often are, but as to their being falsetto is another matter. On all that Burns wrote there is some stamp of the same strong mind ; but he was capable of moulding his style on that of his correspondents, and adapting his sentiments to theirs to such a degree as often to contradict himself. When we compare his letter of the 2nd March to Mrs M'Lehose with that of the 3rd to Ainslie, we are tempted to apply to the former his own line, " 'Tis a' finesse in Rob Mossgiel." But this plastic faculty, the actor's power, the weakness of over sympathetic or electric natures, is wrongly confounded with deliberate deceit ; it is an invariable accompaniment of dramatic genius, which takes its colour from what it works in, " like the dyer's hand." The poet's religious moods were as genuine as those in which he led the chorus of Crochallan : the former were elicited by contact with religious people ; but he never even to them pretends to be orthodox; he is constantly fighting with Clarinda's Calvinism, and trying to undermine her confessor, Kemp. It therefore by no means follows, that, in his offer to meet her "at the Throne of Grace," he was playing the hypocrite: if he did so, it was the worst thing he ever did.

Howbeit, this love-making was his main occupation, till, in February, he had news from Mauchline which naturally distressed and seems less naturally to have surprised him. Jean was again about to become a mother, and this time her father had turned her out of the house. Burns, of course, rushed to the rescue, established her in the neighbourhood with the comforts essential to her condition, and succeeded in reconciling her to her mother; but he was at first incapable of shaking off the spell of the syren, and wrote to Clarinda the somewhat heartless letter about the "farthing candle" and "the meridian sun,"—the former being the woman who was little more than a month later to become his wife, and to be through good and ill report the faithful and forbearing helpmate of the remaining eight years of his life. On February 25th he went to Dumfriesshire and took the farm of Ellisland. " A poet's choice," said Allan Cunningham's father; " Foregirth had better soil;" and perhaps the views of the Nith had something to do with it. The lease was signed March 13th, the day on which Jean's second pair of twins are supposed to have made their appearance. They, however, only survived a few weeks. On the 17th Burns returned to Edinburgh, and on the 22nd had a farewell meeting with his " divine poetess." This, says one narrator, " was the last of the serio-comic episode of Clarinda." It is hardly so; the episode, more serious than comic, had an epilogue; the correspondence continued intermittently, and the renewal of their intimacy, after more than three years of domestic life, resulted in at least one immortal verse.

The poet left Edinburgh on the 24th, having arranged with his publisher, and sent, as we have seen, a share of his profits to Gilbert. He had also applied to Mr Graham for a place in the Excise, the duties of which he hoped to combine with those of a farmer in the same district. His name being placed on the list, he was afterwards appointed to a post of £50 (raised in course of time to £70) a year, which he congratulates himself on having obtained without any hanging on or mortifying solicitation. On the 26th he was in Glasgow, on the 30th riding over the moors between Galloway and Ayrshire. It has been conjectured that he may then have come to the resolve to throw over his poetical grass-widow, and do his duty by the comparatively illiterate girl who for him had given up everything. A letter to Miss Chalmers, April 6th, is however our first distinct intimation of this resolve. On the 28th he admits to his old friend James Smith that he has made another irregular marriage. It was afterwards (May 2nd) solemnised in the house of Gavin Hamilton, as a Justice of the Peace, and on August 2nd solemnly confirmed at the annual communion in Mauchline, when both parties were reprimanded, expressed regret for their conduct, and "Mr Burns," by way of fine, "gave a guinea for the poor." Jean did not sign her name, so her husband did it for her; but only six weeks later he "acknowledges her letter," so the non-signature must have been due to nervousness. In frequent references to the event (especially

that about the Synod in his heart) the poet
takes too much credit for his conduct, but he
always adds that he expects to have no reason
to regret it. "I can fancy how, but I have
never seen where, I could have made it better,"
is his rather ungracious refrain. In a note to
Miss Chalmers on the 16th, he says that his
wife had read nothing but the Bible and his
verses (in singing which he often praises her
voice), but that his marriage had taken him
"out of villainy." Clarinda, however, was of
an opposite opinion, and on the news wrote a
furious letter, calling Burns a "villain"; an
accusation to which, in a dignified reply of
March 1789, he refuses to plead guilty, being
"convinced of innocence, though conscious of
folly." There appears, we must confess, more
of the latter than the former in the whole extraordinary story, the sum of which is that the
poet had entangled himself with two women,
and married the one he loved least, but to whom
he was far the more deeply bound.

VI.—*Sixth Period, Ellisland—July* 1788—
October 1791.
(*Æt.* 29-32.)

Burns left Edinburgh emphatically for good.
His first winter had been, like Byron's one
brilliant London year, over roses all the way ;
in the second he had to walk on withered
leaves. His old temptations had led him into
trouble, even threatened to harden his heart,
and some of his great friends were doing their
best to corrupt his taste. The criticism of the
eighteenth century is by no means so con-
temptible as it is the fashion to represent it ;
the English of Robertson, even the Latinised
style of Blair, was better than the simpleton
Anglo-Saxonism of recent antiquarians ; but it
was not the manner of writing proper to Burns,
and their square and rule were ill adapted for
the measurement of his wood-notes. When a
man adopts a style unnatural to him, he adopts
its most exaggerated or degenerate forms ;
when the author of the " Jolly Beggars " tried
to mimic the verse of Pope, the result was a
reproduction of Hayley. When he expressed

to Clarinda his belief that "the soul is capable
of inflammation," he reminds us not of Steele
but of the Della-Cruscans; he deserves a place
in the "Loves of the Triangles," when he "conglobes a tear." His metaphors are often
laboured; his allegories of "wisdom dwelling
with prudence," etc., are lame travesties of the
"Vision of Mirza." The dedications, acknow-
ledgments, and other letters of the period have
the same taint. In writing to Lords Buchan
and Eglinton he is not at his ease, as he would
have been in conversation with them. It seems
unnecessary to inform the one that he is incapable of mercenary servility, and when he grate-
fully remembers the honour of a suggestion
from the other, which he inly ridiculed, we feel
how near affectation may approach to insincerity. Burns only escaped the latter vice by
timely rescue from an atmosphere that was
becoming unwholesome, and which no high and
most probably unsuitable alliance could have
made otherwise. Burns had all the "honest
pride" of which he says too much, and would
stoop for neither smile nor favour, but to
humour the great people at their dances he
wore a thin mask, and painfully went through

a minuet with hob-nailed shoes. How bad the spoken criticism of his censors must sometimes have been, we may judge by some of the specimens which have been printed : — *e.g.*, Dr Gregory's rejection of "The Lass of Ballochmyle," and his "swashing blows," beating the last bit of life out of the poet's untimely wounded hare; Dr Moore's recommendation to avoid the use of the Scotch dialect; Dr Blair's refusal to allow "Tam o' Shanter" to be printed for the benefit of his family as an appendix to the remains of Michael Bruce ; and George Thomson's suggestion that "Welcome to your gory bed" be softened into "Welcome to your honour's bed," are among the most ludicrous in literature. True genius seldom wants advice ; but the habit of offering it is with some as inveterate as that of gambling or drink. Fortunately Burns seldom paid much heed to the cavils of men who "spun their thread so fine that it was neither fit for warp nor woof," and though, from good-nature, he sometimes permitted his verses to be spoiled, on afterthought a better judgment generally restored them. In his fragment of a Scotch Dunciad, "The Poet's Progress," he calls critics

F

"those cut-throat bandits on the paths of fame,"
and his reception of Alison's " Essay on Taste,"
proves that on occasion he could turn and bite
the biters. On perusing this politely dressed
model of conclusive irony, Stewart innocently
remarks on the mastery of the laws of association shown by the poet.

The lease of Ellisland ran from Whitsunday,
but Burns did not take possession till the
middle of June. His time till the end of
autumn was occupied in getting ready the farm,
and rushing backward and forward over a
distance of forty-five miles, between Dumfriesshire and Mauchline where his wife continued
to reside. Present or absent, his dominant
feeling during this honeymoon, lengthened by
interruption, was that which inspires one of his
most deservedly popular songs, " Of a' the airts
the wind can blaw." When alone he was a
prey to many moods, for solitude never suited
him, and his first impressions of the Nithsdale
folk were unfavourable. " Nothing flourishes
among them," he exclaims, " but stupidity and
canting; they have as much idea of a rhinoceros
as of a poet," and " their whisky is rascally."
Ere the month was over he had, however,

opened up friendly relations, only interrupted near the close of his life, with the Riddells of Glenriddell, and had written the well-known verses in Friars' Carse Hermitage, conceived in a spirit of Horatian content. About the same time he was giving an appreciative study to Spenser, and to Dryden's Georgics of Virgil, criticising amateur verses with which he now began to be pestered, writing a remonstrance to the *Star* against the Anti-Jacobite demonstrations at the centenary of the "Glorious Revolution," and sending to Blacklock his ideas of a model wife, whose "head is immaterial in comparison with her heart."

In the first week of December he brought Mrs Burns to "the Isle," a steading a mile down the Nith, where they remained for about seven months, till everything was ready to enable them to move up to Ellisland. Now, if ever, were the poet's halcyon days. He had to all appearance found a quiet haven, a good landlord, a promising farm, and a loving helpmate. He could look forward to rearing his own crops, walking over the fields, or loitering by the river banks, enjoying his own thoughts and setting his new words to old tunes. Master

of his surroundings, he hoped at last to be
master of himself : his elastic temper let him
put by the shadows of the past, and he brought
into mid-winter the spirit of the spring. His
songs of this period are marked by a more
genuine buoyancy than either before or after.
Beginning with the defiant little lilt, " I hae a
wife o' my ain," he quickly followed it by two
of his most famous lyrics, " Auld Lang Syne,"
in which he turned a tame original into the
national song of peaceful, as " Scots wha hae "
is of warlike, Scotland ; and " The Silver
Tassie," beginning, " Go fetch to me a pint of
wine," a drinking song with the aroma of Lovelace or Herrick. Burns had set before himself
a model domestic life, and for a time maintained
it. He helped Mr Riddell to establish a public
library, had family worship after his fashion,
and went to church for example, though he
found Mr Kilpatrick rather " drouthy." Respected by his servants, esteemed by his neigh-
bours, beloved at home, his ambition was to act
up to his verse, and " make a happy fireside
clime for weans and wife."

The new year 1789 opened brightly : on the
first day he wrote to Mrs Dunlop one of his

longest and finest letters. Soon afterwards an angry gust has recorded itself in the outbreak of ferocity, " Dweller in yon dungeon dark," provoked by his being turned out of a roadside inn, on a bitter night, to make way for the pompous funeral cortège of Mrs Oswald. Burns was a dangerous person to offend, and the quarrelsome lads of the district did well to hold their peace when he threatened to " hang them up in sang like potato-bogles." He was a good disciplinarian, and, while generally indulgent to his servants, came down heavily on dense stupidity or obvious neglect. About Midsummer his delight in chastising wrong-doers found vent in smiting the Philistines with "The Kirk's Alarm," a ringing blast about which he seems to have taken some trouble, one among numerous comments on his theory of literary work. " I have no great faith in the boastful pretentions to intuitive propriety and unlaboured elegance. The rough material of fine writing is certainly the gift of genius ; but I as firmly believe that the workmanship is the united effort of pains, attention, and repeated trial." It would have been well had this passage been impressed on the minds of his imitators, of whom the first of too

many crops had begun to appear. " My success,"
he complains, " has encouraged such a swarm of
ill-spawned monsters to crawl into public note
under the title of Scotch poets that the very
term Scotch poetry borders on the burlesque."
During the whole of this period Burns was
actively engaged on the farm, taking his full
share of hard work, and maintaining perfect
sobriety ; but he found leisure to write several
songs, among them, " John Anderson my Jo,"
and a number of letters from which an antho-
logia of his wit, wisdom, and tenderness might
be constructed. The series addressed to his
brother William would be amusing were it not
for its closing in about a year with a record of
the poor lad's death among strangers. " Form
good habits," and above all " learn taciturnity,"
is the refrain of advice which this comparatively
commonplace member of the family must have
found it as easy as his monitor found it impossible to follow. Towards the close of July
the Excise appointment was conferred, and
shortly after the family left the Isle for Ellisland, where (August 18) Francis Wallace, the
second son, made his appearance; and about the
same time Robert, the eldest, now three years

old, was brought from Mauchline. The few notable incidents of the succeeding months are familiar in connection with the verses to which they gave rise. A September meeting with Nicol and Masterton at Moffat was the inspiration of "Willie brewed a peck o' maut"; the "mighty claret shed" at Friars' Carse, in October, of the famous "Whistle." Mr Douglas seems to have made out that Burns on that occasion was present only in spirit, not in body; but the fact that the verses must have been written five days after "Thou lingering Star" has not failed to evoke comment on the rapidly shifting moods of the "Borealis race," of which he was a consummate type.

Round the dawn of 1790 clouds began to thicken. Ellisland was after all proving as profitless in the poet's hands as Lochlea or Mossgiel. Whether it was owing to want of skill—want of energy it was not—or a luckless choice of soil and situation, he was, as a farmer, destined to one chagrin after another, and had to fall back on his "second line of defence," the Excise, a defence unfortunately exposed to the attacks of enemies from within. There was undoubtedly some irony in his choice of a profession, of which no one was so sensible as himself. He refers to it fitfully in mocking verse and serious prose, now fearing the " Parnassian queans " will disdain him, now manfully asserting, " I would rather have it said that my profession borrowed credit from me than I from my profession;" again complaining that the extent of his ten parishes, compelling him to ride some 200 miles a week, is a strain on his strength. Documentary evidence, especially that recently made public, demonstrates that, during the seven years of his service, he discharged his duty to the Crown admirably well, and under trying circumstances with the utmost possible consideration and humanity. The stale text "*suaviter in modo, fortiter in re*" was never more apt. In dealing with poor old women and other retailers on a small scale of " home-brewed " he strained the law in their favour, and sometimes gave them timely warning. On the other hand, he was so severe on hardened offenders that in one year his decreet perquisites reached the maximum known in the district. The evil of his new business was that it led him to spend so much of his time from home, and to mix so much in questionable society. Towards

Midsummer he was prone to linger in Dumfries at the Globe Tavern, where a "guid willie waught" was not the sole attraction. The landlady's niece, a certain Annie Park, was, we are told, thought beautiful by the guests when they were in a state that made them tolerant in matters of taste. With this Annie of "the gowden locks," the poet contracted an intimacy that inspired what he himself regarded as the best love song he ever composed, "Yestreen I had a pint of wine," and resulted in the birth (March 31, 1791) of his second Elizabeth. The mother, being no more heard of, is supposed to have died. The child was first sent to Mossgiel, and then brought to Ellisland, to be nursed by the much enduring Jean along with her third son, William Nicol, born just ten days later. Burns had again broken loose: "the native hue of his resolution" was blurred over by the red fires of passion, when in a defiant mood he threw off the stanzas beginning, "I murder hate," and ending with a notable proof of his Biblical knowledge. In other directions he was wasting his genius on election ballads, on prologues and addresses for the local theatre, and on furious prose execrations against the Puritans, the Edinburgh police, and things in general. But his genuine inspiration—though he complains of the Muse's visits being "short and far between"—had not deserted him. July gave birth to the elegy and epitaph, among the finest in the language, on Mathew Henderson. In September Captain Grose, an antiquarian Falstaff to whom he had been introduced at Friars' Carse, (the subject of one of the poet's most good humoured epigrams, and of the lines, "Hear Land o' Cakes and Brither Scots"), having got from him three traditionary stories of Alloway Kirk, recommended Burns to put them into verse. The result was "Tam o' Shanter," thrown off in one day's walk along the Nith, in an ecstacy, as Mrs Burns narrates ; but matured into its published form during the three succeeding months. Of this period there are extant several records of friends or strangers who came to visit him ; among them the pleasant pastoral of Ramsay of Ochtertyre with the quotation, "*uxor Sabina qualis*," and that of two English gentlemen who found him angling with a fox skin cap on his head, and a broadsword hanging from his belt.* The next year is marked by little of note, save three instances of the poet's generous sympathy:—his interest in the publication of Bruce's poems, his Ode for the coronation of James Thomson's monument at Ednam, and his interposition in favour of the schoolmaster, Clarke, threatened with dismissal for severity to his boobies—an interference which seems ultimately to have been successful. During the summer Burns had four disabling falls from his horse ; but he produced the elegy on Miss Burnet, the lament for Glencairn, the Banks of Doon, " Bonnie wee thing " in honour of Miss Davis, and began to celebrate, under the name of Chloris, a Miss Jean Lorimer, who from this date till the close of 1795 was his reigning beauty. He wrote besides several letters and some Jacobite songs, the chief of which, " Farewell thou fair day, thou green earth, and ye skies," was a favourite of the poet Campbell. Currie says it is "a hymn worthy of the palmy days of the Grecian muse." At midsummer, Burns had determined

---

* Mr Carlyle does not credit this story, but it is fairly well authenticated.

to leave his farm, and, the roup of the stock having been effected in September, the family flitted to the headquarters of the rest of his life, Dumfries.

VII.—*Period, Dumfries*, 1791—1796.
Æt. 33-37.

a. *The Wee Vennel* (*Bank Street*), *Oct.* 1791—*May* 1793.
b. *The Mill Vennel* (*Burns Street*), *May* 1793—*July* 1796.

Poets have thriven among the hills, nowhere else could Wordsworth, or amid the turmoil of a city, nowhere else could Pope, have found his inspiration ; the atmosphere of a county town is fatal to them. Dumfries, at the close of last century, was by all accounts a bad type of its class : the majority of its industrious inhabitants found relief from the drudgery of their trades in the small gossip of their limited society ; the loungers went " black-guarding " through the streets, or rioting in taverns. In this head-quarter of scandal and dissipation Burns' course was almost inevitably downwards. His whole history was a struggle between the loftiest aspirations, the most refined humanities, and temptations which his will was seldom strong enough to resist. During his last five years, his official duties compelled him constantly to ride in all weathers over moor and vale in search of illicit distilleries, and come into close contact with their contents. His genius opened to him the doors of castle and of cot; in the latter he was exposed to rural hospitality, in the former to the demands of the company gathered to wonder at his wit and rejoice to find it flow freer with the wine. " They would not thank me," he said of the squires and lairds, " if I did not drink with them. I have to give them a slice of my constitution." Thousands of professing Christians, leading far worse lives, have found shelter in obscurity ; but when a great man yields it is proclaimed on the housetops and cried in the market.

The early records of his residence are full of forebodings. His income was inadequate for his growing family, and he began to have reason to complain of the coldness of patrons. " The rock of independence," of which he was wont to talk, was overhung with clouds lit by the meteors of French Revolutionism. In Nov. 1791 he bitterly writes to Ainslie, " My wife

scolds me, my business torments me, and my
sins come staring me in the face." It is at this
period that Clarinda again flashes with a vivid
lustre across the scene. Their intermittent correspondence thickened, and, towards the close
of November, he went to Edinburgh and spent
a week mainly in her company. To their farewell meeting, on the 6th December, there are
several fervent allusions. From Dumfries, on
his return, we have on the 15th: "This is
the sixth letter that I have written since I left
you, my ever beloved." Shortly after he sends
the verses, " Ae fond kiss and then we sever,"
with the quatrain,

> " Had we never loved sae kindly,
> Had we never loved sae blindly,
> Never met, or never parted,
> We had ne'er been broken hearted,"

which, quoted by Byron, admired by Carlyle
and Mr Arnold, is the quintessence of passionate regret. More than a year elapsed, during
which Mrs M'Lehose had gone to the Indies,
and, finding her husband surrounded by a troop
of small mulattoes, had come back again. Then
more letters passed, the final one preserved
being from the poet, dated Castle Douglas,

25th June 1794, in which he professes to be perplexed as to the manner in which he is to address her; "the language of friendship will not suffice," &c. Then he reflects on the fickleness of fame; "she does not blow her trump now as she did." "Yet," he adds, "I am as proud as ever, and wish in my grave to be stretched to my full length, that I may occupy every inch of ground I have a right to." Here —not in the rendezvous of March 1788—closes the episode of Clarinda, unless we bring together two later references that originally lay far apart. One is from a letter of the poet to Mary Peacock, companion of the friend in whose house the lovers first met, of date 6th December 1792. "This eventful day recalls to my memory such a scene! Heaven and earth! when I remember a far distant person!" Then he gives the song—

"Ance mair I hail thee, thou gloomy December,"

. . . .

" Parting wi' Nancy, Oh, ne'er to meet mair."

The other is found in a leaf of an old woman's diary of 1831 on the same anniversary, "This day I can never forget. Parted with Burns in the year 1791 (forty years ago) never more to meet in this world. O, may we meet in heaven!" Μεῖζον ἢ κατὰ δάκρυα. The writer survived till 1841, reaching the age of 82.

In Burns's miscellaneous correspondence of this period there is little of conspicuous interest. The early stage of his intimacy with Maria (wife of Walter Riddell of Woodley Park), a brilliant West Indian of nineteen, at whose house he was for two years a frequent guest, is marked by an introduction of her book to his Edinburgh printer. In September 1792, acknowledging to Alexander Cunningham a diploma conferred by the Royal Archers, he writes one of his half dozen most remarkable letters, brimming with banter like Falstaff's, then growing savage as Timon, in an attack on the "religious nonsense," which he declares to be "of all the most nonsensical," asking, "why has a religious turn of mind always a tendency to narrow and illiberalise the heart?" and then putting the whole storm to rest by the exquisite verse inspired by Miss Lesley Baillie,

> " The very deil he couldna scathe
>   Whatever wad belang thee ;
> He'd look into thy bonie face
>   And say, ' I canna wrang thee.' "

In the same month the Thomson correspondence begins, one of the poet's earliest contributions to their joint undertaking being "Ye banks and braes and streams around." The first volume was published in July 1793, and shortly afterwards came the refusal of remuneration. In March we have an interesting literary link in a letter to Miss Benson of York, afterwards Mrs Basil Montague, Carlyle's ill-requited patroness, and a request to the bailies of Dumfries to be made a freeman of the town, the granting of which enabled his sons to be well educated in the grammar school at small expense. In April 1793 an exuberant humour overflows in his last letter to his old friend Ainslie, signed Spunkie, with a notable satire on pedants, who are advised to go about with bundles of books bound to their backs. Towards the close of the year he writes, to Mrs Dunlop, of Cowper's "Task" "a glorious poem : bating a few scraps of Calvinistic divinity, it has the religion which ennobles man."

The subject of Burns's religion might lead us into deeps beyond the range of the Satires, and supply material for a distinct chapter. His views, seldom clearly formulated, are not always

G

consistent; within limits they vary with varying
moods: but they are in the main those of an
anxious sceptic, as opposed to either extreme
of positive or negative dogmatism. His prevailing reverence in treating sacred subjects has
been justly admired: but, while his light words
have been gathered up against him, the extent
to which he deliberately departed from the
"Orthodoxy" of the mass of his countrymen
has been studiously slurred over. Burns knew
his Bible well, and made frequent use of it; but
we have no reason to believe that, after manhood, he ever read it otherwise than, as a great
modern critic has told us to read it, "like any
other book." "This letter," cries his most
recent biographer, "seems to savour of Socini-
anism." The word, often used in Scotland to
conjure up the devil of intolerance, is equally
applicable to almost all the leading writers of
the eighteenth century; the only conspicuous
exceptions being Cowper and Johnson. Burns
was, as far as he had realised to himself his own
position, a Deist, and held that the mission of
Christ was to redeem man from himself, rather
than from any "wrath to come." "School-
divinity," he in mockery exclaims, "raves

abroad on all the winds." . . . "On earth discord! a gloomy heaven above, opening her jealous gates to the nineteen thousandth part of the tithe of mankind! and below an inescapable and inexorable hell, expanding its leviathan jaws for the vast residue of mortals. O doctrine, comfortable and healing to the weary wounded soul of man!" On points yet more radical he gives an uncertain sound. *E.g.* "We know nothing, or next to nothing, of the substance and structure of our souls. . . . Are we a piece of machinery, or do those workings argue something within us above the trodden clod? I own myself partial to such proofs of those awful and important realities, a God that's made all things, man's immaterial and immortal nature." . . . "Can it be possible that when I resign this feverish being I shall still find myself in conscious existence? . . . If there is another life, 'tis only for the good. Would to God I as firmly believed it, as I ardently wish it." . . . "All my fears and cares are of this world; if there is another, an honest man has nothing to fear from it. Every fair, unprejudiced enquirer must in such degree be a sceptic. As for immortality, we want data to go upon. One thing frightens me much, that we are to live for ever seems too good news to be true." "If there be a life beyond the grave, which I trust there is, and if there be a good God presiding over nature, which I am sure there is, thou (Fergusson) art now enjoying existence in a glorious world."

> "'Tell us ye dead,
> Will none of you in pity disclose the secret
> What 'tis you are and we must shortly be?'

A thousand times I have made this apostrophe to the departed sons of men, but not one of them has ever thought fit to answer the question. O that some courteous ghost would blab it out! It cannot be. You and I, my friend, must make the experiment by ourselves, and for ourselves."

Stretching out his arms to these vast voids, crying aloud in the wilderness, beating at the bars of the iron gates, Burns had no care to pose as a protagonist about a disputed text, or to ride the whirlwind of a tea-cup storm over an antiquated ceremonial. His clear, strong mind—none clearer or stronger of his age or nation—tore right through those comparatively trivial counterscarps of discussion, and battered about the citadel ; raising the questions of the existence of a beneficent, omnipotent Being, and the hopes of a future life. On the last he is tossed, like a ship at sea : on the first he seems to find an anchor. His ethical standard is, in prose and verse alike, explicit. " Whatever mitigates the woes or increases the happiness of others, this is my criterion of goodness, and whatever injures society at large, or any individual in it " (in which category he is careful to include the whole animal creation), " this is my measure of iniquity." Again, " Of all the qualities we assign to the author and director of Nature, by far the most enviable is to be able to wipe away all tears from all eyes. What sordid wretches are they who go to their magnificent mausoleums with hardly the consciousness of having made one poor honest heart happy." Burns's Creed is that of Pope's " Universal Prayer"; his Religion is condensed in the couplet—

> " The heart benevolent and kind
> The most resembles God."

His Millennium was no miraculous cataclysm, no late fulfilment of the wonderful old dream of deliverance from Nero, but the realisation of the slowly dawning golden age—

"When man to man the warld o'er
Shall brithers be for a' that."

The poet's literary activity during these years was, with the exception of a few prologues and epigrams, restricted to his songs, which he continued to pour forth as from a well of living waters. He had planned a long poem on a legend of the Bruce, but never found himself in a vein or at leisure to accomplish it; fortunately so, had it led him to blank verse, in which he always failed. To the years 1792, 1793, belong, among others, the lyrics, "The Deil's awa' wi' the Exciseman," "O saw ye bonnie Lesley," "Gala Water," "Poortith Cauld," "Lord Gregory," and "Scots wha hae," the last inspired in the course of an excursion to Galloway with Mr Syme—a friendly stamp collector, who occupied the ground floor of the house in Bank Street. The following year gave birth to "The Minstrel of Lincluden" expanded into "The Vision," beginning, "As I stood by yon roofless tower" (for there are two poems of the same name), "My Love is like a red, red Rose,"

" It was a' for our rightful King," * which, if it be Burns', is his noblest contribution to Jacobite minstrelsy, and about the same date—passing from pole to pole of politics—the Ode on Washington's birthday. In the interval, the family, increased (November 21st, 1792) by the addition of a daughter (who died in the autumn of 1795), had removed to their second and larger Dumfries residence, a self-contained house in the Mill Vennel, in which were born the fourth son, James Glencairn (1794), and the fifth, Maxwell, who came into the world on the day and at the hour of his father's funeral. Meanwhile during these years the poet had twice got into trouble, owing to an amiable indiscretion in the first instance ; in the second to a misdemeanour.

Burns' politics are on the surface somewhat puzzling. He was a Jacobite and a Jacobin, not in succession but simultaneously, and attempts have been made to reconcile the apparent contradiction by asserting that he was not much in earnest on either side. This view, based on a note to one of his songs,

---

* This poem never seems to have been heard of before its appearance in Johnson's Museum.

"except when my passions were heated . . . my Jacobitism was merely by way of *vive la bagatelle*," is adopted by Scott; and Alexander Smith denies the genuineness of both political sentiments, saying the one sprung from his imagination, the other from his discontent. The poet's own apologetic expression, however, loses its force when we remember that most of his best work was due to passion; and his commentators forget that Burns could only write well on matters on which his heart was set. He had only contempt for the squabbles and corruptions of a county election where "lobster-coated-puppies" were ranged against well-to-do-tradesmen, with their ragged regiments hooting at each other across the street: hence his ballads, &c., on all local and practical affairs might well be dispensed with. His arrows only stuck when they came from a bow at full tension; his bullets only hit the mark when, as in the German fable, they had been dipped in the huntsman's blood. No doubt modern Jacobitism, like devotion to anything that is past, must draw largely on the feelings, and the spirit of Jacobinism is whetted by a sense of injustice. But Burns has written too

much and too well of both to permit his regard
for either to be set down to a love of "fine
phrases." Verses like these—

> " Great Dundee who smiling victory led,
>   And fell a martyr in her arms."
>
> .   .   .   .   .   .
>
> " Bold Scrimgeour follows gallant Graham,
>   Auld Covenanters shiver ;
>   (Forgive, forgive, much wronged Montrose !
>   Now death and hell engulf thy foes,
>   Thou liv'st on high for ever.)"

those with the refrain, " There'll never be peace
till Jamie comes hame," and (if it was his),
" Now a' is done that man can do," are no more
the outcome of shallow sentiment than " Let
us pray that come it may," is of personal pique.
" Politics are not Poetry," said Goethe, and
wrapped in his own classic art, and the prob-
lems of all time, wrote at his Meister and
Xenien with the echoes of Jena about his ears.
But Goethe was a man apart ; his maxim expresses only a half truth ; it may suffice for
calm philosophers, or the gilt gingerbread of
sickly sentimentalism, but poets who are men
of like though fiercer passions than their race,
the class whose souls are " fiery particles," will
be fervid politicians, but of a peculiar, and as

regards their immediate surroundings, perhaps a useless kind. It is of the essence of poetry to attach itself to commanding Personalities, to Romance and to Ideals. The practical government of compromising parties has not elicited a single verse worth reading. The poet looks over the heads of Whig and Tory to legends of the setting, or promises of the rising sun, he celebrates Arthur and Barbarossa, or he heralds the millennium of Shelley, or he falls, as Byron did before he enrolled among the Carbonari, at the feet of a Napoleon. By dint of a sham audacity, even the sanguinary charlatan who travestied the last, has enlisted the homage of our greatest poetess. Over the house of Brunswick it has never been found possible to be poetically enthusiastic. The very countenances of the Georges were enough to gorgonise the Muses. In all the arts they deliberately patronised mediocrity and neglected genius. The great minister of the first and second, Sir Robert Walpole, "the poet's foe," grew dunces faster than Pope could slay them. The great minister of the third, the elder Pitt, was, during the noblest part of his career, practically at war with his sovereign,—the obstinate

farmer whose policy had lost to us one continent and embroiled us with another. The King
was a more hopeless theme for song than his
son, the fribble, in training to become "the first
gentleman in Europe." The poet's letters,
whether of defiance or apology, public or private, to the *Star* newspaper or to Mrs Dunlop,
are full of hardly-suppressed disgust at the self-
complacent "reign of Heavenly Hanoverianism."
No wonder his fancy reverted to the Stuarts,
whose names from that of their glory, the first
James,—the great King and good poet whose
assassination retarded for a hundred years the
civilisation of his country,—to that of their
shame, the sixth, had been indissolubly linked
with minstrelsy and chivalrous adventure. The
ill-starred enterprises of the exiled race, ap-
pealing at once to the poetic sympathy with
fallen greatness and the poetic love of tradition,
gave birth to the host of stirring or pathetic
ballads on which Burns fed. He grants that
the issue tried at Culloden was decided well, but
it does not hinder him from weeping with the
Highland widow over her slain sons; he
theoretically admits that "Sacred Freedom's
cause" was that of the Covenanters, but he

passes over the matters of Episcopacy to celebrate " our greatly injured lovely Scottish Queen," and echo the charge of the Græme at Killiecrankie.

The same temperament which led him to dwell on commanding Personalities and Romance in the past, also led him to look with favour on the imposing figures and aspirations that seemed, in the present, to hold out hopes for the future. Various estimates have been made as to the extent to which the revolution in English verse that marked the close of the century was affected by French politics ; but there is no doubt they had points of contact and affinity ; nor was it possible that Burns should have remained callous to a movement to which in his " green unknowing youth," even Wordsworth designed to offer his aid. He settled in Dumfries about the date of Mirabeau's death ; when the most moderate liberals still looked with favour on the uprising of a people against centuries of misrule. Somewhat later Jemappes was still regarded as a triumph of defensive warfare, and twelve months more elapsed before Danton had flung down the head of a king as his gage, and Burke had taken

it up in his paroxysms against the regicides. It
is hard for us after ninety years of disenchanting
history to realize the fascination of " Liberty,
Equality, and Fraternity," before the reign of
terror had shown the dangers of the first, and
experience the unreality of the second. Burns
was not slow to manifest and even to parade
his sympathies. Towards the close of February
1792, we are told that he seized a smuggling
craft, bought four of her guns,* and sent them
as a present to the National Assembly, and
that, on their being intercepted, the incident,
with others, as his proposing the health of
George Washington at a banquet, went against
him. In any case, rumours got abroad that he
not only held but had freely expressed revolu-
tionary opinions. The Government of the day
was nervous and alert; remembering Wilkes,
alarmed by Paine and the " Friends of the
People," they did not hesitate to employ spies,
and were ready to accept " delations " of " the
suspect." The Board of Excise, with or without instigation, ordered an inquiry to be made
into the conduct of their gauger : hearing of

---

* This has been by some dogmatically denied, but the incident is unlikely to have been invented.

which he, anticipating dismissal, sent off an excited letter to Mr Graham, giving the lie direct to the allegations against him. This was followed by another, January 1793, somewhat calmer in tone, but going into painful details of exculpation, and profuse in professions of loyalty to the " sacred keystone " of our constitution, the king. As far as pains and penalties went the storm blew over, but hope of promotion was at an end, and Burns felt that he had been through the Valley of Humiliation, no salutary discipline for a soul like his, and had to submit to an insolent reprimand. " Mr Corbett," he writes, in a letter to his generous champion, Erskine of Mar, " was instructed to enquire on the spot, and to document me that my business was to act, *not to think*, and that whatever might be men or measures it was for me to be silent and obedient." Incredible as it may appear, this *ne plus ultra* of Bumbledom has been recently defended on the ground that the poet, being " in the public employ," had no right " to dabble in politics," *i.e.*, he was to be debarred from expressing his regard for two republics, with both of which we were at peace, because the Tories happened to be then in power. Burns was bound, with all good citizens, to abstain from seditious courses, but his office, held, we take it, *ad vitam aut culpam*, could not bind him always to agree with the Ministry, nor had he sold his soul and body, or his liberty of speech, for £70 a-year. He ran the risk of every candidate for patronage in offending his possible patrons, but the censure of the Board was an impertinence, and that he felt it to be so the noble close of the letter to Erskine, in which we have the best account of the matter, clearly demonstrates. After this business the poet's first resolve was to hold his peace, "to jouk and let the jaw gae by:" but he chafed under his chains, and sometimes made a noise in rattling them. To use his own image, he felt sore, like Æsop's lion under an ass's kick. During the spring '93, the bitterness breaks out in occasional letters, notably in his answer to the admonitions of the now respectable Nicol, and the recently published Political Catechism— addressed to Cunningham—items of which have naturally attracted attention. The writer of this and the nearly contemporaneous lines, "You're welcome to despots, Dumourier," must have ceased to expect anything from Pitt or Dundas.

It is the clenching sarcasm of a man smarting under the sense of neglect, and sick of hope deferred, whose fair-weather friends were treating him as popular people treat everyone under a cloud. Suspected politics, added to doubtful religion, were too much to bear, and they looked black upon him and fought shy of him. To be thought bad is apt to make a man bad : to be excluded from the society of equals is to be driven to that of inferiors. Fatigue and despondency alternating with fits of restless irritation, Burns, too much impressed with the maxim, "Better be the head of the commonalty than the tail of the gentry," sought relief among the lower ranks, where he found a shallow sympathy and countenance in his now besetting sin. "Occasional hard drinking," he writes to Mrs Dunlop, "is the devil to me. Against this I have again and again bent my resolution, and have greatly succeeded. Taverns I have totally abandoned : it is the private parties among the hard-drinking gentlemen . . . that do me the mischief." On the morning after this letter was written, when the Rev. Mr M'Morline came to baptise his child, he found that Burns had never been in bed, having sat

up all night in his own house, with some boon
companions.

The next year, 1794, opened with a course of
indulgence that twice proved disastrous. On
the first occasion, having proposed a toast
" May our success in the war " (the early stages
of which he always condemned) " be equal to
the justice of our cause," in presence of a fire-
eating officer, he narrowly escaped being dragged
into a duel. The name of this " lobster " is
preserved by the fact of his encounter with the
poet, to whom, when the French really became
aggressive, it fell to write the most stirring of
our challenges of defence. " Does haughty
Gaul invasion threat " will survive Captain
Dods. On the second occasion, in consequence
of his joining in a freak with other over-heated
guests, coming from the dinner-table to Maria
Riddell's drawing-room, he lost for a time the
esteem of her family, and, what was of more
moment, of herself. Kissing, which "goes by
favour," should never be public, and her indignation, aggravated, it may be, by a latent sense
of the disparity of their ranks, was proportioned to her affection for the man to whose
genius she has left the finest contemporary

H

tribute. Next morning the poet, duly con-
trite, addressed the lady in cries of prose and
verse that might have melted a stone, but
she remaining obdurate, Burns, who could
never brook repulse, suddenly passed from
apology to lampoon. This completed the
alienation, and made him regarded as beyond
the pale, a *mauvais sujet*, with whom there
was no dealing. The quarrel was ultimately
made up, but not before his friend, the Laird of
Carse, unfortunately involved in it, had died
and been lamented in the elegy, "No more ye
warblers of the wood." The only remaining
event of the year worth recording is a visit
from his old acquaintance, Josiah Walker,
whose sententious comments on the occasion
afterwards roused the wrath of Christopher
North. Nor is there much in the next, but
the gathering of the clouds on the entrance
to the Valley of the Shadow. Care, remorse,
and embarrassment had done their work in
undermining a strong constitution. "What a
transient business is life," he writes (January 1)
to Mrs Dunlop, "very lately I was a boy; but
t'other day I was a young man, and I already
begin to feel the frigid pulse and stiff joints of

old age coming fast over my frame." Walking with a friend who proposed to him to join a county ball, he shook his head, saying, "that's all over now," and adding the oft-quoted verse of Lady Grissel Baillie. His prevailing sentiment was that of his own couplet, characterised as the concentration of many night-thoughts—

"The pale moon is setting beyond the white wave
And Time is setting wi' me O."

Yet, ever and anon, his vitality re-asserted itself, and out of the mirk there flashed the immortal democratic creed—

"Is there for honest poverty
That hangs his head and a' that?"

In March we have a glint of sunshine; he was reconciled to Maria, again received her letters, criticised her verses, and took heart to make a last appeal to Mr Heron for promotion. In September, the death of his daughter again broke his spirit and accelerated the close. His hand shook, his pulse and appetite failed, and he sunk into an almost uniform gloom : but to the last it was lit with silver streaks. From the very Castle of Despair he wrote, " Contented wi' little and canty wi' mair:" over the dark surface of the rising waters there ripples the music of the lines—

" Their groves o' sweet myrtle let foreign lands reckon,
  While bright beaming summers exalt the perfume,
  Far dearer to me yon lone glen o' green breckan,
  With the burn stealing under the lang yellow broom."

In January 1796, the poet, on his return from a gathering at the *Globe*, fell asleep in the open air and caught a chill, developing into a rheumatic fever, with which he was during the early months intermittently prostrate. On his partial recovery, in April, he wrote to Thomson, " I fear it will be some time before I tune my lyre again. By Babel's streams I have sat and wept. I have only known existence by the pressure of sickness, and counted time by the repercussions of pain. I close my eyes in misery, and open them without hope. I look on the vernal day, and say with poor Fergusson—

" Say wherefore has an all-indulgent heaven
  Life to the comfortless and wretched given."

May was a month of unusual brightness, but cutting east winds went against him, and, though sometimes appearing in the streets, he was so emaciated as hardly to be recognised. His wife being, from her condition, unable to attend to him, her place was supplied by the affectionate tenderness of Jessie Lewars, who hovered about his couch, like the "little fairy," who long afterwards ministered to the dying hours of the matchless German lyrist, Heinrich Heine. To this girl, the sister of a fellow exciseman, Burns addressed two of his latest and sweetest songs with the stanzas—

> "Here's a health to ane I lo'e dear,
>   Thou art sweet as the smile when fond lovers meet,
>   And sweet as their parting tear, Jessie."
>
>   .   .   .   .
> "O wert thou in the cauld blast
>   On yonder lea, on yonder lea,
>   My plaidie to the angry airt
>   I'd shelter thee, I'd shelter thee."

The poet himself was rapidly passing beyond the need of shelter. On July 4th, he was sent for sea air to a watering-place, Brow on the Solway, and there had a last meeting with Mrs Riddell, saluting her with the question, "Well, madam, have you any commands for the other world?" He spoke without fear of the approaching close, but expressed anxiety for his wife and children, and the possible injury to his fame from the publication of unguarded

letters and verses. "He lamented," we quote
from the lady, "that he had written many
epigrams on persons against whom he entertained no enmity, and many indifferent poetical
pieces which he feared would be thrust upon
the world. . . . The conversation was kept up
with great evenness and animation on his side.
. . . I had seldom seen his mind greater or
more collected." On the 10th, when his landlady wished to let down the blinds against the
dazzling of the sun, Burns exclaimed, "O let
him shine, he will not shine long for me." His
peace of mind was unhappily distracted by the
inadequacy of the allowance granted to officers
on leave for illness, and by a letter inoppor-
tunely arriving from a Dumfries tradesman
pressing for the payment of an account. This
drew forth two piteous appeals—one to Thomson, the other to his cousin at Montrose—for
the loan of small sums to save him "from the
horrors of a jail:" with the former he enclosed
his last lyrical fragment, "Fairest maid on
Devon Banks." The same day he addressed
Mrs Dunlop complaining of her long silence,
she too having been influenced by the *fama*
of the preceding year. On the 14th, he an-

nounced to Jean his arrival on the 18th. When brought home he was so weak that he could not stand; but he was able to send to his father-in-law his last written lines, saying, "Do, for Heaven's sake, send Mrs Armour here immediately." From the 19th to the end he was for the most part speechless, "scarcely himsel' for half-an-hour together," said Mrs Burns afterwards. At one time he was found sitting in a corner of the room, and, on being put back to bed, exclaimed, "Gilbert, Gilbert." Early on the 21st he was in deep delirium, broken only by a few sentences, among them a last flash of humour to an attendant volunteer, "John, don't let the awkward squad fire over me."

The practice of lingering over the death-beds of great men to peer and moralize is apt to be either foolish or impertinent. The last utterances of Madame Roland, Goethe, or Byron may be memorable; but we can draw no conclusion as to their lives, or the truth of their views of life, from the despairing agonies of Cowper, the celestial vision of Pope, or the serene composure of Hume. The last moments of Burns were stormy, as his life; an execration on the agent who had sent him the dunning account—and the mighty Spirit passed. On the 25th, his remains were carried through Dumfries amid throngs of people asking, "Who will be our poet now?" and buried with local honours. Shortly after the turf had been laid on the mortal vesture of the immortal power, a young lady with an attendant climbed at nightfall over the kirk-yard stile, and strewed the grave with laurel leaves. It was Maria Riddell, who had forgotten his epigrams and still adored his memory. Burns died poor, but scarcely in debt, owing but a few pounds to his friendly landlord, whose only fault with him was that he did not have enough of his company. A subscription started for his family soon raised for their relief the sum of £700, which enabled them to preserve intact his little library and tide over evil days. The poet had a hard struggle for bread, but a tithe of the stones of his monuments would have kept himself and his in affluence through all their lives. Scotland has had sweet singers since his death, one of them (Tannahill) with almost as tuneful a voice in rendering the beauties of external nature; but only two great writers—Scott and Carlyle. Neither combined his lurid and pas-

sionate force with the power of musical expression. In these respects his only heir was the future lord of English verse, the boy who was about to leave the shadows of Lach-na-gair for the groves of Newstead.

III

RETROSPECT AND SUMMARY

IF the purpose of these records of the poet has been in any degree fulfilled, there is little need to ask further what manner of man he was, or to add a sermon to the half-triumphant, half-tragic text : triumphant in that it was given him to mature his faculties and achieve enduring work, tragic in that, thinking of his own often defeated struggle, he wrote, " There is not among the martyrologies so rueful a narrative." Reticence is rarely, if ever, found in conjunction with genius. Even Shakespeare " unlocked his heart " in the sonnets, and Goethe in the *Dichtung und Wahrheit*. But Burns is garrulous to excess ; least of all great writers, less than his nearest mate, Byron (who burns blue lights within otherwise transparent windows), did he or could he hide himself. He parades " the secrets of his prison house," joins a carnival unmasked, and with an approach to indelicacy throws open his chamber door. " I was drunk last night, this forenoon I was polygamic, this evening I am sick and sorry," is the refrain of his confession. Scotch to the core in his perfervid heart, he wears it on his sleeve to be pecked at by innumerable daws, and is, in this respect,—*teste* Thomas Campbell,—" the most un-Scotch-like of Scotsmen." On the other hand, he had all the ambition often unhappily characteristic of his race. " Fate," he exclaims, " had cast my station in the veriest shades of life, but never did a heart pant more ardently than mine to be distinguished." His youthful pride was, by his own account, apt to degenerate into " envy." His career was haunted by a suspicion of being patronised or insulted by rank or wealth, which led him too willingly to associate with his inferiors and to court the company of the wild " merry " rather than the sober " grave." " Calculative creatures " he condemns as inhumane ; for errors of impulse he has superabundant charity ; he has " courted the acquaintance of blackguards, and though disgraced by follies " has " often found among them the noblest virtues." Burns' affection

for the waifs and strays of mankind was the
right side of the temperament of which his own
recklessness was the wrong. But his practical
sense, on occasion, asserted itself, in a manner
worthy of the canniest Scot, *e.g.*, his refusal to
stand surety for his brother, his determination
never to bring up his sons to any learned profession, all his correspondence with Gilbert
and Creech. Burns is at his worst, where he
is cautious, almost cunning, as in some of the
Clarinda letters, a few relating to the Armours,
and such passages as that on his return from the
West Highland tour where he talks of women,
as a fowler might do of his game. " Miss ——
flew off in a tangent, like a mounting lark. But
I am an old hawk at the sport and wrote her
such a cool deliberate prudent reply as brought
my bird from her aerial towerings, pop down at
my feet like Corporal Trim's hat." Similarly
in his toast of " Mrs Mac," at Dumfries dinners,
his want of reserve amounts almost to a want
of fine feeling, and justifies the censure that if
woman, as a cynic has said, constituted the
poet's religion, he ought to have dealt with it
more reverently. Equally difficult is it to con-
done some of his vindicative epigrams. "*Judex*

damnatur," who can ignore those aberrations of
" Ayrshire's tutelary saint." The rest of the
tragedy, " half within and half without," is the
commonplace of moralizing commentary—that
of hot blood, weak will, and straitened circumstances dragging down an eagle's flight. When
the devil's advocate has done his worst, " the
dissonance is lost in the music of a great man's
name." Tried in many ways, he was never
tempted to do or to think anything mean. The
theme of his prevailing sincerity has been exhausted by a sharer of many of his mental,
exempted from his physical, faults, Mr Carlyle.
The *finesse* of the poet's flirtations is at least
on the surface. His amiable over - estimates
were genuine to the core. His magnanimity
amounted to imprudence ; his gratitude to all
who ever did him kindness to idolatry. Generosity in almsgiving, a virtue though an easy one
of the rich, impossible to the poor, was not
accessible to Burns ; but he had the harder
virtue, rare in our scrambling world, of cordially
recognising and extolling the men whom he held
to be his peers. His anxiety to push the sale of
other people's books, as evinced in his letters to
Duncan, Tait, and Creech about Grose, Mylne,

and Mrs Riddell, is a reproach to an age when poets are animated by the spirit of monopolists. If he loved praise, he was lavish of it. His benevolence that overflowed the living world was, despite his polygamic heats, concentrated in the intense domesticity of a good brother and son, husband and father. His works have been called a Manual of Independence ; and that his homage to the "Lord of the lion heart" is no word boast, is seen in his horror of debt and almost fanatical dread of obligation : they are also models of a charity which goes far to cover his own, as he made it cover the sins of others. Everyone who knew Burns well in private life seems to have loved him ; but he owed none of his popularity to complaisance. Nothing in his character is more conspicuous than the shining courage that feared neither false man nor false God, his intolerance of the compromises and impatience of the shifts which are the reproaches of his nation. Yet no man was ever more proud of his nationality. The excess of patriotism which led Fergusson to assail the Union and detest Dr Johnson passed on to Burns. Here and there his humour sees a little rant in it, as when he writes to Lord Buchan, " Your much loved Scotia about whom you make such a racket ; " but his prevailing tone is that of his letter to Lord Eglinton, " I have all those prejudices. . . . There is scarcely anything to which I am so alive as the honour and welfare of old Scotia ; and, as a poet, I have no higher enjoyment than singing her sons and daughters." Hence, perhaps, the provincialism of his themes, which Mr Arnold with his "damnable iteration" of " Scotch drink, Scotch religion, and Scotch manners" perversely confounds with provincialism of thought.*   Hence, rather than from

---

* *V.* Introduction to Ward's " English Poets," p. xli. After the remark, "the real Burns is of course in his Scotch poems," Mr Arnold proceeds, " Let us boldly say that of much of this poetry, a poetry dealing perpetually with Scotch drink, Scotch religion, and Scotch manners, a Scotchman's estimate is apt to be personal.   A Scotchman is used to this world of Scotch drink, Scotch religion, and Scotch manners ; he has a tenderness for it ; he meets its poet half way.   In this tender mood he reads pieces like the *Holy Fair* or *Halloween.* But this world of Scotch drink, Scotch religion, and Scotch manners is against a poet, not for him, when it is not a partial countryman who reads him ; for in itself, it is not a beautiful world, and no one can deny that it is of advantage to a poet to deal with a beautiful world.   Burns' world of Scotch drink, Scotch religion, and Scotch manners, is often a harsh, a sordid, a repulsive world ; even the world of his *Cotter's Saturday Night* is not a beautiful world."   Thereon follow some pages of supercilious patronage of the poet who was, it seems, "a man of vigorous understanding, and (need

his more catholic qualities, the exaggerated homage that his countrymen have paid to his name. The Continent champions the cosmopolite Byron, heavily handicapped by his rank, against England ; Scotland has thrown a shield over the errors of her most splendid son, and, lance in rest, dares even her own pulpits to dethrone her "tutelary saint." Seldom has there been a stranger or a more wholesome superstition, for on the one hand Burns is the great censor of our besetting sins, on the other he has lifted our best aspirations to a height they never before attained. Puritans with a touch of poetry have dwelt on the undoubted fact that he "purified" our old songs. The commonplace criticism is correct, but so inadequate as to leave the impression that he was an inspired scavenger, whose function was to lengthen the skirts of Scotland's "high-kilted Muse," and clip her "raucle" tongue. His work was nobler, that of

I say ?) a master of language," and mockery of his admirers. If the critic's knowledge of Burns may be gauged by his belief that the *Holy Fair* is "met half way" in a mood of "tenderness" for "Scotch religion," his criticism is harmless ; but in perpetually playing with paradoxes Mr Arnold runs the risk of spoiling his own "attic style"—the style of "a man of vigorous understanding, and (need I say ?) a master of language."

I

elevating and intensifying our northern imagination. He has touched the meanest animal shapes with Ithuriel's wand, and they have sprung up "proudly eminent." His volumes owe their popularity to their being an epitome of melodies, moods and memories that had belonged for centuries to the national life : but Burns has given them a new dignity, as well as a deeper pathos, by combining an ideal element with the fullest knowledge of common life and the shrewdest judgment on it. He is the unconscious heir of Barbour, distilling the spirit of the old poet's epic into a battle chant, and of Dunbar, as the caustic satirist, the thistle as well as the rose of his land. He is the conscious pupil of Ramsay, but he leaves his master, to make a social protest and lead a literary revolt. Contrast the "Gentle Shepherd" with the "Jolly Beggars"—the one is a court pastoral, like a minuet of the ladies of Versailles on the sward of the Swiss village near the Trianon, the other is like the march of the Mænads with Théroigne de Méricourt. Over all this masterpiece is poured "a flood of liquid harmony": in the acme of the two-edged satire, aimed alike at laws and law-breakers,

the graceless crew are raised above the level
of gipsies, footpads, and rogues, and made,
like Titans, to launch their thunders of rebellion against the world. Ramsay adds to
the rough tunes and words of the ballads the
refinement of the wits who, in the "Easy"
and "Johnstone" Clubs, talked, over their
cups, of Prior and Pope, Addison and Gay.
Burns inspires them with a fervour that thrills
the most wooden of his race. He has purified
"John Anderson, my Jo," and brought it from
the bothie to the "happy fireside clime": but
the following he has glorified :—

1. Semple (seventeenth century)—rudely—

> " Should old acquaintance be forgot
>   And never thought upon,
>   The flames of love extinguished
>   And freely past and gone,
>   Is thy kind heart now grown so cold,
>   In that loving breast of thine,
>   That thou canst never once reflect
>   On old langsyne."

2. Ramsay (eighteenth century)—classically—

> " Methinks around us on each bough
>   A thousand Cupids play,
>   While through the groves I walk with you
>   Each object makes me gay ;

> Since your return the sun and moon
>   With brighter beams do shine,
> Streams murmur soft notes while they run
>   As they did langsyne."

3. Burns—immortally—

> " We twa ha'e run about the braes,
>   And pou'd the gowans fine,
> But we've wandered mony a weary foot
>   Sin' auld langsyne.
> We twa ha'e paidl'd in the burn
>   Frae morning sun till dine,
> But seas between us braid ha'e roar'd
>   Sin' auld langsyne."

It is the humanity of this and the like that has made Burns pass into the breath of our nostrils. His " voice is on the rolling air "; his arrows in every Scottish heart from California to Cathay. He fed on the past literature of his country as Chaucer on the old fields of English thought, and

> " Still the elements o' sang
>   In formless jumble, richt and wrang,
>   Went floating in his brain."

But, though as compared with Douglas, Lyndesay, &c., his great power was brevity, he brought forth an hundred-fold. First of the poets of his nation he struck the chord where Love and Passion and reality meet. We had had enough

of mere sentiment, enough of mere sense,
enough of mere sensuality. He came to pass
them through a harmonising alembic. To this
solid manhood, to this white heat, to the force
of language which has made his words and
phrases be compared to cannon balls, add the
variety that stretches from " Scots wha hae "
to " Mary in Heaven," from " Duncan Gray "
to " Auld Lang Syne "—a lyric distance only
exceeded by the greater dramatic distance
between Falstaff and Ariel, the Walpurgis
Nacht and Iphigenia,—and we can understand
the tardy fit of enthusiasm in which William
Pitt compared Burns to Shakespeare. He who
sings alike of Agincourt and Philippi, of Snug
the joiner, and the " bank whereon the wild
thyme blows," has doubtless no mate in the
region of " Scotch drink, Scotch manners,
Scotch religion "; but we have no such testimony to the cloud-compelling social genius of
Shakespeare as everywhere meets us in regard
to Burns. He walked among men as a god
of either region. He had that glamour or
fascination which, for want of a better word,
called electric, gave their influence to Irving,
Chalmers, and Wilson, who have left little that

is readable behind them.   Carlyle alone among his successors,—representing the mixture of German idealism, John Knox morality, and the morbid spirit of our sad critical age—Carlyle alone among great Scotch writers, seems to have had this power : but his thunderous prose wants the softness of his predecessor's verse.   Swift, Gibbon, Hume, and Burns are, in our island, the greatest literary figures of the eighteenth ; as Scott, Wordsworth, Shelley, and Byron are of the first half of the nineteenth century.

TURNBULL AND SPEARS, PRINTERS, EDINBURGH.

www.ingramcontent.com/pod-product-compliance
Lightning Source LLC
Chambersburg PA
CBHW032302280326
41932CB00009B/664